TRAIL RUNNER'S GUIDE

JACQUES MARAIS

MapStudio

CONTENTS

© JACQUES MARAIS

TOP 50 EVENTS & TRAILS

OTHER EVENTS & TRAILS

Foreword by Ryan Sandes

'I love trail running because it keeps me grounded and my soul free ...'

Looking back at the past five years I can without a doubt say that trail running has had a life-changing effect on me. I started trail running towards the end of 2006 as a newly qualified quantity surveyor working for a large property development company; a few short years later, I can now call myself a professional trail runner.

I have been lucky enough to run on all seven continents and yes, I get to call Table Mountain my office. Trail running has become a way of life for me, it keeps me energised and inspired. There's no better feeling than running along the top of a mountain, breathing in the early morning fresh air and watching the sunrise.

Trail running is my form of meditation and my escape from reality. There are days when I feel as if I were invincible and could keep running forever; other days my legs burn and my lungs scream for air. Most importantly, every run leaves me feeling good about myself and craving my next fix of endorphins.

My experiences on the trails have taught me a lot about myself as a person and there have been times when I have really had to explore my physical and mental boundaries. I feel privileged to call South Africa my home, as our endless trails are world-class. You can't beat the range and variety of our terrain, the surrounding landscapes, our abundance of fauna and flora, or the fabulous weather.

I am sure after running the likes of Sky Run, the African Otter Trail Run and the Hout Bay Trail Challenge, every one of you will agree wholeheartedly.

See you on the trails!

Ryan Sandes – The Athlete

© JACQUES MARAIS

Whether you think of Ryan Sandes as an ultra runner, an adventure athlete or an endurance racer, in the end it all boils down to him being one of the most outstanding ultra trail runners the world has ever seen.

In less than a decade of competitive running, he has racked up victories in races spanning the globe, dominating the 'Racing the Planet' series. To name a few, Sandes has won the Gobi Desert Challenge, Sahara Desert Challenge, Jungle Marathon, the Last Desert Challenge in Antarctica, the Nepal Challenge and the gruelling Leadville 100-miler in the USA.

More information on Ryan Sandes at www.ryansandes.com

Ryan Sandes – Races around the Globe

© JACQUES MARAIS

'I've run amazing races in every corner of the planet, but if I had to choose one event on each continent, this would be my selection!' – Ryan Sandes

Africa – Otter Trail Run
Europe – Trans Alps Run
Asia – Racing the Planet Nepal
Australia – TNF Australia 100
North America – Leadville 100
South America – Atacama Desert Race
Antarctica – The Last Desert Race

Author Introduction & Contributors

Author Introduction – Jacques Marais

Trail running is my religion. It is my head space, my therapy, my escape into a parallel world fuelled by fresh air and endless horizons, and uncluttered by rules or red tape. The rhythmic thump of my feet on a remote trail reverberates into my very soul, not only exercising my body, but also freeing my mind to deal with the daily grind of life. I may start the day feeling as if a swarm of bees were buzzing in my skull, and return an hour or two later with proverbial flowers blooming inside my head. Your reasons to run may be different to mine … the search for an elusive 'personal best' along a specific route; the reward of a medal at the end of a race; or earning the respect of your peers. And this is fine, too.

For most of the runners I know, the main driving force is way more basic and instinctive, though. It is about sucking down huge gulps of fresh air. Feeling your blood thump deep within your veins. Maybe the glimpse of a genet dashing amid the restios as you round a bend on a windswept trail. Or watching your breath plume into the sub-zero atmosphere on a freezing winter run. Being alone, but never lonely. Running is about reconnecting with Mother Earth, and free-ranging far and wide beyond the crowds. It is about free expression, and I would hate this genre to be swamped by the bureaucracy and conformity surrounding road running and other, overly regulated sports.

Bottom line: you do not need a reason to run. Or an excuse not to. Trail running ultimately remains one of the most uncomplicated sports you can practise in the great outdoors, and hopefully this book will act as a guide to some of the country's most gorgeous trails.

Selecting these trails was not easy; more than 250 submissions from dozens of runners, organisers, destinations and enthusiasts streamed into my inbox over the months it took to put this publication together.

So here's a massive thank you to everyone who contributed to Trail Running Guide. Without you, it would have been impossible for me to scout and run every trail featured, and your on-the-ground input was vital. Apologies to those whose trails I could not use in full: all I can say is – next time. And if we've made a mistake here or there (or left out your favourite trail), please let us know by emailing me on jacques@jacquesmarais.co.za

Main Contributors

Jacques Marais (Cape Town, Western Cape)
Editorial role: Author and compiler; photographer; slave driver
Favourite runs: Wolfberg Arch in Cederberg; trail-finding in the forests of Hogsback
Dream run: Patagonia Adventure Run: Torres del Paine, Los Glaciares and Tierra del Fuego national parks
Shoes: Addicted to my Merrell Seismics; also any number of Salomon and Hi-Tec models
Why I love trail running: Head space; health; exhilaration; best therapy session ever
Real job: Award-winning photographer and author – www.jacquesmarais.co.za

Andrew Booth (Pietermaritzburg, KwaZulu-Natal)
Editorial role: Contributor
Favourite runs: Along the cattle tracks in the uMngeni Valley
Dream run: To circumnavigate KwaZulu-Natal on foot
Shoes: Inov8
Why I love trail running: I'm completely free when I am out there
Real job: Environmentalist and trail run organiser – www.kzntrailrunning.co.za

Peter Kirk a.k.a. Pistol Pete (Cape Town, Western Cape)
Editorial role: Photographer, route recce, mapping
Favourite runs: Anything along the Garden Route and Wild Coast
Dream run: Running the entire coastline of South Africa with a few mates
Shoes: Montrail Streaks – tough, light and comfortable
Why I love trail running: Fresh air, forests, mountains – why run on the road?
Real job: Freelance digital media compiler – peteinct@gmail.co.za

Tatum 'Hobbit' Prins (Tokai, Western Cape)
Editorial role: Whatever I got told to do by the 'slave driver'!
Favourite runs: Outside my back door: up Noordhoek Peak and over Chappies – beautifull!
Dream run: Running in Nepal would do it for me ...
Shoes: Merrell Seismics are the bomb – light, comfy and great grip
Why I love trail running: Peace, exploration, head space, drinking mountain water ...
Real job: Marketing manager (RAM) and event organiser – www.mountainrunner.co.za

Graham 'Tweet' Bird (Knysna, Western Cape)
Editorial role: Contributor
Favourite runs: Forest runs in and around Knysna still have to be the best
Dream run: Every run is a dream run
Shoes: Merrell Seismics – best all-round shoe I know; tar, trail, beach, rocks, kloofs ...
Why I love trail running: On every run, I discover something new
Real job: Multisport athlete and race organiser – www.mountainrunner.co.za

Lisa de Speville (Johannesburg, Gauteng)
Editorial role: Contributor
Favourite runs: Suikerbosrand (south of Jo'burg) and Mnweni Marathon (Drakensberg)
Dream run: Everywhere; anywhere; legs moving, heart pumping, outdoorsy scents
Shoes: Adidas Response TR have been my faves for a decade; also Hi-Tecs and Vibrams
Why I love trail running: Constant change of pace and cadence in response to terrain
Real job: Freelance writer; creator of FEAT (www.feat.co.za); owner of www.ar.co.za

Nicky Swanevelder (Pretoria, Gauteng)
Editorial role: Trail explorer and (wannabe) photographer
Favourite runs: Kings Kloof in Krugersdorp, Hedianga Farm in Pretoria East
Dream run: Appalachian Trail – Springer Mountain to Mount Katahdin, 3 500km of trails!
Shoes: Columbia Ravenous
Why I love trail running: Can't think of a better way to spend a day
Real job: DTP specialist; publisher of RunTrail.co.za – www.runtrail.co.za

Lizé-Marie Marais (Port Elizabeth, Eastern Cape)
Editorial role: Trail research and fact checking
Favourite runs: PE beach runs, Knysna Forest and exploring anywhere new
Dream run: The Inca Trail, but I'd probably have to walk it!
Shoes: Getting into trail, so still using my Asics 2150 more than my Sauconys
Why I love trail running: Addicted to the endorphins – and birds, bees, flowers and trees
Real job: Research and writing; director of Business-Affaires – www.business-affaires.com

Debbie Agenbag (Pretoria, Gauteng)
Editorial role: Contributor
Favourite runs: Num-Num Trail Challenge in the Skurweberg, Mpumalanga
Dream run: Dodo Trail, Mauritius
Shoes: New Balance Minimus and Inov8 Talon 980
Why I love trail running: My escape from the rat race to refresh and recharge all systems
Real job: Owner and event organizer of WildTrail SA – www.wildtrail.co.za

Mark Collins (Knysna, Western Cape)
Editorial role: Contributor and adventurer
Favourite runs: Otter Trail, Featherbed and Robberg
Dream run: Bolivia Full Moon Trail
Shoes: Salomon SLAB
Why I love trail running: Few things in life fulfil me as much
Real job: Co-owner of Magnetic South – www.magneticsouth.net

Ugene Nel (Noordhoek, Western Cape)
Editorial role: Contributor and non-motorised explorer
Favourite runs: Oorlogskloof and Stanley's Mountain Runs
Dream run: Any remote and undiscovered mountain trail
Shoes: Salomon XA Pro 3D Ultra; starting to run with Vibram Five Fingers
Why I love trail running: Nature, fresh air, space – freedom!
Real job: Owner of Quantum Adventures – www.quantumadventures.co.za

Robyn Ferrar (Cape Town, Western Cape)
Editorial role: Contributor and trail runner
Favourite runs: Aonach Eagach Ridge in the Scottish Highlands; the Cape Fold Mountains
Dream run: Himalayan 100-Mile Stage Race
Shoes: Yet to find a favourite; switching between Adidas, Montrail and my old Salomons
Why I love trail running: It's my meditation, my grounding force, my bonding agent to people and places
Real job: Sustainability consultant – www.livingwealth.co.za

From the Streets to the Trails

Most of us view trail running as a god-given right, but for many less fortunate runners, even basic kit and nutrition are but a dream. Programmes such as JAGRunners make sure that development for runners starts at grass-roots level, allowing previously disadvantaged athletes to enter this amazing sport. Think about how YOU can contribute to the sport ...

The Story of Elana Meyer and JAGRunners

I always like to tell the tale of Father Colm O'Connell, a missionary teacher, who travelled to rural Kenya 35 years ago to work at the St Patrick's High School. He soon realised what talented runners some of the boys were when he saw them running to school, and made a commitment to coach them.

Despite a lack of facilities and with only the most basic nutrition, the priest managed to guide more than 20 athletes to the Olympic Games. Many of these runners went on to achieve world records, and Father O'Connell maintained that the biggest reasons for his success came from patience and understanding each individual athlete.

This is the story that inspired and encouraged me to launch JAGRunners in South Africa at the end of June 2008. Like Father O' Connell, many coaches had little coaching experience and no modern training facilities or equipment. Under the guidance of the late Dave Spence, these coaches started training groups of up to a hundred children, and sometimes assisted in training other coaches.

Today, the JAGRunners programme has extended to four provinces across South Africa, with almost 35 coaches training groups of children twice a week throughout the year. Many of the kids have already begun to shine and are representing their provinces. While creating opportunities for these youngsters we have learnt the following:

Step One – Coaching the coach

The coaches are the key to success. Without them, the programme would not exist at all. I have passed super-impressive facilities with no kids running, and then seen muddy arenas where kids are training hard and having fun. Sometimes, kids are still in school uniform and barefoot, but that does not stop them. Therefore, the JAG Foundation cornerstone is a programme focussing on a coach training and mentorship programme, as passionate and caring coaches mean more opportunities for our kids.

Step Two – Introduction to running

The next step is to introduce kids to the joys of running. This is done by organising a fun cross-country event in the area where the kids live. We usually utilise a nearby school or community field, allowing our coaches to recruit kids for their programmes.

Step Three – Building a new running family

Our coaches are trained to make sure JAGRunners programmes run every week on the same days and at the same time. The children start to realise that they have a regular safe environment where they can train and that the coach is reliable and can be trusted. Once the kids have settled into the discipline of regular training attendance, we often see the coach taking on the role of mentor in these youngsters' lives. Friendships are formed and the training group becomes a place of love and belonging.

© JACQUES MARAIS

Step Four – Expanding horizons

Kids love to compete against one another. They live from hour to hour and, if not given the chance to put their training to the test, they very soon lose motivation and become uninterested. Coaches therefore arrange for the kids to attend races, thereby expanding their horizons. These outside experiences, often beyond their limited worlds, open their minds and soon they start dreaming of a better future.

Step Five – Teaching life values

JAGRunners teaches four basic values to kids attending our programmes – sportsmanship, responsibility, honesty and respect. During the training sessions the coach recognises situations pertaining to these values and highlights them in the moment, thus effectively entrenching these lessons in the kids. Our 'Pay it Forward Projects' have been incredible in teaching children that even if you have no money, you have so much to give, thereby inspiring them to become contributing citizens.

Step Six – Be inspired

Athletes like Ryan Sandes have helped to inspire our kids through courses and training camps, and we would value any input from top athletes or ordinary runners keen to give some of their time. To take our children to the top, we help our talented youngsters to connect with good athletic schools and clubs, or assist with bursaries to help pay their fees at these institutions.

Do you want to help? Please check out JAGRunners on Facebook, or go to our website at www.jagfoundation.org.za and see how you can contribute.

Happy running!

Elana Meyer

© JACQUES MARAIS

Elana Meyer CV

Elana Meyer was born on 10 October 1966 in Albertinia. As the second of four children, she discovered her talent for running at an early age and at age 13 she won her first official road race – the Foot of Africa half-marathon. She started competing against the 'Barefoot Wonder', Zola Budd – who dominated South African athletics during the 1980s – soon after this. Elana achieved great success at national level, and was awarded her Springbok colours as a junior athlete.

The defining moment in Elana's career came when she competed in the 1992 Barcelona Olympic Games. This slight girl from the southern Cape was South Africa's best hope for glory, and she won an Olympic silver medal. She created an abiding memory as she and the winner, Derartu Tulu from Ethiopia, embraced, and then draped their respective flags around their shoulders to run a historic victory lap to massive applause.

Showing her versatility, Meyer continued her winning form in the years to come, claiming the African title in the 1 500 metres in consecutive years. More than a decade on the international circuit followed, during which she broke six world records and won both a World Cup and the World Half-Marathon title.

Elana now devotes her time to the development of less fortunate athletes, but is still a competitive sportswoman. More info on her is available at www.jagrunners.blogspot.com

If the Shoe Fits

Choosing a trail running shoe is a decidedly personal process, and the best way to do it would be to 'try before you buy'. This is unfortunately not always practically possible, so we've asked some of the top global trail shoe manufacturers each to select one or two of their models, and tell us why they think these shoes may just suit you to a T.

COLUMBIA Ravenous II

We took everything we know about trail running shoes and applied it to the evolution of the original Ravenous shoe. Featuring our new Techlite® Fit™ system, they're lighter and more advanced than ever before. Firm support under the heel tapers off to softer foam towards the eye stay, creating incredibly smooth heel-to-toe transitions.

Designed for performance from the ground up, the Ravenous features a multi-directional lugged outsole with Omni-Grip® rubber for superb traction on wet, muddy or rough terrain. Minimal overlays and highly breathable mesh on the upper provides lightweight comfort without compromising quality. Engineered forefoot flexibility and a lateral crash zone ensure correct fit that accommodates a trail runner's natural foot motion. More agile and comfortable than ever before, the Ravenous II delivers big-time trail performance in a sleek, low-profile package.

Men's and women's versions available – www.columbia.com

MERREL Mix Master

Merrell's Mix Master all begins with a solid foundation of outdoor performance, innovation and a merging of modern technology. This shoe drew inspiration from multi-sport activities and athletes who want to expand their horizons in trail running, mountain marathons and adventure racing. Its low-profile construction and midsole offer the best of both worlds – the cushioning you need for all-day comfort and control needed for support on all terrain.

They have been engineered so that each step with the added ESS plate provides the necessary foot protection when running and kloofing over rocky landings. Mix Masters have a 4mm heel-to-toe drop, with a rubber toe protector adding cushioning. A welded-on TPU support structure was built for people wanting to tackle more rugged and longer trails. This shoe is all about the fun of going further faster.

Men's and women's versions available – www.merrell.co.za

NEW BALANCE MT1010

This shoe joins our ever-growing minimalist family as a longer-distance style, specifically designed for those runners who want more cushioning on longer runs, but do not want to sacrifice the semi-barefoot feel. The key features on the MT1010 style include the forefoot ROCK STOP protection, as well as the trusty Vibram in the outer sole. Slip it on and you will soon realise that no key features required to make it a top-end trail shoe have been sacrificed.

The MT1010 features a 4mm drop from heel to forefoot, but retains sufficient cushioning to ensure comfort on longer trail runs. With the lower profile, the style is ideal for trail running, as it keeps the foot in touch with its placement on impact and toe off, making the foot more stable on those tricky uneven surfaces.

Men's and women's versions available – www.newbalance.co.za

PUMA Faas 250 Trail

We've re-engineered the successful Faas 250 racing flat and taken it off-road! The Faas 250 Trail gives you the best of all worlds – it is super lightweight; the material used is all weather; and the shoe is designed for no-holds-barred racing.

Expect the Faas 250 to be light and low to the ground, for excellent traction and response over even the most unstable terrain. A water-repellent performance upper keeps your feet dry during trail runs, while a directional lug outsole enhances traction. Best of all, it weighs in at a feather-light 255g.

Men's and women's versions available – www.puma.co.za

SALOMON XT Wings 3

If ever there was a worthy successor to the XT Wings 2 then this shoe is it. The XT Wings 3 is one of the most impressive trail running shoes to hit the global trail running market since the original XT Wings in 2006. The shoe has undergone a complete revamp and is heavily inspired by the S-Lab programme.

It boasts a brand-new Contagrip outersole with high-abrasion rubber and a new Chevron design for better grip, control and durability. There is a new triple-density midsole housed inside a redesigned, geometrically altered chassis to give more stability with less bulk. The rest of the upper is seamless, resulting in an extremely lightweight and comfortable run, with a new mesh increasing breathability while keeping out debris. Overall the XT Wings 3 sets a new benchmark for trail running shoes worldwide.

Men's and women's versions available – www.salomonsports.com

VIBRAM Spyridon LS

Our first trail-running-specific model – the Spyridon LS – provides that perfect balance of 'foot feel' and protection on rugged surfaces. A minimalist Vibram XS Trek rubber sole with an aggressive tread design provides sure-footed grip in all directions, while improving on proper barefoot dynamics. A moulded nylon mesh midsole provides impact protection from stones and debris, dispersing pressure over a wider area.

The Spyridon LS's closed speed lace system accommodates a wider foot or higher instep, while the naturally breathable upper has an adjustable hook-and-loop closure for a secure fit. A velukid microfibre strip on the upper increases the lateral stability, and the TPU Gambit all around the ankle and heel improves the stability and containment of the shoe. Polyurethane printing on the toes and upper increases durability and strength, and 3M reflective applications have been added for dark conditions. A stitched-in polyurethane insole protects skin and foot tissue during longer runs.

Men's and women's versions available – www.vibramfivefingers.co.za

The Minimalist Movement

One of the latest trends in trail running is the move to minimalist (barefoot) running. Popularised by the best-selling book Born to Run*, the idea of running without shoes, or at least in footwear approximating the barefoot feel, has seen a boom in shoes with thinner soles, less cushioning and minimal underfoot protection. Some old-school runners still see this as a fad, but professionals in the field – such as Benita de Witt – fully support the transition.*

The Road to Barefoot

'Why barefoot running?' you might ask. The most basic – and obvious – answer lies in the undeniable fact that the move to minimalism will greatly improve the range of motion in your ankles, feet and toes.

As in the arm and hand, the leg and foot have been designed with numerous tiny joints and bones, enabling the foot to move in all directions. The process of wearing a shoe basically 'splints' the foot into a semi-immovable cage, thereby disabling its ability to move through its full range. In short, this severely limits the function of the foot.

A fully functional human foot is generally wider than the average foot we see today, as this has been constrained by the shoes contemporary humans wear. The former foot is able to perform many different movements which not only makes its owner more efficient, but in turn less prone to injuries. The idea of returning the foot to a 'barefoot' state by walking and running without shoes will again encourage all the joints, tendons and muscles to move through their full range, with a noticeable change in function.

Several benefits come packaged with this move to barefooting:

It strengthens muscles in the feet and lower legs

As soon as the foot claims back its full range of movement, the muscles in the lower leg and foot become activated and start strengthening. A strong foot leads to a strong leg, which in turn leads to a strong body.

It improves proprioception and body awareness

The skin and connective tissue underneath the foot contain loads of tiny nerve endings, all of them connected to the proprioceptors. These receptors give the information to the brain as to where the body is related to gravity, and then activate the muscles in response to this. By wearing rigid shoes, these proprioceptors are deactivated, and the athlete therefore becomes more vulnerable and injury prone.

It aligns the spine and improves posture, allowing the foot and body to move naturally, which just feels good

By aligning the foot and encouraging a full range of movement and corresponding strength, all the joints become properly aligned, including the spine. When the body moves in the neutral position, running feels light and free and more effective.

It restores normal shock absorption through the calf muscle and Achilles tendon

When running barefoot, without a heel, the foot strikes on the forefoot, which immediately transfers the pressure from the ankles, knees, hips and spine. The calf muscle and Achilles tendon act as a natural shock absorber, preventing injuries of the joints.

It improves athletic performance

A front-foot runner is a faster runner. Most elite athletes strike on their front feet (thus activating the calf and hamstrings), which leads to a faster and more efficient running performance.

The amount of information required to facilitate a seamless transition to barefoot running cannot be covered in just a couple of pages, but the bullet points below should help guide you through the process.

The biomechanics of running

Running in 24mm-heel running shoes leads to an extended knee and therefore a long and deactivated hamstring. A dorsiflexed foot in turn equates to long, deactivated calf and will result in:

- Loss of natural shock absorption
- Slower run

Running barefoot – with a flexed knee and shorter, stronger hamstring – means your foot is in plantar flexion, with a shorter, stronger calf, leading to:

- Activation of natural shock absorption
- Faster run from the forefoot

© JACQUES MARAIS

Why do athletes get injured?

- Too quick progress
- Incorrect biomechanics (i.e. over-pronation)
- Incorrect footwear
- Running on camber
- Combining different sports that do not compliment each other

Why do athletes get injured when changing from running shoes to barefoot?

All of the above, as well as:

- Weak foot muscles
- Weak hamstrings and calf muscles
- Overstretched hamstrings and calves

How can you prevent injuries when changing from running shoes to barefoot?

- Correct your biomechanics
- Strengthen up
- Do not stretch your calves or hamstrings
- Follow a training program designed for your body

More information is available at www.vibramfivefingers.co.za and www.bfcc.co.za

© JACQUES MARAIS

Benita de Witt

Benita de Witt, the founder of the Lyno Method®, qualified as a physiotherapist at the University of the Orange Free State in Bloemfontein in 1982. She worked for 13 years as a physiotherapist in sport, before deciding to develop a more holistic treatment method in the field.

Benita's idea was to focus on assessing full body function by testing the lengths and function of fascia trains. She has since 1996 applied this Lyno Method® to all her athletes with some astounding results. In 2010 she shifted her focus to the teaching of the Lyno Method® to physiotherapists, chiropractors, biokineticists and massage therapists.

More information on her work is available at www.lynosport.co.za

Yoga and Trail Running

Yoga has become part of many runners' weekly grind. To some, yoga and running lie on opposite ends of the exercise spectrum, but they actually combine strength and flexibility.

How yoga can improve your running

Strength and flexibility

With the one-dimensional nature of running, if your body is off-balance, it can often lead to repetitive strain injuries. Out on a run, the average body experiences too much tightening and shortening of muscles and not enough restoration and loosening work. Tight muscles tend to get tighter and compensating weak muscles weaker. Yoga can work specifically at balancing strength in the muscles that support and stabilise the skeletal system, along with increasing the range of motion in the joints.

Breath

Yoga's more internal focus will teach you to 'harness' the breath, co-ordinating breath with movement, which brings more awareness of habitual and ineffective breathing patterns, and encourages integration of body and mind. This integration introduces a more intuitive approach to how you manage your body and teaches you to listen and respond to messages the body sends you, helping to prevent injuries before they develop. Yoga's age-old breathing techniques (Pranayama) will help to soothe the nervous system, which in turn reduces tension in the body. A body that is in a contracted state requires more energy for all activities. The relaxation that yoga offers encourages the body to burn energy at a more efficient rate, which we can all benefit from when out on a run.

Balance

The constant drive, competition and the goal-orientated nature of most sports can hinder much needed focus and calm. Yoga emphasizes the process or journey more – 'being' in the moment, out on the trails and in your daily life, really tuning into your body and breathing, exploring sensations and emotions. Yoga at its roots means 'union'; everything in life is interrelated or connected in some way, from the physical body's interrelated muscular network, to the important integration of our body, mind, spirit and surrounding environment. The key to everything in life is balance. Yoga can be the perfect yin to the yang nature of your running.

Series of postures to help bring balance post run

© JACQUES MARAIS

Child's Pose (Wide Knees) *Balasana*
From kneeling, take knees wide, keep big toes together, buttocks to heels. Arms extend out ahead, forehead resting on the mat. Hold for 10 breaths, gently opening the inner thighs, hips, lower back and ankles.

© JACQUES MARAIS

Cow and Cat Pose *Bitilasana and Marjaryasana*
This is a dynamic movement between two postures which will start to limber the spine and neck and bring balance to the hips. Come to hands and knees, wrists below shoulders, knees below hips. Inhale; moving from the tailbone draw the navel down, opening up the collarbones, gazing forwards. Exhale; draw the navel towards the spine, dropping the head to gaze towards the navel, arching the upper back. Continue for 10 breaths.

© JACQUES MARAIS

Low Lunge *Anjaneyasana*
From all fours, step the right foot forward to the inside of the right hand. Ground the front foot, press into the base of the big toe, align knee above the ankle. Inhale; bring the torso upright. Press into the top of the back foot and draw the tailbone under. To extend the stretch into the side waist and deeper into the hip flexor, extend the right arm upwards and slightly over to the left. Hold for 5 breaths, accessing the deeper hip flexor muscles like the psoas. Move directly to Runner's Lunge.

© JACQUES MARAIS

Runner's Lunge
From Low Lunge, bring the buttocks towards the back heel, straighten the front leg, flex the front foot, and keep the thigh engaged. Keep the spine long. Rest the fingertips on the floor alongside the front leg. Keep the hips squared. Bend the front knee slightly if necessary. Hold for 5 breaths, taking the stretch into the back line of the leg and lower back. Move forward into Lizard Pose.

© JACQUES MARAIS

Lizard Pose *Utthan Pristhasana*
From Runner's Lunge, bend the front knee; bring the hands to the inside of the right leg and lower the torso. Come onto the elbows, or as far as the body will allow. Hold for 5 breaths, accessing the hamstring and deep pelvic muscles of the front leg. Return to Child's Pose for 5 breaths and repeat from Low Lunge on the opposite side.

© JACQUES MARAIS

Downward Facing Dog *Adho Mukha Svanasana*
From all fours, wrists below elbows, knees below hips. Tuck the toes, exhale, pressing into the hands, straighten the legs, pressing heels towards the floor, sitting bones to the ceiling, shoulder blades down the back, relax the neck. Hold for 5 breaths while downward facing dog creates space in the back of the body.

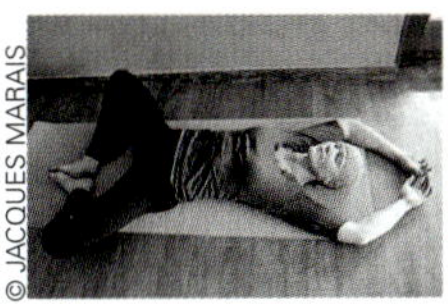

© JACQUES MARAIS

Supine Bound Angle Pose *Supta Baddha Konasana*
Lying on your back, bend the knees, draw the tailbone under, flattening the curve of the lower back, bring the soles of the feet together and allow the knees to drop out to the sides. Bring the arms back above the head, elbows bent. Place blocks as support under the outside of the knees if necessary. Take 10 deep breaths into the abdomen and expanding the ribcage, allowing this restorative posture to release the inner thighs and soothe the nervous system.

Karyn Velleman
Karyn is a practising bodywork therapist and yoga teacher based in Cape Town. She started practising yoga 11 years ago after years of endurance sports (and injuries) and has first-hand experience of using yoga as rehabilitation. Karyn takes a special interest in an athlete's approach to yoga and recognises the need for guidance in terms of safe integration of its many benefits into our daily and weekly routines. She believes that yoga will naturally overflow into your life; it is not just a stretching routine, it's an ancient science in itself, and an essential in the 'toolbox' of life. She takes her yoga everywhere with her, onto the trails, bike, swims, out in the surf and in daily interactions with family and friends. She trained and taught in London and now offers workshops in Cape Town. She can be contacted on info@livebalanced.co.za or Tel (+27 73) 072 6241.

The Thin Edge of the Wedge

Posture therapy and body re-alignment – often combined with kinesiology – is another method of body maintenance for both amateur and professional athletes and has been successfully applied over many years. Jen Rorrison was a provincial and national runner and triathlete, and studied with the legendary Ron Holder. Her own experience of posture therapy helped her manage a chronic sports injury, and motivated her path as practitioner.

Kinesiology and posture therapy: a concise explanation

*'**Kinesiology** (muscle testing) is a method by which the nerve reflexes can be tested in order to find imbalances in the body. An indicator muscle (usually the deltoid muscle, i.e. by pushing down the arm) is used to test weaknesses in the body.*

***Posture therapy** is a technique (using kinesiology) used to align the body in order to reduce pain and prevent injury in running or other activities.*

The human skeleton is genetically asymmetrical (never equally aligned on both sides) and therefore each person's body (by dint of gravity) will always lean either to the left or right depending on the individual (you may notice this yourself by standing in front of a mirror).

Many sports (especially running) involve linear action – a continuous forward motion where the body moves in one plane. Because the skeleton is slightly skew, this may eventually cause pain in one or more areas of the body, adversely affecting the activity. With rest and treatment this may heal, most probably to recur in the same area at a later stage, or defer pain elsewhere because of compensation.

Posture therapy involves the therapist using a technique called kinesiology (a nerve reflex test) to test the functioning of the body between the left and right side. In this way they can find out to which side the person is leaning; the therapist is then able to determine the amount of support needed under the shoe sole on the side of the lean. This ensures the centre of gravity falls in the midline between the feet and thus the body is in equilibrium.

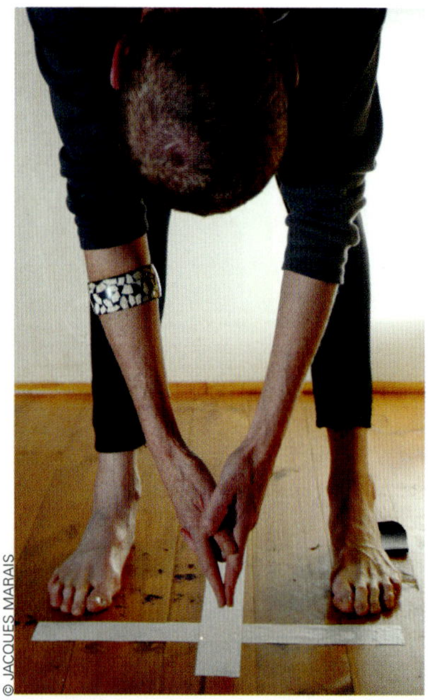

© JACQUES MARAIS

During therapy the person is further balanced by an 'unlocking' technique using pressure points while on the treatment table before retesting the height of the wedge again. Once the final height of the wedge has been established, the person will wear it for daily use and while running for a set period of time (determined through kinesiology).

The wedge counteracts the imbalance, thus creating a new posture, minimizing both pain and the tendency for recurring injury. The height of the wedge and balance of the body are tested regularly to ensure the centre of gravity remains balanced. The height of the wedge may vary from as little as a layer of duct tape to a 10mm wedge, depending on the need for stabilization.

How to apply self-maintenance

To some extent, anyone can balance their centre of gravity through the following method:

- Make a cross with tape on a tiled floor or flat surface – approximately 30cm x 30cm
- Stand with your feet directly either side of the cross
- Hang your body forward with hands clasped in front of you and arms hanging forward in a relaxed way (as shown in picture)
- Position the four fingers of the clasped hands over the centre of the cross
- Now close your eyes and take a deep breath; on exhalation, relax your body fully in the hanging position for 10 seconds to allow the skeleton to reveal its lean
- Open your eyes and you will be able to see whether you are leaning to the left or right of the midpoint
- Add some support to the side of the lean – telephone directory pages are quite good for testing the height needed to support the centre of gravity
- Repeat above process adjusting the height of the support until the body remains at the midpoint of the cross – the centre of gravity is now balanced
- Once the height has been established one can make up a wedge – either with rubber or duct tape or the pages wrapped in duct tape – equivalent to the height needed to support the body
- Position the wedge on the heel under the inner sole of the running shoe
- Repeat the balancing process as often as you feel is necessary; you can test your own alignment daily to ensure the body is in equilibrium before you run

For further details or info, please contact Jen Rorrison on Tel (+27 83) 266 3305.

© JACQUES MARAIS

Jen Rorrison

In 1984 I had to terminate my running scholarship in America due to a chronic lower back injury. After a year of no running and researching what to do, I was treated by the famous chiropractor Ron Holder, who had developed a unique method of posture therapy.

After aligning my running shoes with a heel wedge, and three months of slow running and treatment, I was fully back into competitive running. Another 15 years of high-intensity training and competing in triathlon and running events followed. (I still run with a heel wedge in my shoe.)

My fascination with this process was in how logically and simply the body can be aligned. I developed a passion for the treatment, did a kinesiology course, and evolved my own method of helping others with pain and injury.

For the last 20 years I have maintained this passion, treating others and encouraging them to align themselves to maintain equilibrium. I have also taught other therapists this technique as an added tool to their therapy.

I hope to reinforce this knowledge through a text book on posture therapy I'm planning to write within the next year.

The End of the Pasta Party?

Carbo-loading used to be the mainstay of every endurance athlete for the past couple of decades, but is this just one of the many myths perpetuated by outdated research. If anyone else made this statement it would be immediately ridiculed; however, if the man holding forth on the benefits of a high-protein diet is none other than Professor Timothy Noakes, it might be time to sit up and take notice …

The right diet for the body type

We exist at an exciting time in the evolution of our understanding of optimum nutrition for sport. The idea that we need to drink 'as much as tolerable' to 'stay ahead of thirst' has been thoroughly discounted. Instead, science now clearly shows that exercise performance in any event is optimized by drinking according to thirst – drinking either more or less than thirst dictates is associated with an impaired exercise performance.

The evidence for this is presented in detail for the first time in my book ***Waterlogged*** (released in the USA in May 2012). In this, I show that commercial interests rather than good science were behind a false dogma that ingesting fluid at high rates is the only way to maximize athletic performance. What is now under attack is the concept that a high carbohydrate diet and high rates of carbohydrate ingestion during exercise are essential to maximize athletic performance. Not unexpectedly, commercial interests are an important driver of these ideas.

There are perhaps three drivers for the new thinking. First is a re-analysis of the original idea that all of exercise performance can be reduced to one single nutrient – carbohydrate. This is known as reductionism. For if one focuses only on one nutrient to the exclusion of other nutrients, the possibility is that there might be adverse consequences as a result of the nutrients that are excluded from the diet (because of that single-minded focus).

Second is the growing realization that, for some, carbohydrates are not quite as benign a foodstuff as is generally believed. There are those whose metabolism of carbohydrates is abnormal; instead of storing the excess ingested carbohydrate as a muscle fuel (glycogen, which can then be used during subsequent bouts of high-intensity exercise) those with a carbohydrate-resistance (CR) will store that excess fuel as fat.

Even worse, the more carbohydrate they ingest, the more insulin they secrete. The effect of insulin is to reduce fat release from the fat cells of CR athletes, and as a result the carbohydrates actually impair the exercise performance of subjects with CR by 'crippling' their metabolism during prolonged exercise.

Thirdly, there is the realization that humans evolved over a period of 2–3 million years as persistence hunters able to run for many hours without ingesting anything, even water. This ability as hunters was produced by humans used to a high-fat, high-protein diet with rather less carbohydrate than is used by modern endurance athletes. Are humans best adapted to running on fat and protein, rather than on carbohydrate, especially when doing that for which we seem especially well adapted – low-intensity exercise over many hours?

Finally, there is the realization that when athletes run relatively slowly in events lasting more than a few hours, fat metabolism is more than able to provide all the energy they need. Since the body fat stores are essentially unlimited, this means that athletes who are adapted to run on their fat stores can run without the need to continually top themselves up by eating and drinking repeatedly during exercise.

By avoiding repeated intakes of carbohydrate during exercise, fat-adapted athletes do not subject themselves to frequent fluctuations in blood glucose and insulin concentrations a few times every hour that they exercise. (The effects of such fluctuations on the emotional state of athletes during very prolonged exercise are not known.)

We are finally at the stage of realizing that dietary advice for athletes must be specific for each individual. Some will benefit from eating high-carbohydrate diets and by ingesting lots of carbs during exercise; others will benefit from the opposite – low-carbohydrate diets and the ingestion of fat and perhaps protein while avoiding carbohydrate during exercise.

I expect these ideas will become mainstream in the next 5–10 years. In the meantime, athletes must understand that (for some) taking the unthinkable step of switching to a low-carbohydrate, high-fat diet may do more for their performance in ultra-distance events than they could ever believe.

Professor Timothy Noakes

Tim Noakes is the Discovery Health Professor of Exercise and Sports Science at the University of Cape Town. He is a lifelong athlete and is rated an A1-scientist by the National Research Foundation.

In 2008, he was awarded the Order of Mapungubwe by the president of South Africa for 'excellent contribution to the field of sport and the science of physical exercise'. His book *Lore of Running* is considered the global 'bible' of running. He has been married to Marilyn Anne for 39 years, and they have two children, Travis and Candice.

Tim is the co-founder of the Sports Science Institute of South Africa, along with Springbok rugby icon, Morné du Plessis.

Woman Alone

An epic solo run, ride and paddle – circumnavigating the whole of South Africa over a distance of 6 772km – may seem like a foolhardy undertaking for any athlete, let alone a woman facing the elements on her own. Not so for Kim van Kets, who absolutely believes in the good karma of running with a smile on your face.

All you need is faith – and a pathologically positive attitude ...

In nearly 40 years on this planet, I have yet to experience anything to match the pure and unadulterated joy of running in some wild and beautiful place, preferably at sunrise, and knowing I have it all to myself. To revel in the beauty of nature, the strength of my limbs, lungs and heart and the matchless sense of freedom that this heady cocktail produces is an ecstasy second to none.

I have been running for more than half my life, often alone (initially because of snatching running moments while performing the juggling act of being a working mother), and later because I genuinely relish the solitude. Although I am not naïve about the fact that bad stuff happens to good people from time to time, it simply never occurs to me to be fearful about my safety on the trail.

This is partly because – in 22 years of running – I've only experienced absolute goodwill from everyone I've ever encountered. Having said this, I might add that if I feel a strong sense that I should not take a particular route I obey the prompting. I also never listen to an iPod while running, and I instinctively square my shoulders and jut my jaw to ensure I look confident, hardcore and alert. Well, as hardcore as possible, anyway, plus I have a plan combining speed, aggression and surprise. I don't expect that I will ever use it though.

When I set off from East London on 1 March 2011 to begin my 6 772km TRI THE BELOVED COUNTRY journey around the perimeter of South Africa, I took a Tazer with me to make my mother feel better ... I tossed it away after the first week, because the humidity on the Wild Coast rendered it useless, while the kindness of people rendered it unnecessary.

© JACQUES MARAIS

The amazing thing about running and cycling and paddling around the country is that one makes eye contact with everyone you see. You hear the voices, smell the cooking fires and really engage with everyone you pass. No whizzing past at 120km/h with windows closed. In 148 days on the road I never once experienced anything other than the most incredible hospitality, kindness, goodwill and genuine concern for my wellbeing from every South African I met.

I was provided with food, water, directions, encouragement, company, accommodation … an old man in the former Venda took my hand and told me I was as welcome in his village as if I were his own daughter. I was led for hours along the coast in the dark by two young Xhosa men concerned that I would get lost on the cliffs and not reach my destination. I was called a 'Ramkat' by an admiring, but toothless, Kalahari farmer. I was welcomed into farmhouses and given tea in huts. My experience was both humbling and exhilarating and has given me faith and a pathologically positive attitude towards my countrymen and women.

Somehow, even the potentially scary situations no longer hold any fear for me, yet so many women I met on my journey would look at me in amazement and say 'I would love to run, but I am absolutely terrified!' Of what exactly is hard to establish – there seems to be a vague, but universally common fear that other South Africans are waiting to pounce on them, ravage them and take all their stuff. And that the only way to avoid this is to stay inside behind 6-foot walls or locked in an SUV with the windows closed. Considering that my experience proved to be the complete opposite during 148 days on the road, don't you think it's worth the risk of going out to play?

For more info, visit www.kimvankets.com

© JACQUES MARAIS

Kim van Kets

Kim was born in the Eastern Cape. After matriculating, she studied Law at Stellenbosch University and at the University of Cape Town. She is currently self-employed as a legal consultant, corporate trainer, freelance writer and motivational speaker. She works just enough to stay out of the poorhouse and to afford to run in interesting places.

Despite opportunities to marry someone sensible, she is happily married to adventurer Peter van Kets (a 2x Atlantic Rower, the only African to have rowed solo across any ocean and one of the few South Africans to have trekked to the South Pole) and mother to six-year-old Hannah (who wants to be an extreme rock-climbing ballet dancer when she grows up).

Having established that running requires no particular skill other than the ability to endure monotony and discomfort, she has spent a lot of time on the road and trail, and has now been running for more than half her life. The Comrades and Two Oceans were followed by a number of extreme off-road races, including the Addo Elephant 100-Miler, 270km Transkei Ultra, 250km self-sufficiency desert stage race across the Kalahari (KAEM), and so on.

Her most recent and extreme epic was the 6 772km circumnavigation of South Africa in 2011, during which she covered the distance on foot, bike and kayak in 148 days.

To find out more about Kim's new book, email her at kimvankets@gmail.com

Getting Geared

Development in outdoor apparel is a nonstop and ongoing process, but the advantage of trail running as a sporting genre is that the technical gear required will not break the bank. Your most expensive purchase will be shoes, with a hydration pack, breathable top, shorts or tights, a wind-shell and a handful of additional items completing the outdoor ensemble. Obviously you need to compensate for seasonal changes, but throughout most of South Africa the weather will allow you to get away with minimal winter kit.

Summer and Winter Running – Gear Choices

Feet

- Lightweight, sturdy trail running shoes suited firstly to your feet and running style, and then to the environment and terrain you plan to run in. Extreme climates or biosystems may require add-ons such as snow- or sand gaiters, or other measures of protection against thorns, grass seeds and the like.
- Feet-dedicated, breathable socks; many athletes now prefer natural fibres such as mohair or wool. Waterproof sealskin socks may come in handy in wet weather.

Legs

- Summer – lightweight, quick-drying tights or shorts, with a key pocket and an inner mesh lining (compression inners are a relatively new addition).
- Thermal or lycra tights in colder climates; or you could opt for compression garments to assist in protecting you against the elements.

Upper Body

- Inner Layer – Lightweight, quick-drying, breathable and moisture-wicking long- or short-sleeved base layer top.
- Second Layer – Thermal, long-sleeved base layer garment for cold and potentially wet conditions.
- Third Layer – Mid-layer fleece with dynamic stretch for weather conditions when added thermal protection is required.
- Outer Layer – Lightweight, windproof, water-resistant, breathable outer shell for mild racing environments; waterproof, insulated jacket with hood, tape-sealed seams, draw cords and venting for more extreme situations.

Other

- Headwear – Quick-drying peak caps (with drop-down neck flaps and breathing panels for desert conditions); Buff's unique range of headwear, including thermal balaclavas, neck scarves, ear warmers and beanies for winter.
- Gloves – More and more trail runners head out wearing hand protection, both against the elements and to avoid terrain burn when taking a tumble.
- Eyewear – Quality, polarised lenses will protect your eyes from UV rays, dust, snow, sleet and branches; photo-chromatic lenses adjust as light conditions change.
- Wrist Computer or GPS – a non-negotiable item, especially on longer runs where you need to establish exact distance and time on trail; a heart-rate monitor function will allow you to pace yourself, while a GPS function means you won't get lost.
- Hydration Pack – Factors to consider include a stable body fit, ventilated back, water capacity, storage volume and the bite valve quality.

Trail & Event

4 Peaks Mountain Challenge
24km

Province Free State
Region Eastern Free State (Maloti Route)
Closest town Ficksburg
Trail destination Moolmanshoek Private Game Reserve
Series Pure Adventures
Contributed by Michael de Haast and Adrian Saffy

EXPERT'S VIEW

Adrian Saffy is an adventure racer, trail runner, mountain biker, event organiser and weekend warrior. He has competed in many multi-day expedition races around the world, and is considered to be one of the true off-road pioneers of outdoor sport.

My Run

'The event starts with a massive vertical ascent of about 800m over the first 4km; it is imperative that you pace yourself in the early stages of the race.'

Insider tips

Start slowly and make sure that you have good legs for the downhills, as this is where you can make up a lot of time. Take enough water in your bladder as there is no water on the route. (The route is not marked, but the fact that it's circular means you always keep the Lodge on your right-hand side.)'

Gear and apparel

'Sturdy trail shoes are an absolute must as you will be carrying a pack with emergency clothing and provisions. I personally prefer my Salomon XT Wings 2, but any shoe with good underfoot grip and protection will ensure solid traction on the rocks. Do not even think of entering this event without a fully rainproof jacket, extra dry clothing and a first-aid kit.'

Training and Pacing

'The 24km run is in effect equal to an ultra-marathon, so don't think you can take this one on if you have a tar-mac marathon under the belt. Even elite athletes may be out in the elements for four hours or more, so make sure you are 100% fit and injury-free before you tackle Thule 4 Peaks.'

THE DESTINATION This race exists to enlighten all those who think the Free State is flat. Think again, and challenge yourself at this unique, extreme mountain race. The picturesque Moolmanshoek Private Game Reserve hosts the Thule 4 Peaks Mountain Challenge, with the route traversing a course along the Witteberg Mountains watershed that shapes an unforgettable horseshoe enfolding the Moolmanshoek valley.

The event is hosted by the Nel family of Moolmanshoek, and many athletes make the race a weekend affair with family and friends. Breathtakingly beautiful mountain-bike rides, great hikes, bird hides, game viewing, horseback rides and 4X4 routes should not be missed.

THE TERRAIN The terrain is not for the faint-hearted, with hiking paths and animal track making up some of a 24km route that is mostly off-track. The route combines steep hills and descents with great ridge running, specifically between the second Pyramid and up to before the Jakobsberg descent. The course used during the event is not marked, but easy enough to navigate with marshals and clear signage at key junctions.

DIRECTIONS It is very easy to get there from Johannesburg (about 320km by road), Durban (450km by road) and Bloemfontein (250km by road). Very clear directions from all major centres can be obtained on the Moolnmanshoek website - www.moolmanshoek.co.za

ACCOMMODATION Most athletes make use of the camping facilities at the Langesnek Leadership Centre that is part of Moolmanshoek Private Game Reserve. The Lodge has 16 rooms that are superbly fitted out and ideal for those who are not into camping but still want to be part of the event.

FAST FACTS

Grading Difficult to extreme mountain terrain
Duration Anything from 3–9 hours
Configuration Circular route of 24km
Start point Main Lodge, Moolmanshoek
GPS co-ordinates 28°37′58″S, 27°59′56″E
Terrain A few animal tracks, but mainly no trail
Map Supplied by race organisers
Trail markings Unmarked route
Facilities Basic huts and tents along trails; water is available in the river year-round
Cell reception No coverage in valley, but some signal on higher ground
Beware Hydration is critical; keep a look-out for snakes and loose rocks
Time of year All year – summers are hot and dry, winter cold and beautiful
Local info www.moolmanshoek.co.za / Tel (+27 51) 933 2220 or 933 3729
More info www.pureadventures.co.za / Tel (+27 82) 566 5668

THE TRAIL The 4 Peaks is arguably the toughest 24km in South Africa, with a vertical accent of over 1800m, and it is the massive altitude gain over the first 4km that will get under your skin. Start off from the Main Lodge on a circular route, with four distinctive peaks lying in wait as you set off to traverse Moolmanshoek valley.

Slog into gravity onto the first Pyramid and then settle into your rhythm as you drop down steeply, resting your legs before negotiating the second Pyramid shortly thereafter. Follow the fence line to the top of this extremely technical section; an enjoyable and free-ranging ridge run awaits you as you continue towards the distant foot of Jakobsberg.

Start ascending again towards the halfway point at High Ridge and on towards the intimidating Visierskerf, the most challenging section of the race. Traverse along the back of this landmark, where the camber of the mountain and the extreme terrain here make it the undeniable crux of the event. Once around 'The Kerf', you will be faced by the highest point along the route at Sikonyela's Hat.

Get your breath back and concentrate along the slow descent (or rather fast if your legs are still in good shape) into the dongas below. Once through these erosion ruts, a short and relatively flat section will bang you back towards the starting point. The total distance may only be 24km, but you will most probably never again think of 24km in the same way.

GRADIENT PROFILE

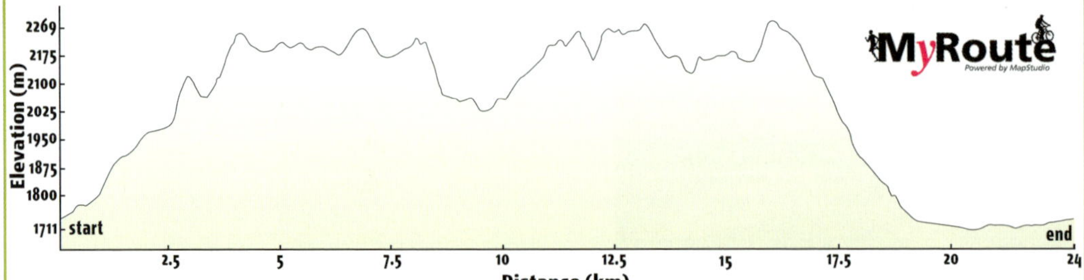

To view maps and gradient profiles go to **www.myroute.co.za**

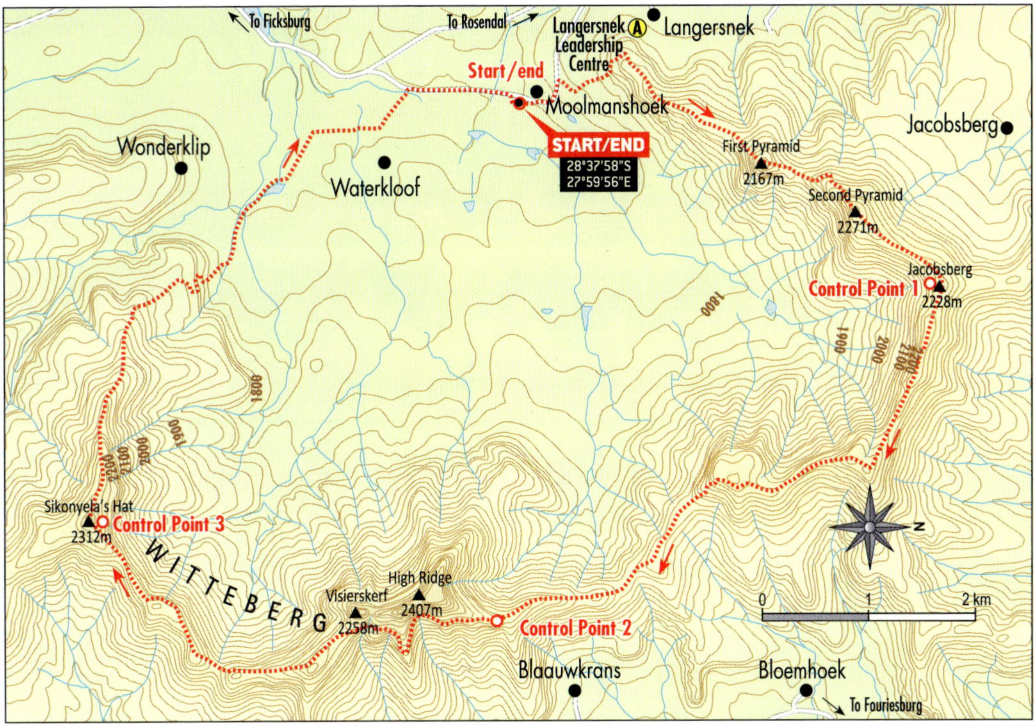

EVENT FACTS

Event name Thule 4 Peaks Mountain Challenge
Venue Moolmanshoek Private Nature Reserve
Distance from Bloemfontein / Johannesburg 250km / 320km
Time of year Mid-September
Entries Limited to 200 athletes; first come, first served
Enter as Solo
Cut-offs Will be enforced (runners to be briefed before the race)
Distances 24km
Average duration 5–9hrs
Entry info www.pureadventures.co.za

THE EVENT This is a family affair at a grand location catering for young and old, with everything from a kids' treasure hunt to game drives and horseback riding for those not participating in the race. A fun MTB race on the day after the event will furthermore showcase some of the most breathtaking scenery in South Africa.

Thule 4 Peaks is a self-supported and self-navigational race. The circular route makes it a good entry-level event, but do not be fooled – this is extreme mountain running and equivalent to an ultra-marathon. Also unique is the fact that Thule 4 Peaks is an unsupported race, with every athlete required to carry all the required safety gear and water.

Event Only

Addo Elephant Trail Runs
76km and 44km

Province Eastern Cape
Region Sundays River Valley
Closest town Start Kirkwood, finish Addo
Trail destination Addo Elephant National Park
Series Stand-alone event
Contributed by William Robinson and Laura Forster

THE DESTINATION Addo Elephant National Park – now the third largest national park in South Africa – has grown to conserve a wide-ranging and biodiverse landscape. The burgeoning 180 000ha conservation area encompasses a range of habitats, from the semi-arid Karoo veld near Darlington Dam to the rugged Zuurberg Mountains, the Sundays River valley and a section of the coastline between the Sundays and Bushman's River mouths.

The park also includes the Bird and St Croix island groups, and provides sanctuary to 500+ elephants, lion, buffalo, black rhino, spotted hyena, leopard, a variety of antelope and zebra species, as well as the unique and endemic Addo flightless dung beetle.

THE TERRAIN Singletrack trail and jeep tracks wind through the thick indigenous bush of the valleys, and glimpses of duiker, kudu, warthog and eland sustain you as you soak up the beautiful ache that exemplifies long-distance running. Completing the Addo Trail is an experience that will stay with you for a lifetime, a rare opportunity to immerse yourself in this magical region of the Eastern Cape.

Both distances offer runners a mixed bag of valley and mountain running, which naturally serves up some conversation-stopping ascents and reciprocally technical downhills. These are interspersed with long, flowing and beautifully runnable trail, traversing the broad fynbos-covered backs of the Zuurberg Mountains, and through the shady riverine forests hugging the valley floors.

Fast, fit runners will enjoy these sections and relish the true freedom of running. Underfoot, the runner experiences a mixture of rocky jeep track and smooth singletrack, with some dirt road running for good measure. Unless it's a drought year, wet feet are a fact of life on certain sections of the trail where streams are crossed along the route. With the race held during the late summer or early autumn, these are generally welcome chances to dip in and cool off before soldiering on.

DIRECTIONS Follow the N2 from Port Elizabeth towards Grahamstown, turning left onto Exit 761 (R335) towards Motherwell. Turn left again on St George Street (R335) and continue for around 50km to Addo Elephant National Park. GPS co-ordinates are as follows:

Addo Kabouga Gate:
33°22'39.18"S, 25°27'32.88"E
Zuurberg Mountain Village:
33°21'4.74"S, 25°44'40.62"E
Addo Rest Camp:
33°26'42.24"S, 25°44'44.28"E

ACCOMMODATION The national park itself boasts various accommodation options to suit just about any taste or budget, from caravans and safari-style tenting to self-catering chalets, guesthouses or luxury lodges. For more options, visit www.sanparks.org.za or www.kirkwood.co.za

EXPERT'S VIEW

William Robinson has won gold medals at provincial championships in road cycling and road running. He has represented South Africa at world championships in duathlon and trail running. Besides two wins in the Addo 76km, he has won several of the Cape classics including the Hout Bay Trail Challenge, the Table Mountain Challenge, and the Puffer.

My Shoe

Brand ~ Montrail
Model ~ Mountain Masochist
Rating ~ Lightweight performance trail shoe which balances excellent durability and protection

GRADIENT PROFILE

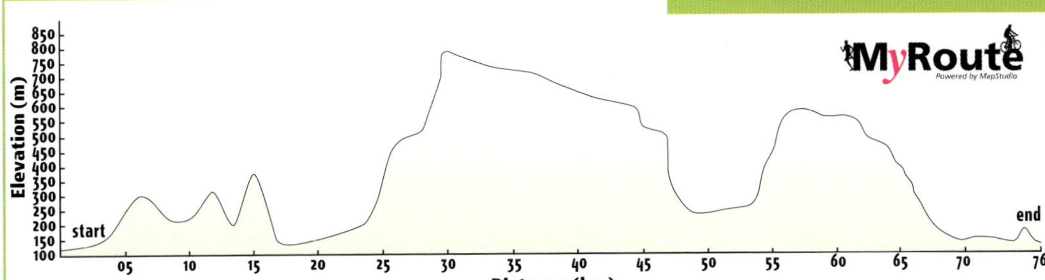

To view maps and gradient profiles go to **www.myroute.co.za**

FAST FACTS

Grading Difficult to extreme
Duration 7–15hrs (76km), 4–12hrs (44km)
Configuration Point to point; marked and fixed route
Start point Addo's Kabouga Gate
GPS co-ordinates 33°22'39.18"S, 25°27'32.88"E
Terrain Rugged jeep track; some singletrack
Map www.extrememarathons.com/addo
Access requirements Route restricted to event only
Trail markings Chevron tape, metal boards and orange stickers
Facilities Refreshment points every 8–11km
Cell reception Pockets of coverage along the route
Beware Extreme temperatures; no water between checkpoints; snakes
Time of year March
Local info www.sanparks.org.za
More info Website – www.extrememarathons.com / Tel (+27 83) 309 7755 or (+27 44) 690 3420

THE TRAIL The hiking trails within Addo have been designed with hikers in mind, and include a one-hour Novice Trail as well as an intermediate four-hour hike to a natural pool on the Doringnek Trek. The two-day Alexandria Hiking Trail is a favourite with overnight hikers, and starts in a magical coastal forest alive with turacos and ancient podocarpus yellowwood trees. You will experience everything from sand dunes to sea cliffs along the route, with a range of fascinating archaeological sites to explore along the way to the finish at Langvlakte Valley.

THE EVENT With only 300 places on offer, this is not a race many people will experience in their lifetime. The lucky runners who get their names on the list start off amid the citrus orchards of Kirkwood, from where they progress into dense riverine forest and sub-alpine ridges characterising the Zuurberg section of Addo.

Both events start – usually at 06:00 sharp – at the new Kabouga Gate of Addo Elephant National Park, then wind their way over the hills and into the Sundays River Valley. The shorter 44km run meanders up a steep gravel track to finish at the picturesque Zuurberg Mountain Village, while the 76km runners continue into Addo itself to finish at the Main Rest Camp.

Enjoy the undulating jeep tracks in the cool of the morning. After about 25km (12km on the short route), you reach a series of drifts which, depending on how much rain has fallen, may hold a substantial amount of water. (None of these 20m submerged sections are more than knee-deep though). Some may be traversed with a bit of bundu-bashing, but keeping your feet dry is hardly worth the effort.

Once you clock in at the 32km mark (long route), you'll tackle the first major climb of the day, and it is a mean one. The jeep track rises straight up out of the valley, and even the most stubborn runners will be sensible and walk this. The main pitch is followed by a short contour which provides some respite, with the next hairpin signalling the start of the final 5km drag to the top of the plateau.

EVENT FACTS

Event name Addo Elephant 76km / 44km Trail Runs
Venue Addo Elephant National Park
Distance from Port Elizabeth 80km
Time of year March
Enter as Individual
Distances 76km / 44km
Average duration 7–15hrs (76km route)
Entry info www.extrememarathons.com

This is very taxing, but once you reach the top you have 15km of relatively easy running and with uninterrupted panoramas all round. After a steep descent down to a farm, you hit single-track for the first time as you begin the second major ascent of the day along the horse trail through a forested kloof towards Zuurberg Mountain Village.

When the terrain gets steeper, the zigzags begin, winding up until eventually you pop out above the tree line and into the lodge. The 44km runners are now done, but the full 76km route continues onto 19km of gravel road en route to the Addo Rest Camp. A gentle cruise down Zuurberg Pass is rather fun, but the final few kilometres are a slog. Be ready for one final sting in the tail on the approach to the finish along a few switchbacks through the dense Addo thickets.

Although the trail is clearly marked, the stunning views, your immersion in the bush, and the interaction with fauna and flora will offer welcome distractions. Every 8–11km you will also reach welcome refreshment stations, stocked with bottled water, energy drinks, cola, tea, coffee, soup, boiled potatoes, jam and peanut butter sandwiches, fruit, and sweets to help you on your way.

This being a wilderness run, safety is your first responsibility – stay on the marked route at all times, carry a space blanket and a whistle, and pack a torch if you expect to be on the route after 18:00. Sweepers and marshals with radio comms will ensure that everyone has a safe and enjoyable run.

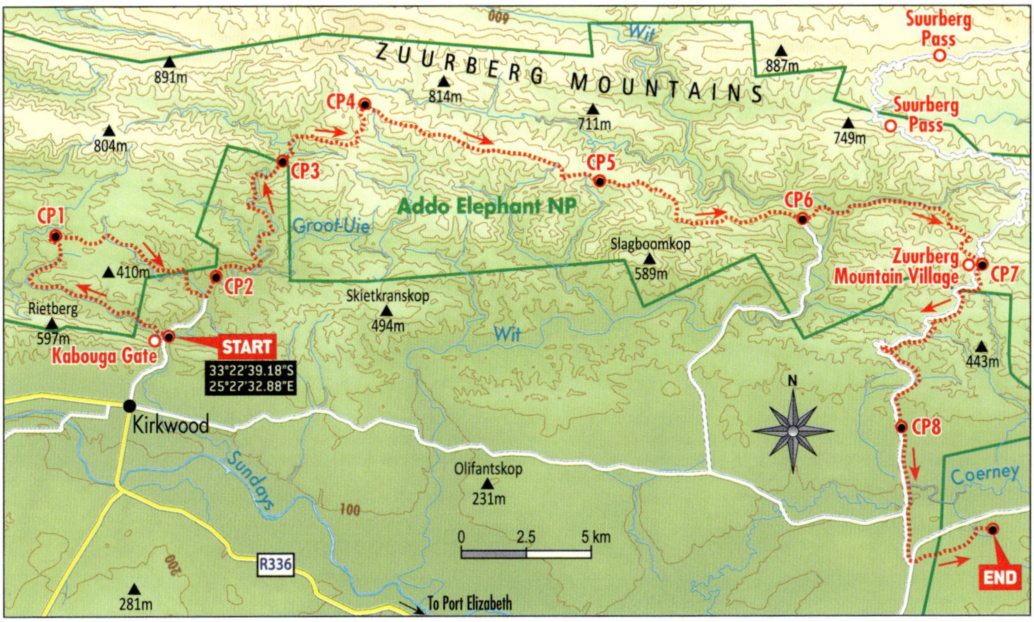

AfricanX Trail Run
32, 33 and 25km (90km)

Province Western Cape
Region Overberg
Closest town Kleinmond
Trail destination Overstrand and Kogelberg Biosphere
Series Stand-alone event
Contributed by Stillwater Sports and Dawid Visser

THE DESTINATION The small coastal town of Kleinmond is situated inside a UNESCO-declared biosphere about 90km east of Cape Town between Betty's Bay and Hermanus. The 100 000ha UNESCO-registered Kogelberg Biosphere Reserve is home to the most complex biodiversity on our planet. The Cape Fold Mountains and highland valleys are home to over 1 880 different species of plants, of which 77 species occur nowhere else on earth but in Kogelberg!

THE TERRAIN The three stages of the AfricanX Trail Run include all the various terrain options that the Overstrand and Kogelberg Biosphere have to offer. The terrain varies from beach running to spectacular hidden singletrack high in the Kogelberg Mountains, interlinked with a variety of running surfaces including jeep tracks and even the odd stretch of hard-pack roads, as well as a short section of district road to satisfy those with more of a road-running orientation.

DIRECTIONS Follow the N2 from Cape Town past Somerset West and over Sir Lowry's Pass. Just after descending the Houw Hoek Pass, take the R43/Hermanus/Kleinmond turn-off. Continue towards Hermanus, past the Shell Garage until you see the Kleinmond turn-off to your right. Turn right past Arabella and continue towards Kleinmond. As you approach Kleinmond (GPS **34°20'15.7"S, 19°02'26.2"E**), you will see the Race Village on your left-hand side.

ACCOMMODATION When booking your race you can choose to organise your own accommodation or opt for the race organizer's tented accommodation that will then be included in your race cost. As you start and end in Kleinmond every day, your accommodation, meals and entertainment will remain in the same place for the duration of the race.

If you choose to enter the race without accommodation, it is recommended to contact the Hangklip-Kleinmond Tourism Bureau at 028 271 5657 or visit www.ecoscape.org.za

THE TRAIL With the exception of Cape Nature Trails, the two beach sections and the boardwalk and beach path in Kleinmond, the ProNutro AfricanX Trail Run routes go through privately owned property and non-commercialised MTO areas which are closed to the public for everyday running.

The first day's 32km starts in Betty's Bay, and after a beach run to warm up the legs, the route begins with the infamous Harold Porter climb! The trail takes runners into the mountains where a mind-blowing 6km singletrack awaits. This trail will include technical uphill sections, fynbos and even a canopy run through an indigenous forest in the Cape Nature Area before descending back down towards Kleinmond. The stage will be concluded by a 7km footpath along the ocean which leads runners back to the finish at the Kleinmond Day Camp.

Day two was traditionally the 'marathon' day of the AfricanX and, although the distance has been reduced to 33km, it remains the longest stage of the event. Runners should prepare themselves for the toughest climbs of the event through the beautiful MTO forest areas of the region. The day begins on Honingklip farm and follows the route through the MTO forest area and onto the hiking and horse trails at Arabella. After the descent, runners will return along the 6km beach run to the finish.

Day three starts at Arabella and this 25km stage will be the easiest of the race. Runners will enjoy magnificent views of the ocean, valley and the town of Kleinmond. After the mountain running, the trail starts heading down towards Kleinmond via one of the largest protea farms in the country, offering the runners a special experience.

EXPERT'S VIEW

Dawid Visser is a Cape Town-based trail runner. In 2011 Visser and team-mate Rohan Kennedy walked off with the title of ProNutro AfricanX Trail Run men's winners.

My run

'I have run various races, road and off-road, and this is one of the most enjoyable of all. Although it's an off-road race the terrain caters for every type of runner so even the "roadies" can enjoy it. There are some very technical areas, but luckily there are also a few gravel roads to cancel out the pain and enjoy the scenery.'

Insider tips

'The biggest lesson I learned in this race is to keep hydrated. Run with a hydration pack from day one, and the extra weight of fluids that you will consume will help in recovery and you will feel 100 times better than the person trying to save weight on the first day. It's multi-stage racing; think ahead to the next day!'

Gear and apparel

'I know that finances are tight, but paying for physio or being booked off due to a twisted ankle will be way more costly – mentally and financially. Get some trail shoes; believe me, they make a difference and your feet will thank you after the first day! Good grip and cushioning are important in trail shoes. I prefer lower profile so that I can feel the terrain, while my AfricanX partner Rohan enjoys extra cushioning more. Test all your gear before the race to make sure that nothing irritates you, because it will just get worse as the days get longer.'

Training and pacing

'If you feel that you are running too hard on day one, you probably are, so hold back and enjoy the view. Even the top guys walk on certain hard parts so don't feel bad to catch the odd walking spirit. Enjoy, enjoy, enjoy! This is the main aim of the game. Don't get caught up in the racing, but stick to your own game plan. I learned the first year that if you don't run at your own pace you will pay the next day – it's not a one-day 10km race.'

FAST FACTS

Grading Intermediate to difficult
Duration Three days
Configuration Each stage will follow a cloverleaf format point to point
Start point Betty's Bay
GPS co-ordinates (Race Village) 34°20'15.7"S, 19°02'26.2"E
Terrain Singletrack and jeep tracks, beaches and district roads
Map www.stillwatersports.com
Access requirements Most sections of the route are restricted to the race only; if you plan to scout the area, obtain your permits when you enter these areas
Trail markings Temporary markings only – red arrow on yellow background
Facilities Exact locations of support stations are announced prior to stages
Cell reception Yes
Beware Slippery and loose rocks; heat and snakes during summer; sloping shores and strong currents during high tide on the beach run
Time of year Middle of March for the race; all year round for leisure running
Local info website www.ecoscape.org.za / Kleinmond Tourism, Tel (+27 28) 271 5657
More info website www.stillwatersports.com / Tel (+27 86) 138 3591

THE EVENT The ProNutro AfricanX Trail Run presented by New Balance is a three-day stage race. Taking place in and around the picturesque town of Kleinmond, teamwork forms an essential part of this trail run, as participants will have to rely on each other's experience and expertise in order to complete the route.

Teams of two will be seen battling it out on a route varying from 25km to 35km each day. The three routes have been planned in such a way that the participants will have the opportunity to tackle a different breathtaking scenic route each day, allowing them to enjoy the full diversity of the world-renowned Kogelberg Biosphere. This trail run stage race will follow a cloverleaf format, which means that runners will finish in Kleinmond on each of the three days.

Entries are limited to 300 teams (600 runners). Entries open 12 months prior to the event and close two weeks before the event (that's if the entry limit has not yet been met).

EVENT FACTS

Event name ProNutro AfricanX Trail Run
Venue Kleinmond Main Beach Day Camp
Distance from Cape Town 80km
Time of year Mid-March
Cut-offs 17:00 each day, but will only be enforced in case of extreme weather or health conditions
Enter as Teams of two
Distances 32, 33 and 25km (90km over three days)
Average duration 2.5 hours for the leaders, up to 7 hours for the back markers each day
Entry info www.stillwatersports.com

GRADIENT PROFILES

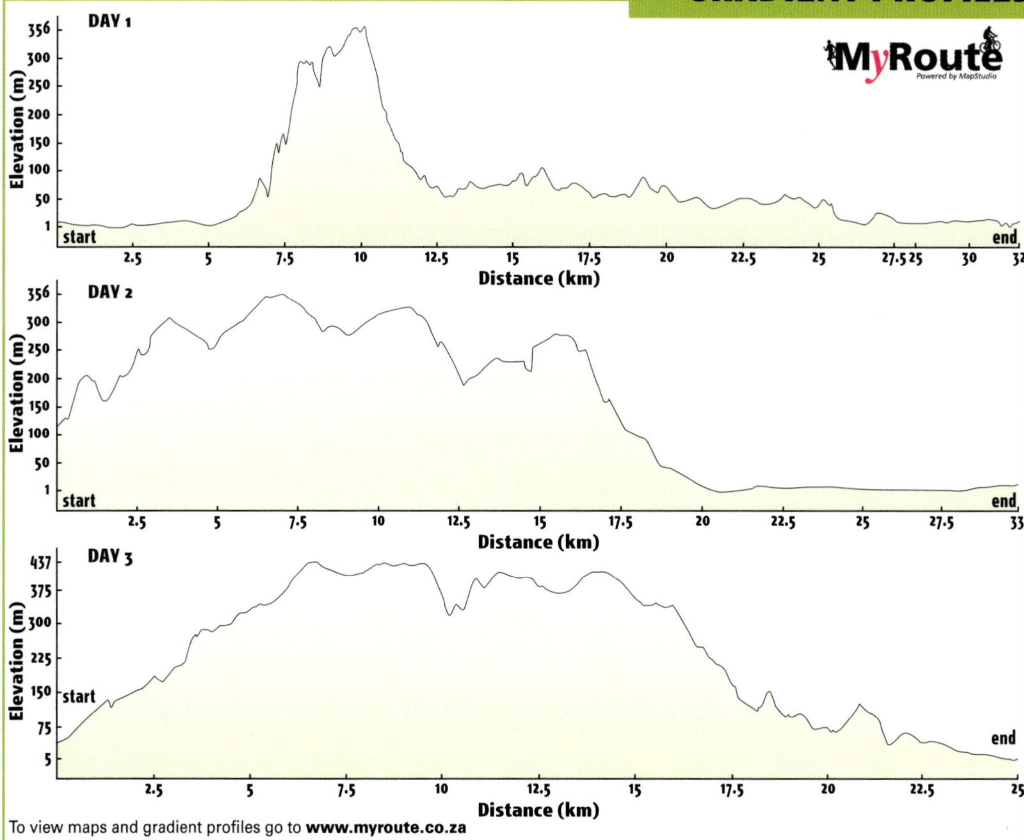

To view maps and gradient profiles go to **www.myroute.co.za**

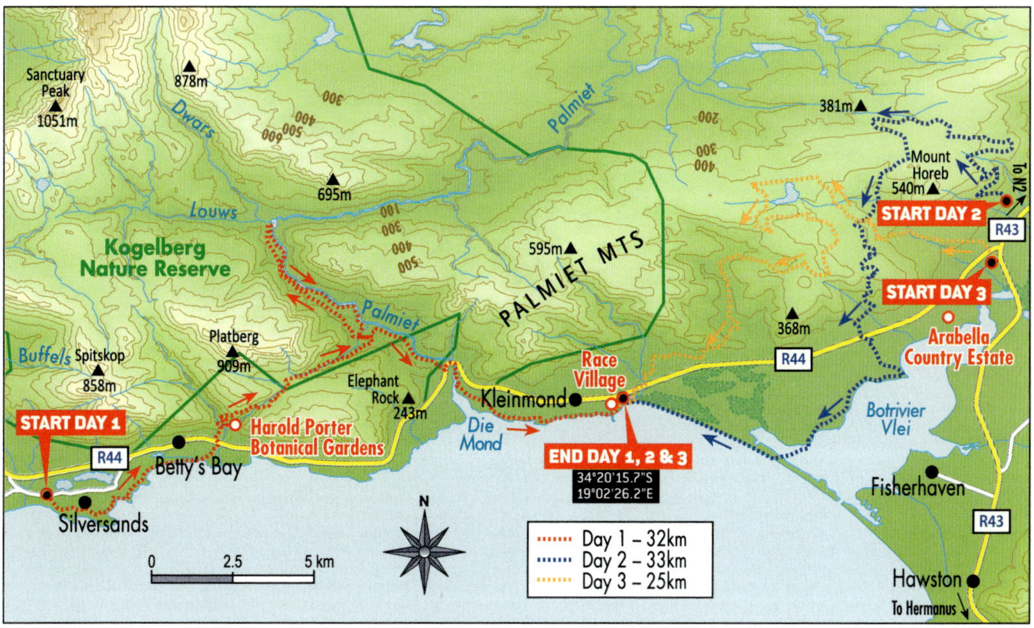

Baviaanskloof Trail Run

Trail & Event

40km

Province Eastern Cape
Region Tsitsikamma and Baviaanskloof
Closest towns Willowmore, Patensie
Trail destination Baviaanskloof Nature Reserve
Series Stand-alone event
Contributed by Peter Marriott

EXPERT'S VIEW

Peter Marriott has completed three Ironman, three Comrades, four Rhodes Trail Runs, has provincial colours for triathlon and duathlon and national colours for duathlon, and finished twelfth in the 2009 Baviaanskloof Trail Run.

My run

'To describe the route profile is not difficult, but running it is very difficult; suffice it to say that after a short, sharp climb early on to wipe the sleep out of our eyes there is a very steep climb to the plateau, although I can't recall ever reaching anything remotely plateau-like. The climb was over rocky, very uneven and unstable scree, or it could have been that by then my oxygen-deprived legs were also contributing to my instability. Then there is a steep descent through the bush – literally.

'The joy of finishing the run, showing off my new battle scars and sharing war stories with fellow trail runners was awesome, but being part of the Baviaanskloof Trail Run, to my mind, priceless'.

© JACQUES MARAIS

THE DESTINATION The Baviaanskloof Nature Reserve, a World Heritage Site and part of the Baviaanskloof Mega-reserve, lies roughly 120km west of Port Elizabeth and is one of the largest wilderness conservation areas in the country. Seven out of the eight South African biomes are present in the 260 000ha reserve and over 500 000ha conservancy area. The 'Valley of Baboons' is a true wilderness, and wildlife residing in the area includes baboon, bushbuck, tortoise, kudu, bush pig, caracal, mountain zebra, leopard, black rhino and Cape buffalo.

THE TERRAIN Hemmed in by the Kouga and Baviaanskloof mountain ranges, this unspoiled valley awaits exploration. With rugged rocky mountain peaks dropping steeply into ravines forested with lush riverine vegetation, fynbos plateaus, semi-arid plains, waterfalls, caves and precipitous mountain passes, the ever-changing scenery is spectacular.

The gnarly twist and swerve of the R332 traverses the valley between Willowmore in the west and Patensie in the east. A network of hiking trails and 4X4 routes operated by private farms criss-crosses the valley.

DIRECTIONS The recommended route to Geelhoutbos is via Willowmore. Follow the N9 south from Willowmore and take the R332 turn-off to Nuwekloofpas, Rietrivier, Studtis and Sandvlakte to Geelhoutbos.

Access into the Baviaanskloof from Port Elizabeth is along the R331 through Hankey and Patensie.
As it is recommended to approach Geelhoutsbos from the Willomore side if you do not have a 4X4 vehicle you can either head via Steytlerville to Willowmore, or, alternatively via Kareedouw, Avontuur and Uniondale to Willowmore. GPS co-ordinates are as follows:

Race start: **33°36'46.0"S, 24°15'26.0"E**
R332 turn-off from N9: **33°19'14.6"S, 23°27'37.8"E**
Eastern entrance: **33°44'25.6"S, 24°36'52.2"E**

ACCOMMODATION There are several accommodation options within the Baviaanskloof area, ranging from self-catering farm cottages to camp sites, catering for all budgets and comfort levels. Spending time at Rooihoek and other hideaway spots along the way is a must. Contact Baviaans Tourism on (+27 44) 923 1702 or www.baviaans.co.za

FAST FACTS

Grading Intermediate to extreme
Duration 3.5–7 hours (40km)
Configuration Circular
Start point Geelhoutbos
GPS co-ordinates 33°36′46.0″S, 24°15′26.0″E
Terrain Rugged jeep track to no track
Map www.baviaansrun.za.net
Access requirements Route restricted to race
Trail markings Flags
Facilities Runners are expected to be self-sustaining; minimal support will be provided en route
Cell reception None
Beware Extreme heat, dangerous fauna
Time of year Mid-September
Local info www.baviaans.co.za

THE TRAILS The many hiking trails and 4X4 routes in the Baviaanskloof Wilderness will keep you running for at least a week. The terrain is rough and the going very tough, especially in summer when the temperatures soar to the high thirties.

On the 24km multi-day Rietrivier Hiking Trail (www.makkedaat.co.za) you can spend the night in a cave; from Doringkloof (www.doringkloof.co.za) a 4X4 route takes you right over the Kouga Mountains and Bo-kloof's Waterkloof Hiking Trail is a short scramble, but the scenery is spectacular and you can always follow up with their 16km Uitslag 4X4 route (www.baviaans.co.za/bokloof/).

GRADIENT PROFILE

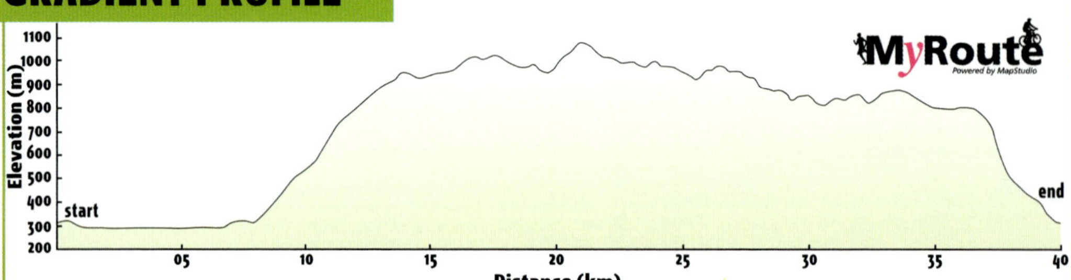

To view maps and gradient profiles go to **www.myroute.co.za**

EVENT FACTS

Event name BaviaanskloofTrail Run
Venue Baviaanskloof Nature Reserve
Distance from Port Elizabeth 175km
Time of year Mid-September
Enter as Solo
Cut-offs 4.5hrs at 25km; 7hrs to qualify as a finisher
Distance 40km
Average duration 3.5–7hrs
Entry info www.baviaansrun.za.net

THE EVENT The Baviaanskloof Trail Run was designed for seriously adventurous trail runners who want to take on this unspoiled, rugged terrain and experience the unique privilege of running with legends of the animal kingdom such as the Cape cobra, black rhino and Cape buffalo. The entire route is in a section of the wilderness area of the Baviaanskloof Nature Reserve that is closed to the public. There is no access at all to this area outside of race day.

The race starts and finishes at Geelhoutbos on the western side of the Baviaanskloof. The route is approximately 40km and covers some of the roughest, most rugged, inhospitable and unforgiving terrain in the Baviaanskloof. This punishing and demanding route will take runners through a remote wilderness inhabited by two of Africa's wildest and most fearsome wild animals – the Cape buffalo and the black rhino – so this run is not for the nervous or faint-hearted. This is potentially a dangerous environment.

The run has a high point of 1 122m and a cumulative ascent of over 1 400m. There is a seven-hour cut-off to complete the course and to qualify as a finisher. There is also a mandatory cut-off at the top Check Point (approximately 25km into the race) of 4.5 hours. Runners who arrive at the Check Point after the cut-off must abandon the race.

The race is limited to 100 runners and places are allocated on a first come, first served basis. It is not recommended for unfit runners or for those who are not prepared to cover rough terrain. Sections of the route are on uneven ankle twisters and very rocky terrain.

The first stage is along a twin track through riverine forest, and the second stage takes the runners over a very rough twin track up a reasonably decent climb that generally sees all the runners reduced to a walk. The third section follows a ridge and is a combination of rough twin track and no track at all, and the fourth and final section drops the runners from the ridge sharply down to the bottom of the kloof. This is the notorious scree section.

On completion of three Baviaanskloof Trail Runs a runner will be recognised as a 'Legend of the Baviaanskloof' and receives a very special, significant and unique memento of the achievement: a framed limited edition, numbered and signed Alan Ainslie print of a black rhino. Each presentation has a plaque identifying it as a 'Legend' award.

© JACQUES MARAIS

Berg & Beach Trail Run

23km and 27km

Trail & Event

Province Western Cape
Region Overberg
Closest town Hermanus
Trail destination Fernkloof and Walker Bay nature reserves
Series Quantum Country Classics
Contributed by Ugene Nel

© JACQUES MARAIS

EXPERT'S VIEW

Ugene Nel is an adventure racer, trail runner, mountain biker and event organiser, sponsored by First Ascent (www.firstascent.co.za), SPUR (www.spur.co.za) and VIBRAM (www.vibram.co.za). He has competed in multi-day expedition races around the world, and has completed the gruelling 2 400km 'Freedom Challenge MTB Race across South Africa' three times.

My run

'Day one starts with a slight downhill before the sand-stone track spills out onto the flat, hard beach. One can see the end from the start – if you get my drift. If the lagoon mouth is open, it makes for an exciting crossing, 5km from the finish. The mountain trail of Fernkloof Nature Reserve is solid underfoot with ever-changing vistas – bliss out on the views.'

Insider tips

'Take drinking water on both days. There is none on the beach, although there may be some fresh streams in the mountain.'

Gear and apparel

'Some folk run in barefoot shoes, but I prefer my Salomon XA Pro 3D trail shoes on Day 2. A 10-litre running pack should give you enough carry capacity and will fit your compulsory safety gear.'

THE DESTINATION Hermanus has the status of being the best land-based whale-watching destination in the world, with southern right whales visiting Walker Bay from June through to December. The town is also blessed with rugged mountain ranges, the pristine Klein River Lagoon estuary, fantastic beaches and plenty of other outdoor adventure activities.

THE TERRAIN Walker Bay stretches from the Klein River estuary to De Kelders at Gansbaai. This section is about 1 000ha in size and has a coastline of 17km featuring a long beach, known as Die Plaat, with white sands and rocky limestone outcrops. Immediately northwest of the reserve is the scenic Klein River Lagoon, with Fernkloof Nature Reserve blanketing 1 800ha along the adjacent Kleinrivier mountain ranges rising above Hermanus.

DIRECTIONS Follow the N2 from Cape Town past Somerset West and over Houw Hoek Pass, then take the R43 to Hermanus. Once in town, look out for Fir Avenue (GPS **34°23'52.1"S, 19°15'59.7"E**) on your left; the trail head is at the entrance to Fernkloof Nature Reserve.

ACCOMMODATION Accommodation options can be found at www.hermanus.co.za

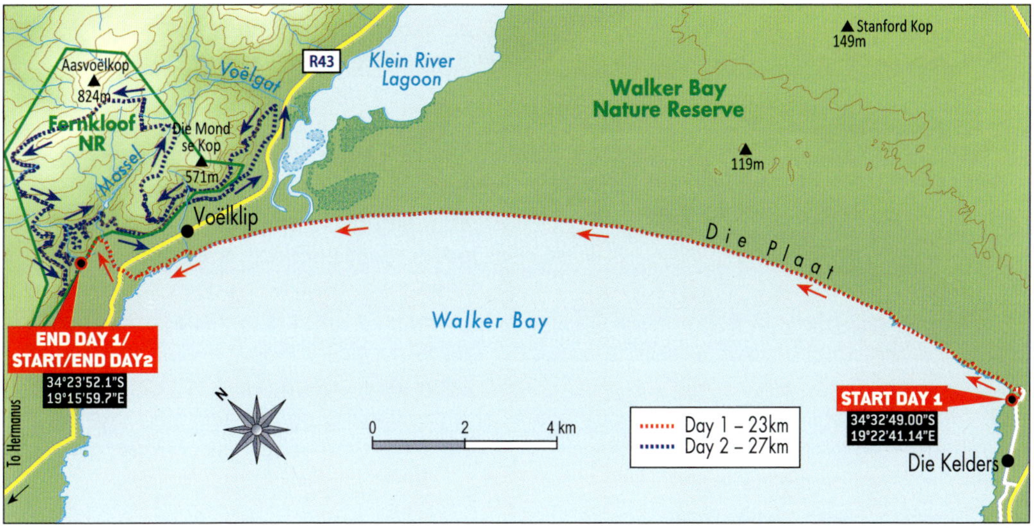

GRADIENT PROFILES

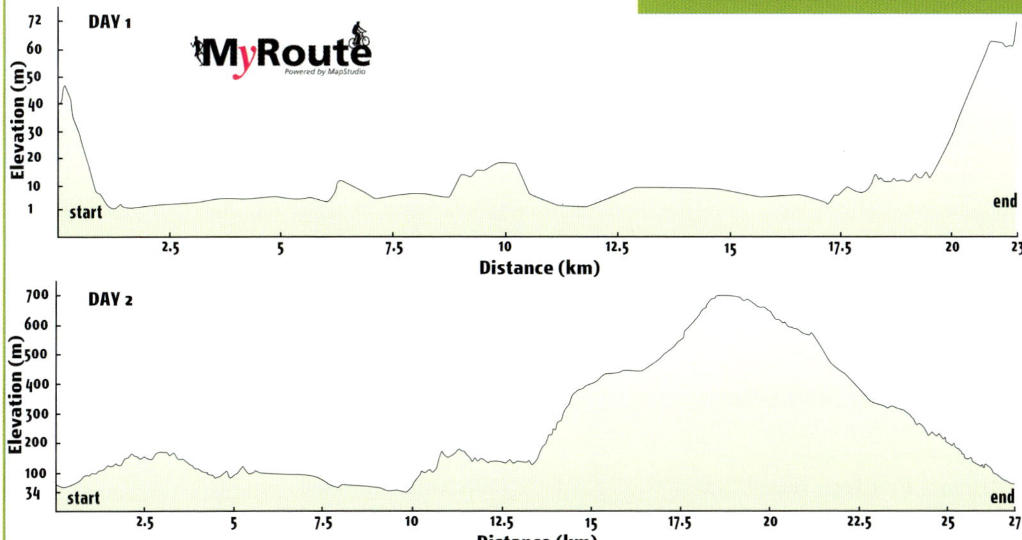

To view maps and gradient profiles go to **www.myroute.co.za**

FAST FACTS

Grading Intermediate to difficult
Duration 6–8hrs over two days during the race, or your own time
Configuration Various return or circular options
Start point Die Kelders
GPS co-ordinates 34°32'49.00"S, 19°22'41.14"E
Terrain Gravel roads, lots of singletrack, beach and river mouth crossing
Map Available at Fernkloof Nature Reserve Office
Access requirements Free, but please make a donation
Trail markings Some trail markings on wooden stakes
Facilities NO water tables during the race; full ablutions at start
Cell reception Yes, except behind mountain at furthest point
Beware The weather can change in an instant; watch out for fog
Time of year October for race; otherwise choose between winter rains or summer winds
Local info www.fernkloof.com or www.hermanus.co.za
More info www.quantumadventures.co.za / Tel (+27 82) 658 3078

THE TRAIL Fernkloof Nature Reserve boasts a network of more than 60km of trails, providing runners with ample opportunity to enjoy the amazing mountain ranges. Various trails offer unequalled views over Walker Bay, the Hemel en Aarde Valley and Maanskynbaai.

THE EVENT The Berg & Beach Trail Run must surely rate as one of the most scenic trail runs in the country. Day 1 follows a 23km coastal route through Walker Bay Nature Reserve, followed on Day 2 by a 27km mountain run in Fernkloof Nature Reserve. Entries are restricted to 200 runners.

The first day's 23km run starts along an old 4X4 track along the cliffs above the bay for 4km before dropping onto the beach. After a few rocky sections, the beach opens up and runners will be wedged between the dunes and the tide on hard-packed sand. A two-hour tide window ensures ample time even for slower runners to beat the high tide, with a good chance of spotting both whales and the endangered African black oystercatcher en route. Unlike many other beaches, this one is flat with hardly any camber, making running an absolute pleasure.

Runners may have to cross the river mouth (safety marshals and inflatable boats will be in place), and must therefore ensure they have a small dry bag to keep phones, etc. dry while crossing. The run continues along the beach for 3km, then follows the cliff path and the course of the Mossel River to the finish back at Fernkloof.

The 27km mountain run on Day 2 starts along a short dirt road, then bangs onto a superb singletrack hiking trail for 99% of the remainder. The first 10km sees quite a bit of climbing, but mainly follows the contour line to the first checkpoint 6km from the start. You then ascend via ravines thick with indigenous forest, before contouring for the next 4km to the famed 'switchbacks'. This short, steep section will reward you with spectacular views of Hermanus and Walker Bay.

EVENT FACTS

Event name Berg & Beach Trail Run
Venue Fernkloof Nature Reserve
Distance from Cape Town 127km
Time of year Beginning of October
Enter as Solo
Cut-offs Will be enforced – runners to be briefed before the race
Distances 23km and 27km
Average duration 2–3hrs and 3–4hrs
Entry info www.quantumadventures.co.za

Braamfontein Spruit

18km

Trail Only

Province Gauteng
Region Johannesburg
Suburb From Emmarentia to Sunninghill
Closest town Johannesburg
Trail destination Braamfontein Spruit
Contributed by Lisa de Speville

THE DESTINATION The Braamfontein Spruit – or just 'The Spruit' in local lingo – is the first place to head if you're looking for a long, local trail run; but remember to invite friends along if you plan to run outside of the Emmarentia Dam and Johannesburg Botanical Gardens area (these two spots together are affectionately known as Emmies).

Emmies is the southernmost point for Spruit activities. It's a hive of activity over the weekends with runners, walkers, mountain bikers, dog walkers and picnickers dotting the paths and open lawns. A little to the north, Delta Park is a substantial 104ha of woodland and grassland. This too is a popular spot, especially for runners, bikers and dog walkers. The trails linking these two large park areas and everything onwards, heading north, are a trail runner's playground.

The Spruit is patrolled daily by mounted River Rangers (www.riverrangers.org.za). They observe and report on environmental issues like sewerage spills, illegal dumping, littering, water pollution and informal settlements. They also notify authorities of fallen trees, fires, flood damage, the spread of invasive vegetation and the illegal pumping of water out of local rivers.

Keeping safety first, always aim to run with two or more friends, especially on the section after Craighall, which is less utilised than the Emmies and Delta sections. Leave valuables behind and only use the trails in daylight. Politely move over for bikers.

THE TERRAIN If you run north, the trail has a slight downhill gradient as it follows the river. The trail is well used and it offers easy running throughout; there are few places to stub your toes. The trail mostly keeps to the Spruit. It winds through open lawns and grassland and it is tree-lined and shaded for much of the total distance.

DIRECTIONS Hop onto the trail at any number of access points. Parking is your deciding factor. Primary locations are:

Johannesburg Botanical Gardens – any of the parking areas; we recommend the parking area off Olifants Road, near the Emmarentia Dam wall

Delta Park – there's parking outside the Environmental Centre; access the entrance to the park at the end of Road No. 3, Victory Park

Sandton Field and Study Centre – Louise Avenue, Parkmore (the entrance is closest to the corner of 14th Street)

Riverside Shopping Centre – corner of Cambridge Road and Bryanston Drive, Bryanston

The Trail Head

Like a hop-on, hop-off bus route, you can join and leave The Spruit at any point along its length. If you run the whole route from the southernmost tip of Emmies (near the Judith Road / Beyers Naude intersection) to Witkoppen, you're looking at an 18km route.

FAST FACTS

Grading Easy
Duration As you wish; the A to B route from Emmies to Witkoppen Road is around 18km
Configuration Circular routes within the parks; A to B or out and back
Start point Various – anywhere along the length of the trail
GPS co-ordinates 26°09'4.80"S, 28°00'9.48"E (parking at the Johannesburg Botanical Gardens)
Terrain Smooth, easy-going singletrack; flat running
Map Marked with red dots (hiking trail) in a regular street mapbook; various available online
Access requirements Open to everyone; no fees
Trail markings Signboards indicating the sections of the Gardens
Facilities Toilet facilities at the Johannesburg Botanical Gardens (near the dam), Delta Park Environmental Centre, and shopping centres like Riverside (corner Cambridge Road and Bryanston Drive, Bryanston)
Cell reception Throughout
Beware Be careful if crossing the Spruit after it has rained; although vagrants usually pose no threat, bike hijackings are not uncommon
Time of year All year
More info www.jhbcityparks.com (Johannesburg Botanical Gardens and Delta Park Environmental Centre)

THE TRAIL In some places there are trails on both sides of the river, but in general the trail lies to the left of the river as you follow it. Heading north, the route has a lovely, slightly downhill gradient. If you run south, towards Emmarentia, you're in for a little less freewheeling. There are very few hills in either direction – humps really, not hills.

The most popular section is between Emmarentia and Craighall (where the trail crosses Jan Smuts Avenue). Here you'll see many other runners and bikers.

The trail is very straightforward and there are few options so you can't get lost, but there is one tricky spot. Heading north, after crossing Jan Smuts Avenue at Craighall, you'll pass Rattray's Weir and then the bottom of Old Parktonians Sports Club. The trail here is river left. You'll come to an area with a big grassy uphill (and power lines, leading on to Republic Road) to your left with a fenced-off house and dead-end ahead. Take a trail that leads to a river-crossing point. It's rocky here and, depending on the water level, you can make it across without getting your feet wet.

Now, running on river right, you'll edge away from the river, which flows through gated, private property. You'll run uphill and then downhill, approaching a palisade fence surrounding a grassy area (the road here is Iona Drive). Walk along the fence to the right and go through the pedestrian gate. This trail leads you straight into the trees – follow the trail to the left, next to the little stream. This section, with its bike jumps, is well used by bmx-ers. This little stream meets the Spruit after about 250m. Cross the Spruit (rocky crossing) and get back onto the trail on river left. From here the route is straightforward again.

Additional running options include a loop on the many trails within the Johannesburg Botanical Gardens (Emmies) and a loop within Delta Park. If you're really into exploring, run the Spruit from the top of Albert's Farm on the southern side of Northcliff, in the suburb of Greymont. Here you're on the Montgomery Spruit, which joins the Braamfontein Spruit before Rustenburg Road.

GRADIENT PROFILE

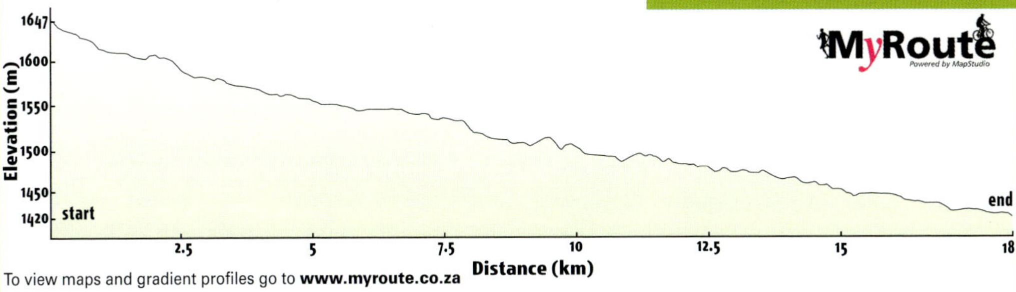

To view maps and gradient profiles go to **www.myroute.co.za**

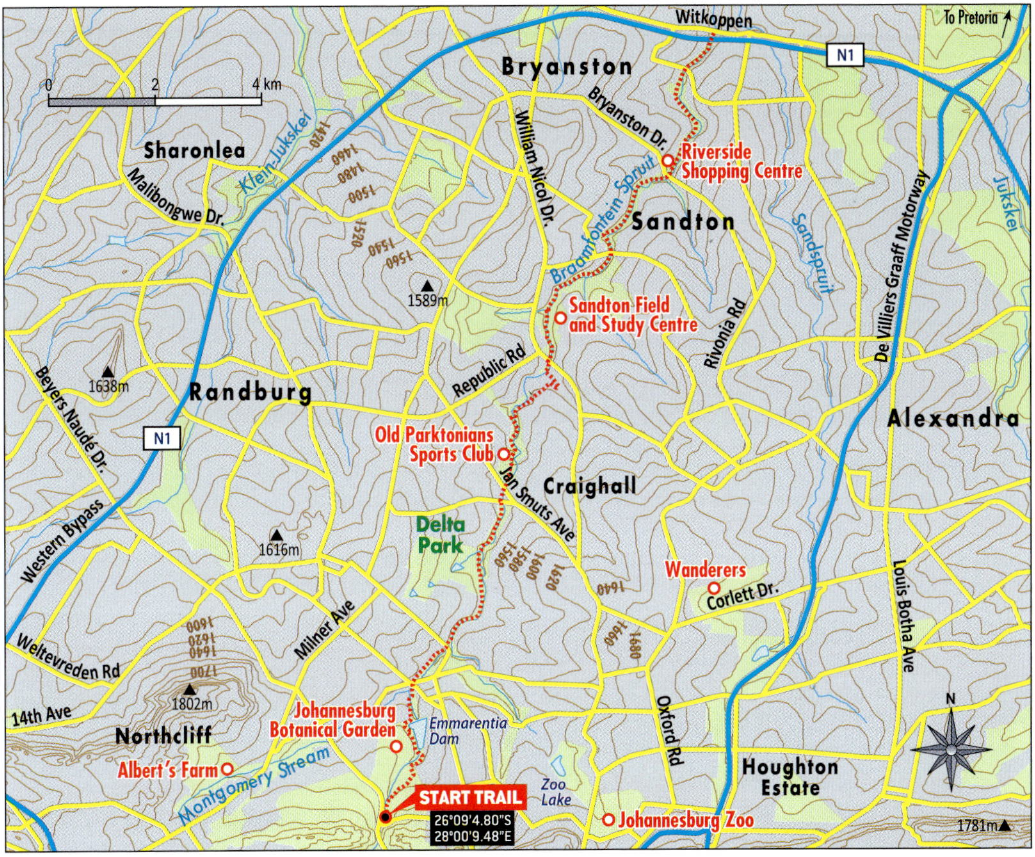

EXPERT'S VIEW

Lisa de Speville is the owner and editor of www.AR.co.za, South Africa's adventure racing website. She is also the creator and organiser of FEAT (www.featsa.co.za), an annual evening of fast-paced and inspiring talks by adventurers. Lisa is an adventure racer, orienteer and trail runner. She has been a passionate participant in these sports for well over a decade and in this time she has completed many ultra-distance, multi-day and staged races.

Trail & Event

Clearwater Trails and Sardine Classic

10km, 25km and 45km

Province KwaZulu-Natal
Region South Coast
Closest town Port Edward
Trail destination Clearwater Trail Centre and Old Pont Resort
Series Stand-alone event
Contributed by Natalie Abbott

© JACQUES MARAIS

THE DESTINATION Bordered by the dramatic Umtamvuna River gorge, Port Edward is the southernmost town on KwaZulu-Natal's South Coast and regarded by many as the 'Gateway to the Wild Coast'. It is on the outskirts of this laid-back town, among indigenous forests and coffee plantations, that you will find Clearwater Trails.

THE TERRAIN The tranquil little town of Port Edward is surrounded by subtropical coastal forests and banana and coffee plantations. Port Edward claims to have the smallest desert in the world, called the 'Red Desert'. The area lies some kilometres west of town and measures only 11ha. It looks like a miniature version of the Arizona desert. Man-high hills and valleys of naked red soil build a striking contrast to the lush, subtropical vegetation of the surrounding area.

DIRECTIONS Travelling south on the R61, continue till you get to the only traffic lights in Port Edward, where you turn right onto Izingolweni Road. Continue for about 2km till you reach the Old Pont Road on your left. Turn left and continue for 2km. Old Pont is the last resort at the bottom of the road.

ACCOMMODATION One hundred grassed, shady camping and caravan sites are available at the Old Pont Resort (www.oldpont.caravanparks.co.za). Accommodation can also be found at www.clearwatertrails.co.za

GRADIENT PROFILE

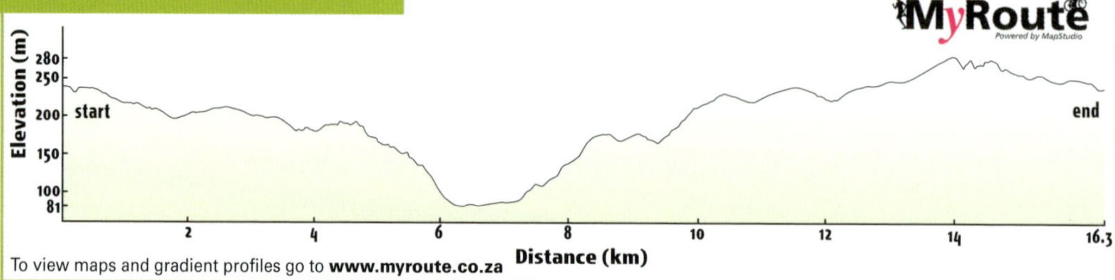

To view maps and gradient profiles go to **www.myroute.co.za**

THE TRAILS Clearwater Trails have a marvellous mix of terrain, with singletrack, jeep track and gravel roads offering options to remain on moderate gradients or attempt steep downhill sections and, of course, the ascent back up and onto the ridge. All the trail options are set against the alluring backdrop of the Indian Ocean, and they all pass through Beaver Creek Coffee Estate and 'Coffee-Bean Uphill' before ending at the Clearwater Cabins.

The classic view of the Umtamvuna estuary will slow you down before you head on to the 'Spook House Downhill', the awesome 'Red Desert' or the cool single-'track through the rolling grassland above the D595, with its magnificent views of the river gorge and waterfalls in the nearby Umtamvuna Nature Reserve.

THE EVENT The Sardine Classic, with different run options, is suitable for the whole family, though it is fairly challenging with respect to the terrain. It also boasts a beautiful setting near the coast, with other nearby attractions, making it the perfect weekend getaway.

FAST FACTS

Grading Easy to difficult
Duration 30mins to 3hrs
Configuration Interlinked circular routes
Start point Clearwater Trail Centre
GPS co-ordinates 31°02'45.5"S, 30°10'08.8"E
Terrain Farm roads, singletrack, dirt roads, mountainous and steep
Map Available from the Trail Centre
Access requirements Open year-round; day permits from Trail Centre
Trail markings White-painted rocks with colour co-ordinated mountain bike symbols and arrows
Facilities Restaurant, self-catering accommodation and ablutions on site
Cell reception Average to full coverage along most sections of trail
Beware Fairly rocky areas (on more extreme routes) and the occasional tractor and other farm vehicle at work
Time of year All year round
Local info www.southcoasttourism.co.za / Port Edward Tourism Office, Tel (+27 39) 319 1193
Local info www.clearwatertrails.co.za / Tel (+27 83) 549 6710

EVENT FACTS

Event name Sardine Mountain Bike Challenge and Trail Run
Venue Old Pont Resort and Clearwater Trail Centre
Distance from Durban 160km
Time of year Beginning of June
Enter as Solo
Cut-offs None
Distances 10, 25 and 45km
Average duration 30–60min, 2–3.5hrs and 2.5–5hrs
Entry info www.bundubasher.co.za

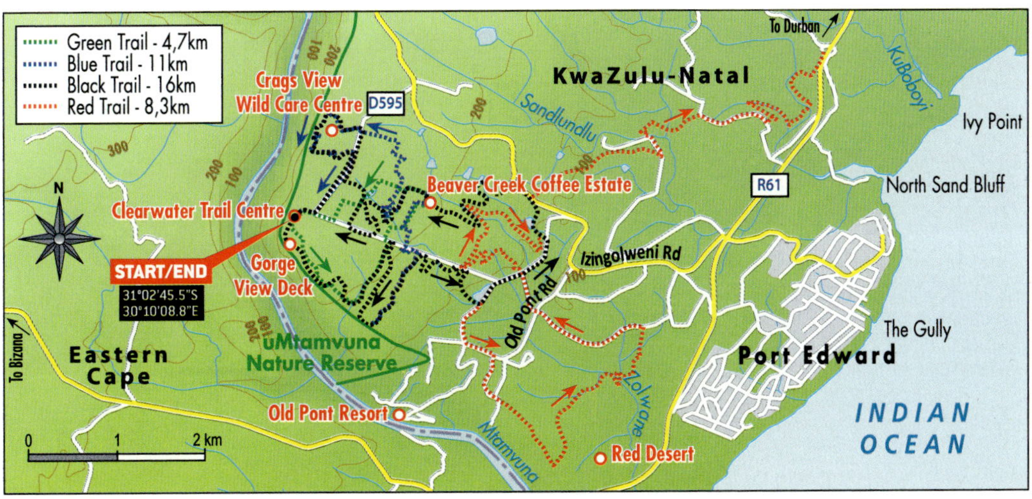

The Cradle Mayhem Three-day Trail Run

65km, 7km or 20km

Trail & Event

Province North West
Region Bojanala
Closest town Hartbeespoort
Trail destination Van Gaalen Cheese Farm
Series Cradle Mayhem
Contributed by Gavin Grobbelaar

THE DESTINATION Once you reach the rural surrounds of the magnificent Hartbeespoort Dam with the sheer cliffs of the Magaliesberg towering behind it, you will find it hard to believe that you are only 30 minutes from the hustle and bustle of Johannesburg and Pretoria. On arrival at the Van Gaalen venue, revel in the old-world setting of this typically Dutch (and quite famous) cheese farm.

THE TERRAIN Easy and fast-flowing singletrack leads along a flat, sometimes sandy, route to the foot of the surrounding hills. The route is easy enough for any relatively fit runner, although there is a wake-up call after the first 3–4km where the trail heads into the mountains after a stretch of sandy jeep track.

The Cradle can get very warm, especially later in the day, while early mornings during autumn will be fresh. The further into the Cradle one goes, the rockier and more technical the terrain becomes. Freak downpours will make conditions underfoot very slippery.

DIRECTIONS The race starts at Van Gaalen Cheese Farm (GPS 25°47′16.3″S, 27°46′19.6″E), about 10 minutes outside Hartbeespoort village and about five minutes from Pecanwood Golf Estate. The farm is situated just off the R560, about 3km north of Skeerpoort – a map is available on www.vangaalen.co.za

ACCOMMODATION The region is a hub for tourism activities and acts as a gateway to the many game lodges in Limpopo as well as the Sun City Resort. Accommodation options cover the full gamut of choices – www.hartbeespoortonline.co.za

EXPERT'S VIEW

Gavin Grobbelaar is a duathlete, Iron Man, adventurer, trail runner, ultra marathoner, entrepreneur and event organiser. He has placed 6th at the World Long Course Duathlon Champs and raced Iron distances and triathlons around the world.

My shoe

Brand ~ Asics

Model ~ Fugies

Rating ~ Light, great underfoot, responsive and durable for a light neutral shoe

FAST FACTS

Grading Intermediate to difficult
Duration 3 days
Configuration Cloverleaf
Start point Van Gaalen Cheese Farm
GPS co-ordinates 25°47'16.3"S, 27°46'19.6"E
Terrain Flat, flowing, technical singletrack, steep and rocky in places
Map Available from Van Gaalen Cheese Farm office
Access requirements A permit can be obtained from the Van Gaalen Shop or office
Trail markings Signs and arrows
Facilities Camping with ablutions; all amenities in Hartbeespoort village
Cell reception 100% coverage
Beware Midday heat, puff adders and rocky descents
Time of year Early May for race; summers extremely hot and winters freezing
Local info www.hartbeespoortonline.co.za
Local info www.mayhemsports.co.za /Tel (+27 11) 047 1820

THE TRAIL The trail head is located on the well-known Van Gaalen Cheese Farm, with all trails leaving from the main farm office and shop where you also obtain your permit. Not all trails run during the Cradle Mayhem are accessible to the public, as some cross privately owned farms, but there is an abundance of trails showcasing some of the best running in the Highveld region. Some routes are shared by runners and mountain bikers, and safety is not an issue.

All Cradle Mayhem routes set off from Van Gaalen, nestled between the Magaliesberg on one side and the Cradle of Humankind on the other. The Hartbeespoort Dam is situated centrally between these two ranges, with the trails traversing private land across a total of 10 farms.

Stage One of the Cradle Mayhem Three-day Trail Run follows the Skeerpoort River, cutting through thick reeds and bush forming a corridor and canopy. Expect a flat profile with very little climbing, but as this is a night run with some technical aspects, runners will have to stay alert.

Stages Two and Three – as well as the single day event – head into the Cradle of Humankind, a World Heritage Site right on the urban edge of the PWV. Routes follow old ox-wagon trails used by the miners, the old 'Dagga Pad' (a road used by marijuana smugglers in days gone by) as well as some new trails along natural contours, cut by Eric, the owner of Van Gaalen. With three big climbs totalling 450m of climbing on the second day, runners will need to push hard as recovery possibilities are few and far between along the technical, rocky singletrack descents. Runners set off on a jeep track with soft sand to warm up for the nitty-gritty along the Cradle slopes, with an immediate, extreme ascent up Pofadder, possibly the steepest climb of the day.

Climb for 3.5km (an ascent of 250m) until the Hartbeespoort Dam and rolling hills of 'The Cradle' pop into view. Two more climbs await before you hit the 'Dagga Pad' with its sheer, 10m drop to the right. After this, a flat section combines soft sand, stones and singletrack to lead you back to camp. The final day is run in the same direction, but with fewer severe climbs, with the final return along the Skeerpoort River into the finish on Day Three.

© PETER KIRK

THE EVENT From a total mileage perspective, this event rates as an entry-level stage race aimed at runners keen to compete in their first multi-day trail run. The race routes and terrain will, however, test the experienced athlete looking for a challenge. The single-day race on the final stage allows all levels of athletes to take part and enjoy this beautiful area.

EVENT FACTS

Event name The Cradle Mayhem Three-day Trail Run
Venue Van Gaalen Cheese Farm
Distance from Pretoria 47km
Time of year Early May
Enter as Solo
Cut-offs Yes (runners to be briefed at race)
Distance 65km (10, 35 and 20km); 7km or 20km
Average duration 3 days
Entry info www.mayhemsports.co.za

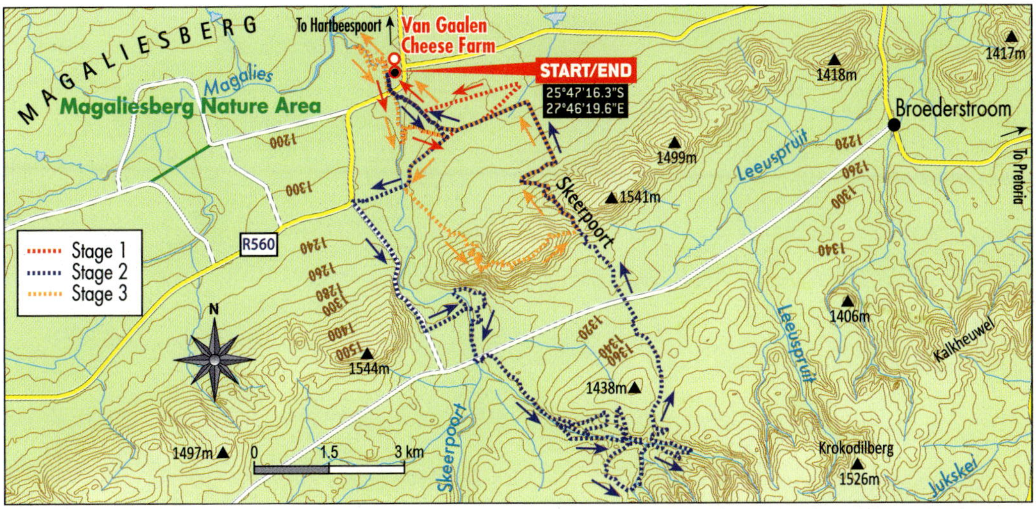

GRADIENT PROFILES

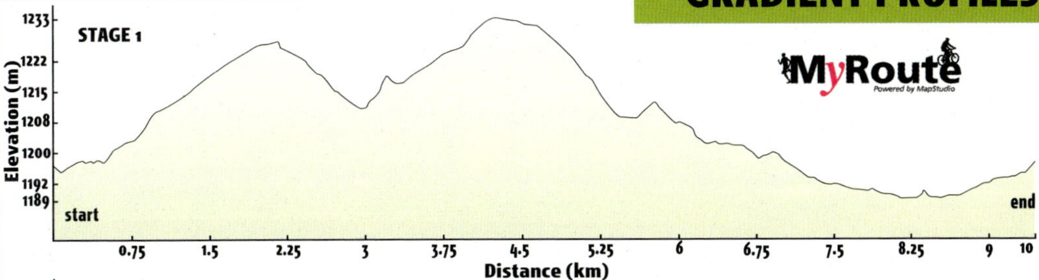

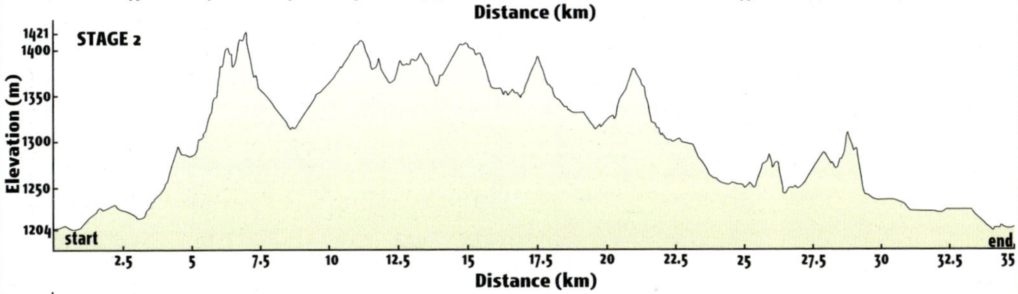

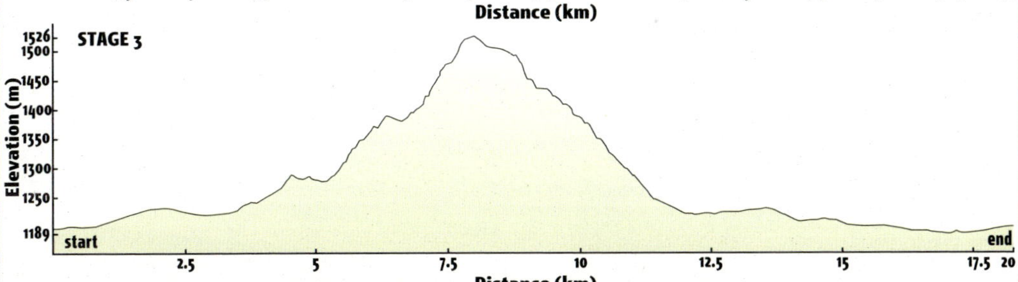

To view maps and gradient profiles go to **www.myroute.co.za**

Cumberland – Talbot Trail Run Series

Trail & Event

14km and 7km

Province KwaZulu-Natal
Region KZN Midlands
Closest town Pietermaritzburg
Trail destination Cumberland Nature Reserve
Series Talbot Trail Run Series
Contributed by Andrew Booth

© JACQUES MARAIS

EXPERT'S VIEW

Andrew Booth is primarily a trail runner, but a road-running family history means he cannot resist great South African tarmac ultras such as the Comrades and Two Oceans. He started organising trail runs in KZN in 2009 and launched www.kzntrailrunning.co.za, which now coordinates a dozen events in and around the uMngeni and Dusi valleys.

THE DESTINATION Cumberland Nature Reserve is a little-known gem just outside Pietermaritzburg in the general vicinity of Wartburg. The area is characterised by steep cliffs dropping onto acacia-wooded plains and bush thickets that line the majestic uMngeni River below. Atop the cliffs one will find open grass plains inhabited by the elusive oribi antelope.

When the reserve was established in 1996 by the Behn family, much of the area had been mined for sand, leaving open scars invaded by alien vegetation. A rehabilitation programme has resulted in spectacular grassland inhabited by not only oribi, but herds of plains game, too.

THE TERRAIN A network of trails runs along the cliff edges, with breathtaking views into the most wild and pristine part of the uMngeni valley. Several trails lead down to and along the river as well, but most of the running is along a relatively flat plateau. Steep ascents and descents are obviously on the cards when venturing down to the river.

While the tracks are generally open and allow for fairly free running, a few rocky sections require a spot of scrambling, with short, steep hills bringing most runners down to a walk. There are a few jeep tracks and gravel roads for those who like running in nature but are not that keen on technical singletrack.

DIRECTIONS Follow the N3 north from Durban, take the Ohrtmann Road off-ramp in Pietermaritzburg and keep right. Cross the highway, pass the next set of traffic lights and turn right into Manning Ave at the second set of lights. Cross Baynespruit stream, go through the first set of traffic lights, then turn left at the Shell Garage. Travel up the hill for 2km, then turn right onto the Table Mountain Road. Travel for another 2km before turning left onto the D408. Follow the D408 all the way into Cumberland and follow the signs to the trail head (GPS 29°30'47.81"S, 30°30'36.90"E).

ACCOMMODATION The reserve offers options varying from camping to rustic bungalows. The secluded Krantz Hut has an outside shower overlooking the uMngeni Valley, and it's only 25 minutes' drive from Pietermaritzburg.

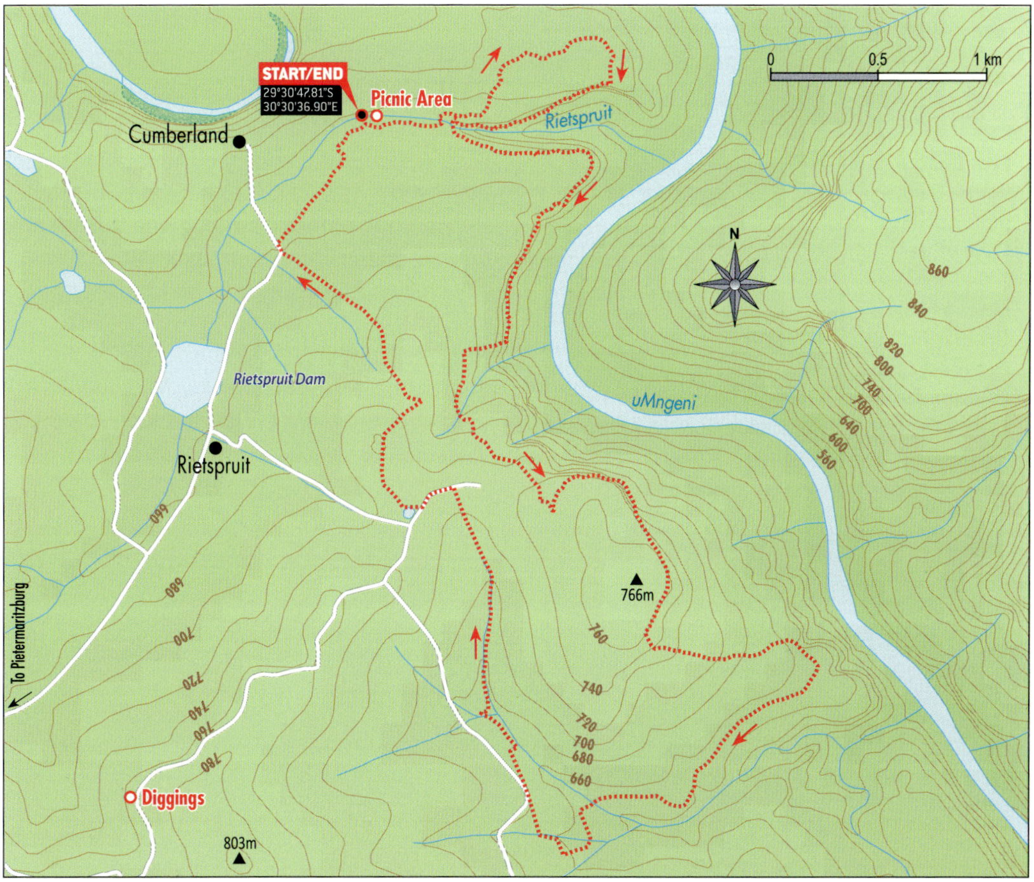

FAST FACTS

Grading Intermediate
Duration 45min to 2.5hr
Configuration Circular
Start point Cumberland Nature Reserve picnic area
GPS co-ordinates 29°30'47.81"S, 30°30'36.90"E
Terrain Gravel road and singletrack
Map Available at trail head
Access requirements Payable at trail head
Trail markings Tags and chalk arrows mark the trail (during the race)
Facilities Ablutions and picnic facilities available at start/finish area
Cell reception No signal along sections of trail
Beware Cliff-top trail sections
Time of year September to November (after the first rains)
Local info Tel (+27 33) 001 7538
Local info www.kzntrailrunning.co.za

THE TRAIL The picnic site at Cumberland serves as the trail head and this is also where the race starts and finishes. The short and long courses set off together and split at the 4km mark. The first 1.5km of the course is run on jeep track with a stream crossing that will get your shoes wet; there is a slow swing bridge alternative for those who want to stay dry and are not worried about time.

From here, the route narrows onto singletrack meandering along the cliff for 2km, with a few technical sections where the sandstone has eroded unevenly. Just before the short/long course split, there is a steep climb along a clay track that becomes very slippery when wet. While the short course meanders through avocado orchards on a neighbouring farm, trail runners on the long course continue along the cliff tops.

A steep descent through open grassland links onto a jeep track along a stream tributary to the uMngeni River. The track leads onto the neighbouring farm and onto a steady, grassy climb through the sugar-cane fields before entering the short-course avocado orchard to loop back to the picnic area for a comfortable downhill finish.

EVENT FACTS

Event name Talbot Trail Run Series – Cumberland
Venue Cumberland Nature Reserve, Pietermaritzburg
Distance 14km, 7km
Time of year Summer Series in November, Winter Series in June
Enter as Solo
Cut-offs No
Event organiser Andrew Booth (KZN Trails)
Average duration 30–90min (7km); 1–2.5hr (14km)
Entry info www.kzntrailrunning.co.za

THE EVENT The sheer beauty of Cumberland – and its proximity to Pietermaritzburg – makes it one of the most popular trail events in KwaZulu-Natal. It suits both experienced trail runners and beginners, with a course that is 100% runnable, yet technically challenging enough to be interesting.

Rookies to trail running should tackle the short course, but reasonably fit runners will have no problem with the long route. Walkers are welcome on either course.

GRADIENT PROFILE

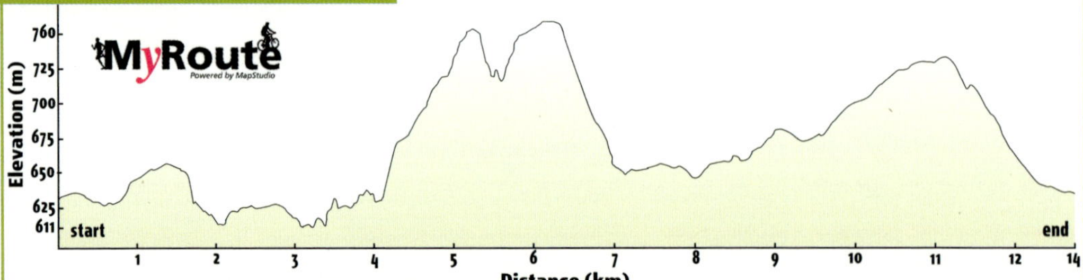

To view maps and gradient profiles go to **www.myroute.co.za**

Diamond Dash

5–7km, 10–12km, 17–20km

Trail & Event

Province Gauteng
Region Northern Gauteng
Closest town Cullinan
Trail destination Seringveld Conservancy
Series Diamond Dash
Contributed by Landie Greyling

©PETER KIRK

THE DESTINATION The Diamond Dash Trail Run is found in the 18 000ha Seringveld Conservancy, which is situated about 15km northwest of Cullinan. The Seringveld Conservancy was established in 1997 by a group of concerned residents who recognized the need to protect the exceptional natural and historical heritage of the area. Casa Riparia (The River House) is situated next to a scenic dam in Tweefontein Spruit on Goodland Estate, the latter nestling within the peaceful Seringveld Conservancy. This is the place to come and experience the peace and tranquillity of the bush.

THE TERRAIN The Seringveld is part of the southernmost outlier of the Waterberg geology and flora, and is characterised by deep, sandy soils. Several rocky ridges traverse the area, as do several spruits, all with a mix of wetlands and small irrigation dams along their courses. The region comprises mixed woodland with characteristic sandveld trees, as well as fragments of natural grassland. The environment is largely unspoiled, although some sand quarries, cultivated lands and intensive animal production are encountered.

DIRECTIONS The turn-off from the M10 for Goodland Estate is opposite the turn-off for De Tweedespruit, and is an easy 15km drive northwest of the well-known diamond-mining town of Cullinan. GPS co-ordinates are as follows:

M10 turn-off **25°33′57.1″S, 28°31′08.4″E**
Casa Riparia **25°33′55.1″S, 28°29′14.7″E**

ACCOMMODATION Goodland Estate offers various accommodation options – contact Jansie at tel (+27 82) 520 2232 (www.goodland.co.za). There are several guesthouses and lodges in the nearby area, all offering great accommodation.

FAST FACTS

Grading Easy to intermediate
Duration 20–120mins
Configuration Circular
Start point Goodland Estate or Cullinan
GPS co-ordinates 25°33′55.1″S, 28°29′14.7″E
Terrain Jeep tracks, singletrack footpaths, rocky, tough climbs
Map No
Access requirements Contact www.seringveldtrails.co.za for access on non-race days
Trail markings Red arrows and bright orange tags
Facilities Limited water and food tables during the race mean runners should be self-sufficient; ablutions and refreshments on site
Cell reception 90% coverage
Beware Heat, rocks and snakes
Time of year Autumn and spring for the races, but the trails are open all year
Local info www.dinokeng.co.za
More info www.diamonddash.co.za /Tel (+27 82) 820 9488

THE TRAIL The route incorporates three calf-busting climbs, followed by some technical descents and a mix of fast sections along undulating single- and jeep track. It's a true all-round test of trail-running ability, and runners will revel in the tranquil bushveld setting, abundant bird life and game such as the rare roan antelope. The infamous scramble up to the first koppie is generally a hot topic after the event.

All trails take runners through the natural habitat of animals like waterbuck, zebra, wildebeest, kudu and impala. Much of the course is on established footpaths, smooth jeep track and contouring mountain paths, all providing varied and challenging terrain. The races have been carefully designed and selected to offer exciting new routes with testing downhills and climbs. The Seringveld Trail Park was launched in November 2011 to offer runners the opportunity to run Diamond Dash race trails under their own steam. Visit www.seringveldtrails.co.za for information.

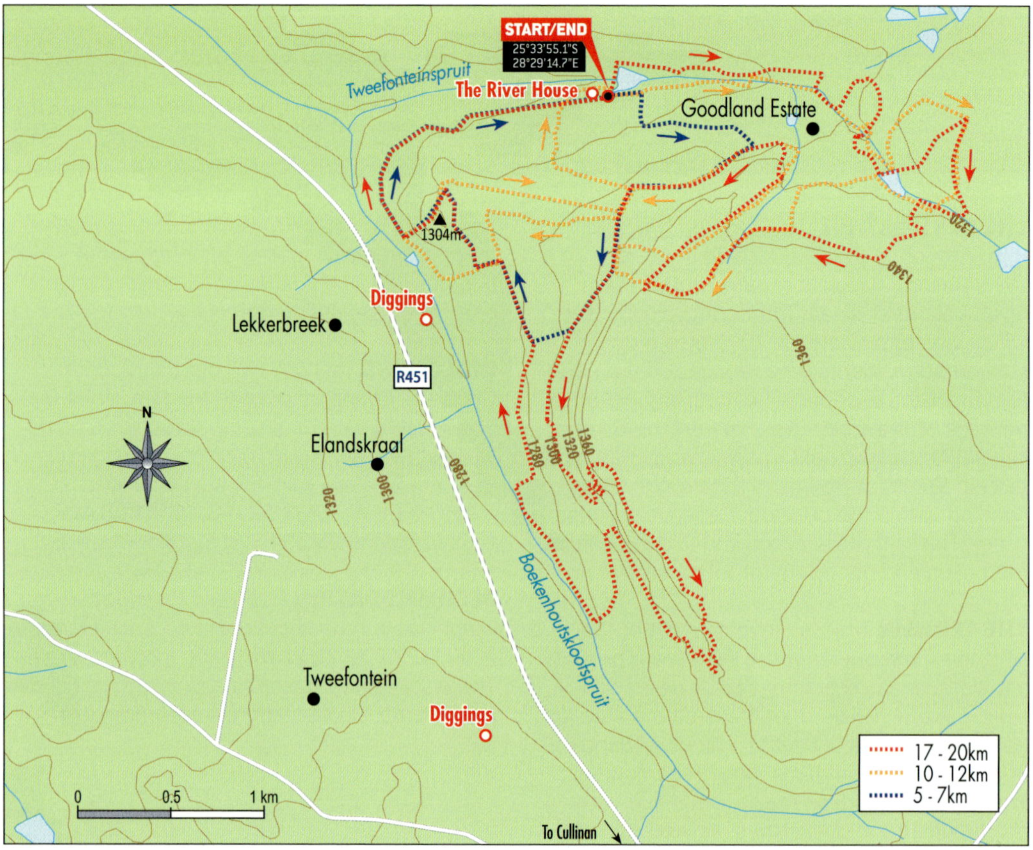

EVENT FACTS

Event name Diamond Dash
Venue Goodland Estate
Distance from Pretoria 40km
Time of year Spring and autumn
Enter as Solo
Cut-offs No
Distances 5–7km, 10–12km and 17–20km
Average duration 20–40min, 40–80min and 75–120min
Entry info www.diamonddash.co.za

THE EVENT The bushveld Trail Run events normally take place in autumn and spring. The start venue is at the beautiful Goodland Estate (www.goodland.co.za). Three races with different distances cover everything from short sprints to medium-distance trails. These vary across each event to ensure new and exciting challenges, from a short 5–7km trail to longer events mixing jeep- and singletracks through varied and mountainous terrain. Routes are well designed to allow competitive runners to take the lead without being held up on singletrack.

This is one of the best organised trail run events in Gauteng, with accurate time-keeping and complimentary coffee and rusks before the race starts. Entries are limited to 500 runners.

GRADIENT PROFILE

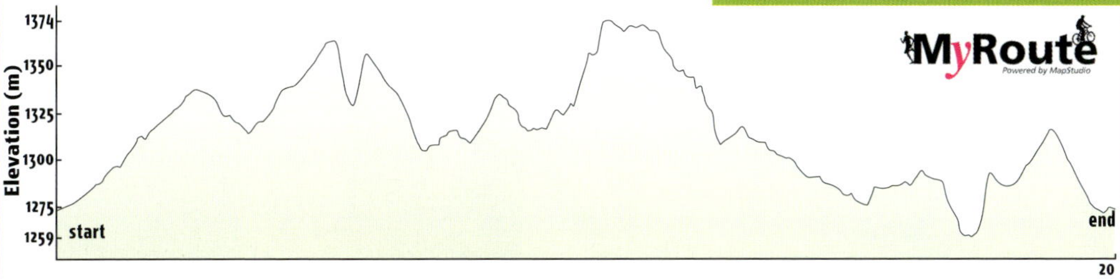

To view maps and gradient profiles go to **www.myroute.co.za**

© PETER KIRK

EXPERT'S VIEW

Landie Greyling is one of South Africa's top trail running athletes. Since starting trail running in 2008, she has achieved over 30 podium wins in SA and the USA.

Insider tips

'This is a challenging route, providing a good variety of open running, boulder hopping, steep climbs and technical descents. Sun block, a running cap, good sunglasses and a small hydration pack are recommended.'

Training and pacing

'It would be good to squeeze in one or two trails in the week to focus on the technical skills, plus at least one hill session, and then focus on some distance on the road. Start at your own pace, but make sure you are well positioned after the first kilometre where the singletrack begins.'

Trail & Event

Dryland Traverse
8km, 26km, 29km and 21km

Province Western Cape
Region Little Karoo
Closest town Oudtshoorn
Trail destination Cango Caves and Swartberg Nature Reserve
Series Stand-alone event
Contributed by Chantel Nienaber

© JACQUES MARAIS

EXPERT'S VIEW

Chantel Nienaber Chantel Nienaber is a trail runner, sponsored by Salomon and Hammer Nutrition. She has completed numerous multi-day stage races and endurance events. In 2011, she won the Wild Coast Wild run, as well as the Dryland Traverse – Mixed Team division.

My shoe
Brand ~ Salomon
Model ~ Speedcross 3 and SLAB 4
Rating ~ You can put brand-new Salomon shoes on and comfortably run a multi-day event

THE DESTINATION The Swartberg Nature Reserve, a proclaimed World Heritage Site, lies between the Great and Little Karoo, jutting for 121 000ha along a long and narrow mountain range. Winding between these two biomes, you will find the historic Swartberg Pass, built by Thomas Baines, at dizzying heights of up to 1 585m.

THE TERRAIN The prologue to the race starts within the deep, dark and dank crevices of the world-renowned Cango Caves. The race itself circumscribes the imposing Swartberg Mountains from south to north and back again. For most of the way, runners will negotiate singletrack, traversing the foothills and valleys, passing monuments and crossing rivers and rugged ridges.

The Swartberg is an area of climatic extremes, with freezing winters, often with snow and below-zero temperatures, while the summer heat can peak at highs of up to 40°C!

DIRECTIONS The Dryland Traverse sets off from De Hoek Mountain Resort, situated along the R328 connecting Oudtshoorn to Prince Albert (it is 35km from Oudtshoorn). GPS co-ordinates are as follows:

De Hoek Mountain Resort **33°22′06.8″S, 22°10′37.0″E**
Cango Caves **33°23′36.1″S, 22°12′53.2″E**

ACCOMMODATION A tented village provides race accommodation at the venue, but if you prefer to arrange your own, check the recommended venues on www.drylandtraverse.co.za

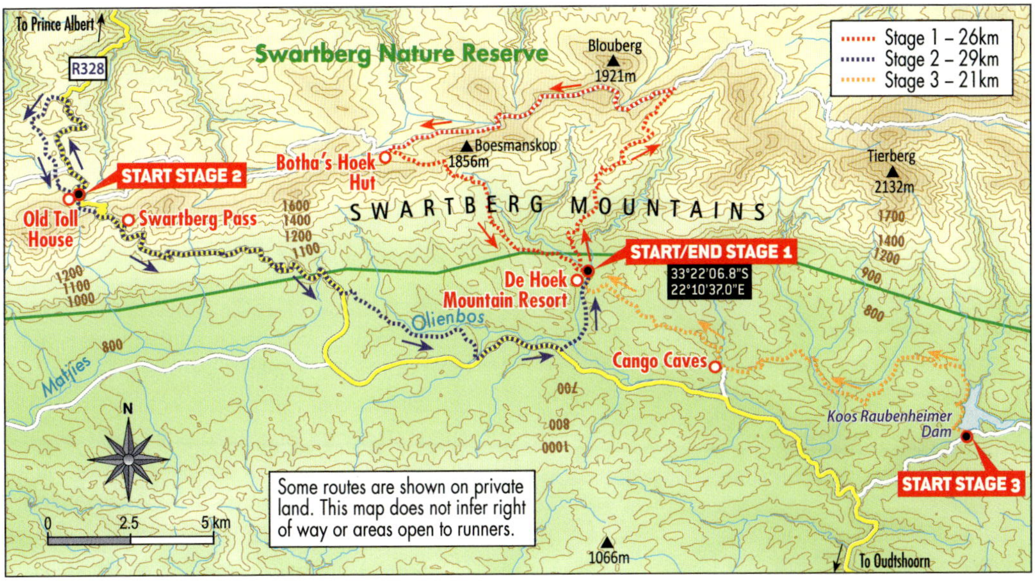

GRADIENT PROFILES

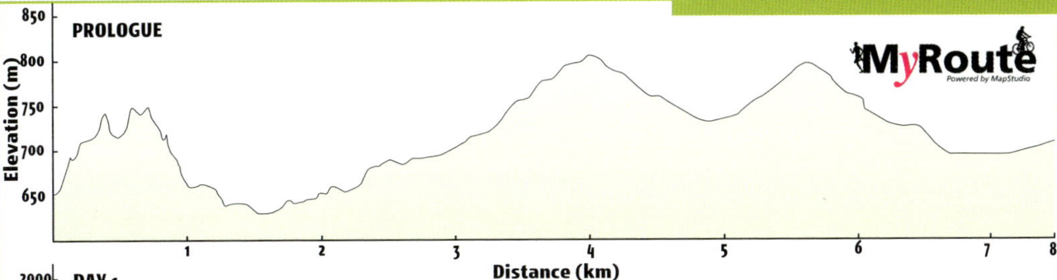

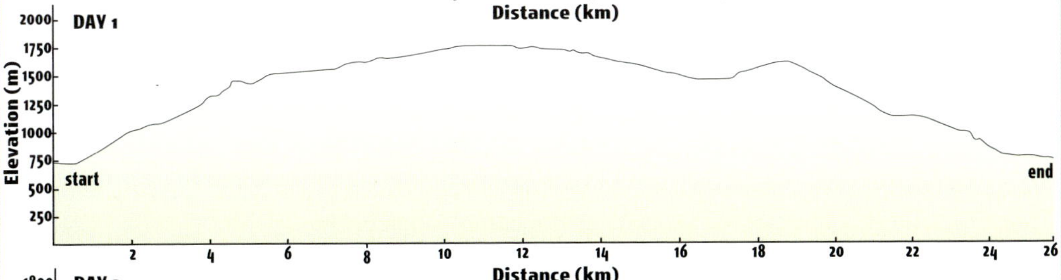

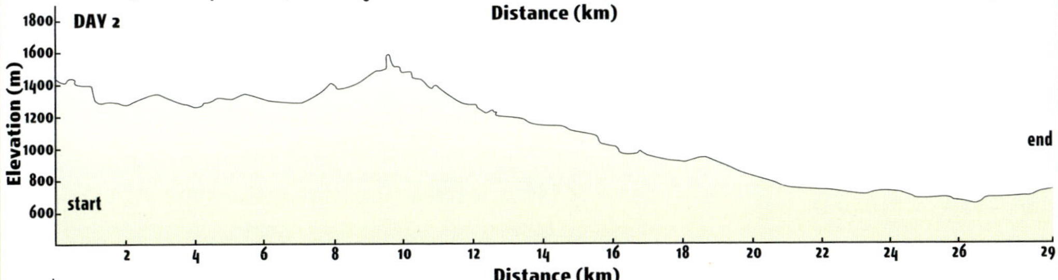

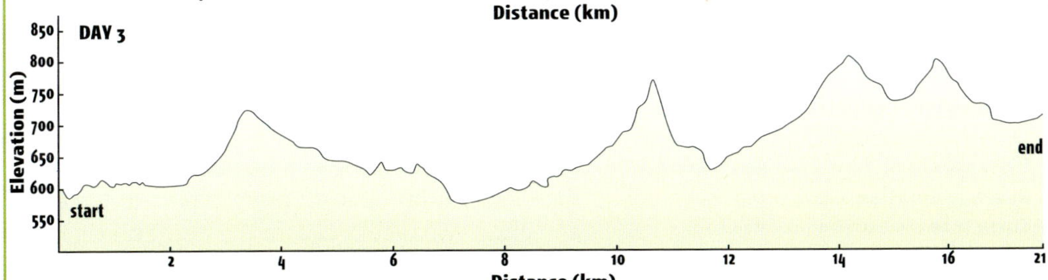

To view maps and gradient profiles go to **www.myroute.co.za**

FAST FACTS

Grading Intermediate to difficult
Duration Three days (plus a prologue)
Configuration Cloverleaf
Start point De Hoek Mountain Resort
GPS co-ordinates 33°22'06.8"S, 22°10'37.0"E
Terrain Mountainous with singletrack, jeep tracks and gravel roads
Map Refer to website
Access requirements Trails only open on race day except for those in Swartberg Nature Reserve; CapeNature permit needed
Trail markings Permanent CapeNature markers (temporary tags during race)
Facilities Water points en route; all amenities at race village
Cell reception Minimal coverage
Beware Extreme temperatures
Time of year Early November for race; spring or autumn for trails
Local info www.capenature.co.za and www.oudtshoorn.com
More info www.drylandtraverse.co.za / Tel (+27 82) 379 2627

THE TRAIL The 8km night prologue starts in the Cango Caves, going through Van Zyl Hall, past Devil's Chimney and the 'preekstoel', and exits via the old entrance. The route to De Hoek Mountain Resort follows superb singletrack along the foothills of the great Swartberg Mountains.

The first stage of 25.7km starts and ends at De Hoek. The route heads upwards and onto rather technical singletrack on the old Gouekrans hiking trail, now closed to the public. The first 8km climbs from 700m to about 1 650m, but amazing views will greet you at the first water point. Unspoilt undulating jeep track takes you to Botha's Hoek hut (the second water point). This 9km stretch feels like running on the back of a dragon, with panoramas from the Little Karoo valleys in the south to the arid plains of the Great Karoo in the north. The plunge back to De Hoek starts with an exciting zigzag section of singletrack.

The second stage starts at the old Toll House at the top of the Swartberg Pass, twisting back to De Hoek after 28.7km. The trail descends northwards before hitting the only singletrack of the day. A challenging 4.5km snakes to the top of the pass and the first water point before the huge downhill starts. The Swartberg Pass drops over 9.7km of winding gravel road to the second water point. The route then crosses farm lands and a final 3km of tar back to De Hoek.

The final day's 21.2km third stage sets off from the Raubenheimer Dam wall. The trail runs around the dam before entering the secret valley of 'Die Kombuis'. From here, runners traverse swathes of ancient agricultural land before heading back to the Cango Caves and onto the last 8km stretch to De Hoek along a fun section of singletrack.

The unequalled views from the Swartberg Mountain top, the singletrack through the foothills and the eerie silence beneath the earth's surface make for an extraordinary experience! About 50% of the route is open to the public throughout the year; the rest is only accessible during the official race – make sure of access before you try and run it.

EVENT FACTS

Event name Dryland Traverse
Venue De Hoek Mountain Resort
Distance from Cape Town 470km
Time of year Early November
Enter as Solo or teams of two
Cut-offs Yes (runners will be briefed at race)
Distances 8km, 26km, 29km and 21km
Average duration 3 days (+ prologue)
Entry info www.drylandtraverse.co.za

THE EVENT The Dryland Traverse takes place in November to miss the heat of summer and the unpredictable winters of the Swartberg Mountains. The route is challenging, but well balanced, with scenic trails, undulating jeep track and historic passes over a prologue and three stages totalling more than 80km and with a total vertical ascent of 2 964m. Entries are limited to 300 teams (600 runners). Entries open 12 months prior to the event and close two weeks before the event (that's if the entry limit has not yet been met).

Featherbed Trail Run
11km and 14km

Event Only

Province Western Cape
Region Garden Route
Closest town Knysna
Trail destination Featherbed Nature Reserve
Series Stand-alone event
Contributed by Mark Collins

© JACQUES MARAIS

THE DESTINATION Every year Knysna celebrates the Pick n Pay Oyster Festival – South Africa's biggest sporting festival with more than 70 sports, culinary and cultural events – in a 10-day extravaganza during the Cape winter months. The Salomon Featherbed Trail Run is the Oyster Festival's official trail run and rates as a unique trail running experience.

THE TERRAIN The Coelacanth Route includes some technical rockwork and a seriously inclined ascent before it reaches the start of the Sea Horse Route. Both routes then follow a sandy, rolling trail through some low coastal forests and fynbos. Short sections of jeep track and servitudes link the trails until the route returns along the old railway line into town.

DIRECTIONS The trail head is accessible only by ferry boat departing from Cruise Café (GPS 34°02'20.52"S, 23°02'25.74"E); this is also the venue for registration and the finish line. Both the restaurant and Featherbed Ferry Terminal are well signposted from Waterfront Drive in Knysna.

ACCOMMODATION Options in Knysna during the Oyster Festival are in high demand, so make sure you book well in advance – www.knysnafeatherbed.co.za

FAST FACTS

Grading Easy to intermediate
Duration 50–120mins
Configuration Point to point
Start point Featherbed Nature Reserve
GPS co-ordinates 34°02'20.52"S, 23°02'25.74"E
Terrain Singletrack, rolling dune trails, jeep track, abandoned railway line
Map Download from www.magneticsouth.co.za
Access requirements Entry to event only
Trail markings Directional arrows
Facilities Refreshments at finish line; ferry trip and meal included in entry fee
Cell reception 90% of route
Beware Rickety railway bridge
Time of year July
Local info www.knysnafeatherbed.com or www.visitknysna.co.za

THE TRAIL Sea Horse Route participants board a Unimog-powered 'truck train' on which they are transported up to the start of their event atop the Knysna Heads, but as an added bonus they get to watch the start of the Coelacanth racers from the comfort of their carriage seats.

The Coelacanth participants are assembled north of the restaurant and set off first. After a quick 800m loop around the duiker-breeding enclosure they join the coastal trail, which follows the water's edge out onto the Heads. The route takes them through a tunnel, onto a pebble beach, up a stone stairway and across a spectacular rock arch before the climbing proper starts.

This forested incline tops out at the start of the Sea Horse Route, and from here both events follow the same trail back towards Knysna. The route criss-crosses the ridge line, one moment offering panoramic views of Buffalo Bay in the west and the next moment broad glimpses down over the estuary's blue waters in the east. A sandy, helter-skelter descent onto the railway line chutes the runners to the finish line at Cruise Café.

EVENT FACTS

Event name Salomon Featherbed Trail Run presented by PETZL
Venue Featherbed Nature Reserve
Distance from George 70km
Enter as Solo
Time of year July (the Tuesday of the Knynsa Oyster Festival)
Distances 11km and 14km
Average duration 50–120min
Entry info www.magneticsouth.net

THE EVENT The Featherbed Trail Run is offered in three departures: a Morning Run, an Afternoon Run and a very popular Night Run. Choose from two routes: either the 14km Coelacanth Route (442m of elevation) or the 11km Sea Horse Route, which climbs a more manageable 282m. Although the routes differ little in distance, the easier Sea Horse Route excludes the brutal climb up the mountain.

EXPERT'S VIEW

Mark Collins has competed as an international adventure racer, with three top-six finishes in the Adventure Racing World Series (ARWS). His passion is sport in the wilderness and he spends all his free time exploring the wilder regions of the Southern Cape.

My shoe
Brand ~ Salomon
Model ~ SLAB
Rating ~ Lightweight performance trail shoe balancing excellent durability and protection

GRADIENT PROFILE

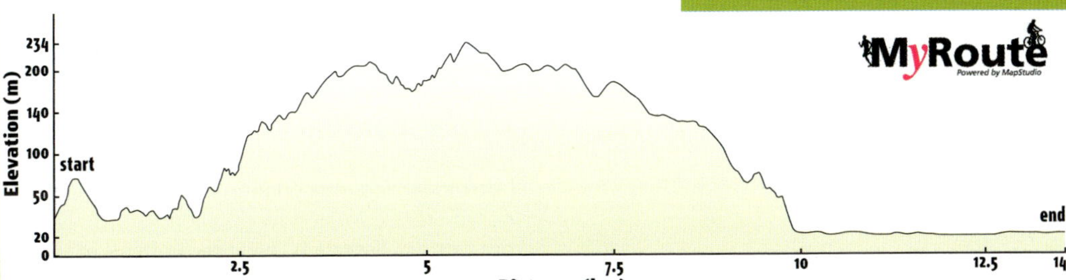

To view maps and gradient profiles go to **www.myroute.co.za**

© KELVIN TRAUTMAN

Golden Gate Challenge

Event Only

27km, 27km and 17km (71km)

Province Free State
Region Thabo Mofutsanyana
Closest town Clarens
Trail destination Golden Gate Highlands National Park
Series Bonitas Wild Series
Contributed by Heidi Mocke and Filippo Faralla

EXPERT'S VIEW

Filippo Faralla spent many years running on roads before completing his first trail run, the Mont-Aux-Sources Challenge, in 2004. His passion and enthusiasm for trail running has taken him to the Antarctica Marathon, the Canadian Rockies 125km Death Race, New Zealand's Keppler Challenge and the TransRockies in the USA. However, the Drakensberg still remains his favourite wilderness to run through.

My run
'The variety of terrain sets this trail run apart, and the runner has to contend with steep climbs, technical singletrack, ridge-line running, fast, technical descents, open grasslands, river crossings and high-altitude running.'

My shoe
Brand ~ Solomon
Model ~ Speedcross 3
Rating ~ Lightweight performance trail shoe that performs well on technical trails

Insider tips
'The most important thing to remember is not to judge this race on the distances; they might look short but there's a reason for that!'

Gear and apparel
'Fluid-carrying capability (minimum 1 litre), well-fitting trail shoes, a headlamp and minimum emergency equipment are essential.'

Training and pacing
'Participants need to build leg strength to cope with mountain running. It is essential to incorporate hills (up and down), gym and stairs in the runner's training to prepare the legs for this event.'

THE DESTINATION The scenic Golden Gate Highlands National Park boasts a fascinating geological heritage, dating back millions of years to when the area existed as a vast swamp ruled by dinosaurs. Erosion gradually turned the landscape to desert, before wind and water sculpted the dramatic amber cliffs over aeons. Volcanic activity finally capped the region's ranges with soaring basalt peaks.

THE TERRAIN Welcome to real-life 'Cloud Country'. The towering Maloti Mountains serve up lung-busting climbs of note, all at an altitude that will surely make you sit up and take notice. Glorious views come as part of the deal in this premier national park, so runners may find it difficult to concentrate on the amazing trails traversing the ridges.

DIRECTIONS The most direct route from Durban and Gauteng is via Harrismith. From here, follow the R712 to Phuthaditjhaba and the Golden Gate Highlands National Park's entrance gate (GPS 28°30'23.5"S, 28°37'07.2"E). However, it would be a shame to miss out on a quick visit to the picturesque village of Clarens, reached by approaching the park from the opposite side.

ACCOMMODATION You can opt for the race package (including tented accommodation), or book local accommodation instead in one of the nearby rest camps (www.sanparks.org). More options are listed on the race website at www.goldengatechallenge.co.za/accommodation.php

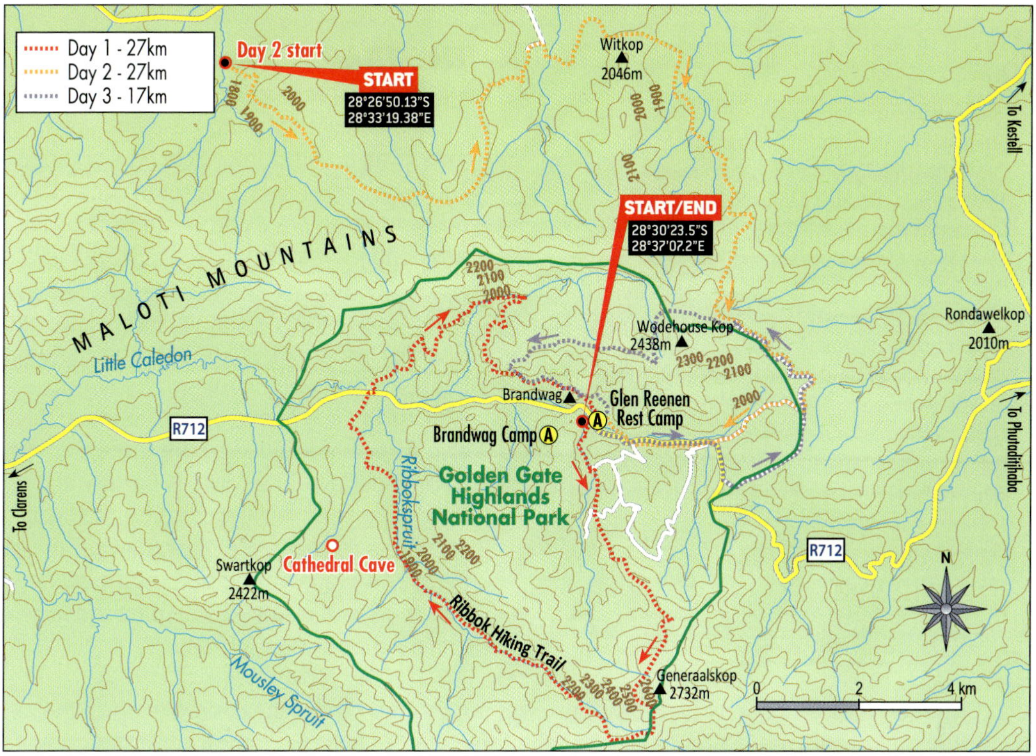

GRADIENT PROFILE

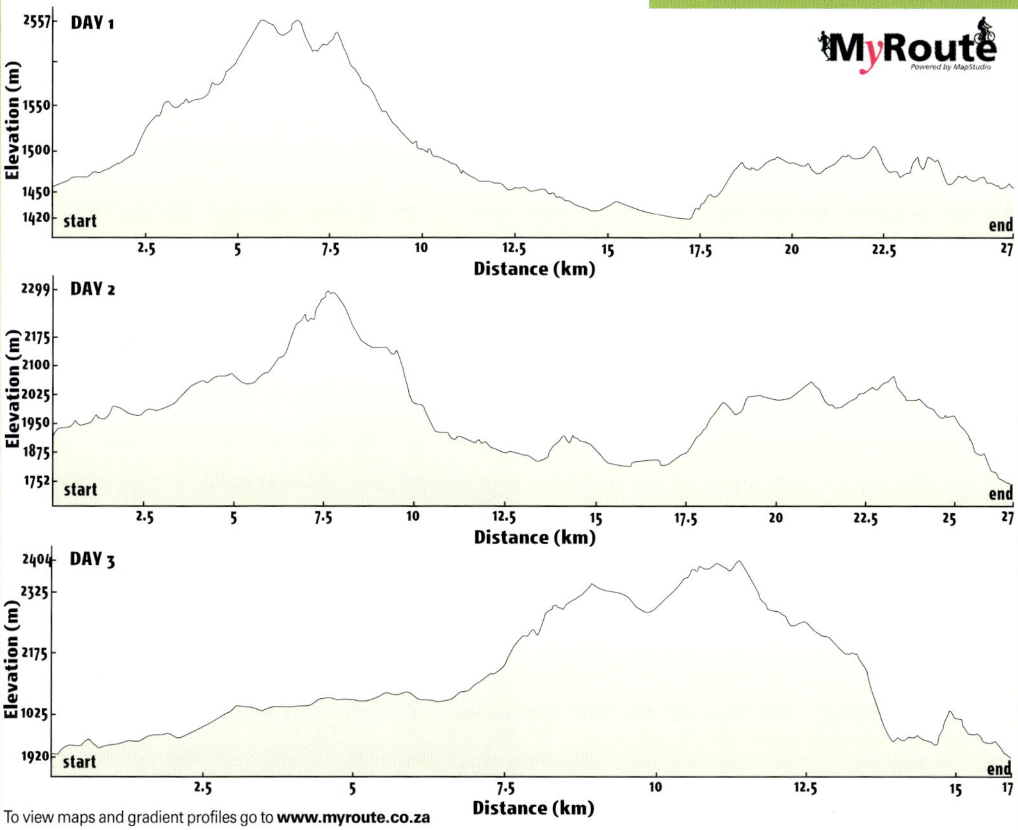

To view maps and gradient profiles go to **www.myroute.co.za**

FAST FACTS

Grading Intermediate to difficult
Duration Three days, 3–7hrs per day
Configuration Circular; cloverleaf setup
Start point Glen Reenen Rest Camp
GPS co-ordinates 28°30'23.5"S, 28°37'07.2"E
Terrain Singletrack and rugged jeep track
Map Available at www.goldengatechallenge.co.za
Access requirements By invitation only; email heidim@wildlands.co.za for info
Trail markings Directional arrows, candy tape, reflective tape
Facilities Refreshment tables every 10km
Cell reception None in some of the valleys
Beware Extreme heat, thunderstorms in the afternoon; cool nights
Time of year Last weekend in October
Local info www.sanparks.org and www.clarens.co.za
More info www.goldengatechallenge.co.za / Tel (+27-33) 343 6380

THE TRAIL The terrain is extremely rocky with steep descents and ascents. Routes consist of hiking trails and jeep track. Day one is completely on singletrack and hiking trails and is very technical. Days two and three are a combination of hiking trails and jeep tracks.

The first day follows the very well-known Ribbok Hiking Trail, 28km of magical stuff but also hard work. Look out for some waterfalls, rock pools, eland, ribbok and also a special addition to the route, Cathedral Cave. The route is narrow and in some places really rocky so watch your step. Two relatively big climbs await; the biggest is Generaalkop right at the start. The route will also take you past the legendary Brandwag Mountain.

On the second day an hour's bus trip will take runners to the other 'unexplored' side of the park. The start is hard – a big rocky climb to the top and into 'Little Serengeti'. Vast mountains, rolling hills and herds of game will accompany you along old jeep tracks and management roads.

The third day has one of the biggest uphills and downhills you'll ever find in a race – you'll be going to the top at 2 438m!

THE EVENT The terrain and altitude make the Bonitas Radox Golden Gate Challenge extremely hard, with big, difficult climbs to be found on each day's route. Entries are by invitation only and should you wish to enter you need to email Heidi on heidim@wildlands.co.za to get an invitation. The race is run over three days and covers 71km inside the Golden Gate Highlands National Park.

EVENT FACTS

Event name Bonitas Radox Golden Gate Challenge
Venue Golden Gate Highlands National Park
Distance from Clarens 42km
Time of year Last weekend in October
Enter as Solo
Cut-offs No, but there are checkpoints along the way
Distances 27, 27 and 17km (71km)
Average duration Three days, 3–7hrs per day
Entry info www.goldengatechallenge.co.za

© KELVIN TRAUTMAN

Goukamma Traverse
5.5km and 18km

Trail & Event

Province Western Cape
Region Garden Route
Closest town Sedgefield
Trail destination Goukamma Nature Reserve (CapeNature)
Series Stand-alone event
Contributed by Amanda Judson Dixon

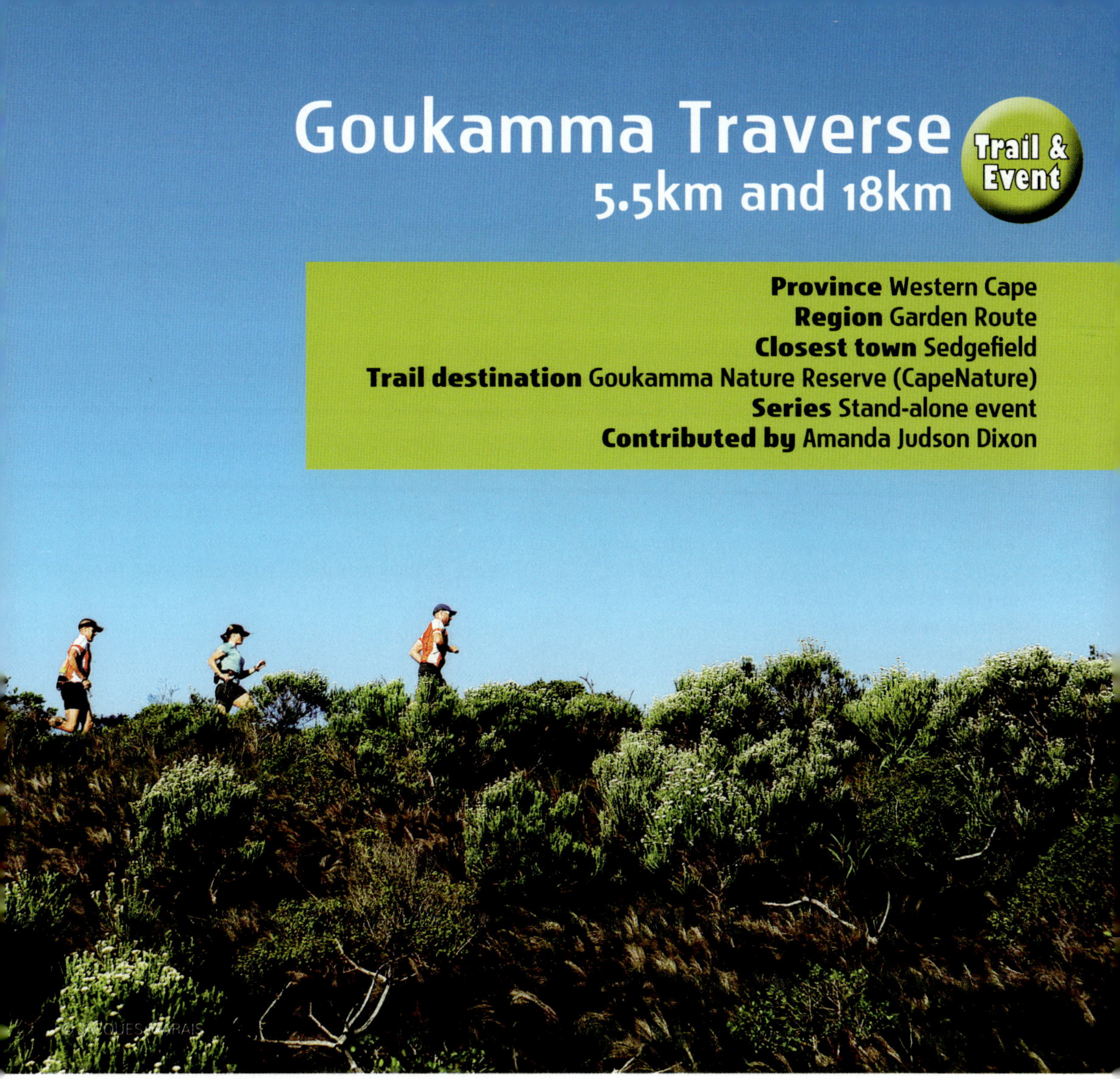

THE DESTINATION Sedgefield is an ideal family destination in which to relax and enjoy the great outdoors. This quaint coastal village nestles within the heart of South Africa's very own 'Lake District', with abundant estuaries, lagoons, lakes and four splendid beaches on which to bliss out.

THE TERRAIN The run will take runners along singletrack for the most part, with short sections of jeep track and an unfortunate 3km of tar towards the finish. About 90% of the route takes runners along ridges and through ancient dune systems, so the substrate is mostly compact dune sand, potentially soft in places. The terrain is varied – steep climbs; flat, winding sections of trail; shady milkwood forests; eye-popping ocean vistas, all highlighted with flourishes of fynbos. Some tracks are stabilized with 'log steps'.

DIRECTIONS Goukamma Reserve is accessed from the east via the Buffels Bay Road, from the N2 between Sedgefield and Knysna. The area is linked by main roads to all major centres, including George (40km), Port Elizabeth (385km) and Cape Town (470km). The 18km run starts remotely to the west of Goukamma River (GPS **34°03'51.60"S, 22°56'31.74"E**). To reach the trail head, follow the Buffels Bay Rd off the N2 for about 8km and turn right into Goukamma Reserve. Continue to the parking area near the ablution block and follow the dirt road and signs to the registration area and river pontoon.

ACCOMMODATION With the start being equidistant from Sedgefield and Knysna, numerous accommodation options await – www.visitsedgefield.co.za

FAST FACTS

Grading Intermediate to difficult
Duration 2–4hrs
Configuration Remote start to finish (18km)
Start point Goukamma River Pontoon
GPS co-ordinates 34°03′51.60″S, 22°56′31.74″E
Terrain Varied, single- and jeep track, compact and soft dune sand
Map Available from Information Office
Access requirements CapeNature access fee
Trail markings Orange arrow route markers during race
Facilities All amenities at start and finish
Cell reception Minimal coverage along remote sections of trail
Beware Extreme temperatures, puff adders, dune mole rat undercutting
Suggested carry Water, energy bar and cell phone
Time of year All year
Local info www.visitsedgefield.co.za / Tel (+27 44) 343 2007
Local info www.slowfestival.co.za /Tel (+27 72) 949 3002 / events@tumbleweeds.co.za

THE TRAIL Trail runners start remotely from the Goukamma River pontoon on the eastern side of the reserve, traversing the reserve from east to west to finish in Sedgefield on the Village Green. With this in mind, runners must arrange transport between these points. Once on the trail, you follow single- and jeep track along an ancient dune systems.

Part of the beauty of this trail run is that you will be ridge-running atop high, grass-covered dunes, with breathtaking views of the ocean to the south and of some of the wide vleis and lakes to the north. It's quite simply a 'wow!' run, capturing the essence and spirit of the Garden Route at its very best.

EXPERT'S VIEW

Amanda Judson Dixon is a trail runner, mountain biker, multi-sport athlete and event organiser. She has previously helped organise and co-ordinate the Land Rover G4 Challenge SA Selections and the Otter Trail African Trail Run, together with brothers Mark and John Collins. She currently owns and organises one of South Africa's premier family festivals – The Slow Festival – in Sedgefield.

My shoe
Brand ~ Salomon
Model ~ XT Wings
Rating ~ Fantastic trail running shoe for the slightly wider foot

© JACQUES MARAIS

THE EVENT The 18km run is not recommended if you are a novice off-road runner. There is also a 5.5km trail run for families, youngsters and ex-couch potatoes. This starts and finishes at the Village Green in Sedgefield.

EVENT FACTS

Event name Goukamma Traverse
Series name Part of the Slow Festival
Venue Sedgefield
Distances 5.5km and 18km
Time of year Always falls on Easter Saturday (during the Slow Festival)
Enter as Solo
Cut-offs No
Event organiser Tumbleweeds Events
Average duration 2–4hrs (18km); 30–60mins (5.5km)
Entry info www.slowfestival.co.za

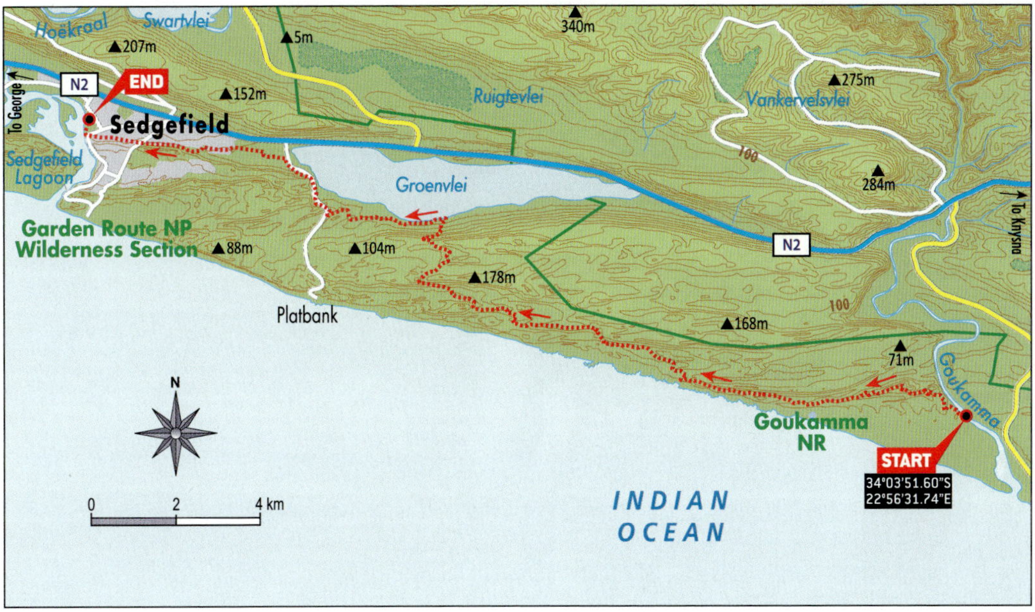

GRADIENT PROFILE

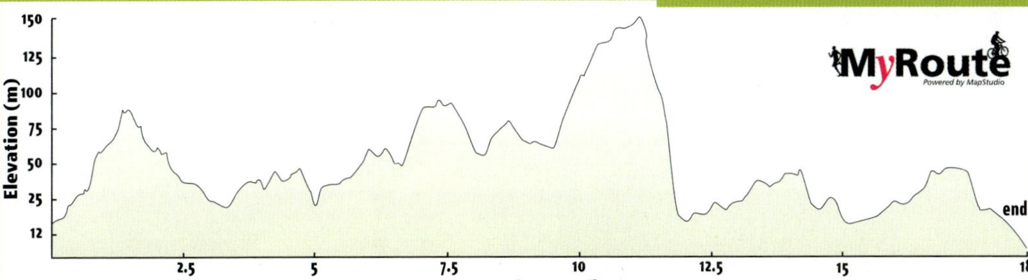

To view maps and gradient profiles go to **www.myroute.co.za**

Trail & Event

Grootvadersbosch Trail Run

30km and 20km

Province Western Cape
Region Overberg
Closest town Heidelberg
Trail destination Grootvadersbosch Nature Reserve
Series Quantum Classics
Contributed by Noel Ernstzen

© JACQUES MARAIS

THE DESTINATION The N2 town of Heidelberg, situated at the foot of the majestic Langeberg ranges, serves as the gateway to the Garden Route. Travel inland from the highway and you will soon find yourself in awe of the Grootvadersbosch Nature Reserve and conservancy. More than 250ha of indigenous forest here constitutes the largest block of intact primary forest outside of Knysna. Adjacent to Grootvadersbosch is the Boosmansbos Wilderness Area, one of South Africa's Natural World Heritage Sites.

THE TERRAIN The trails in Grootvadersbosch Reserve and through the conservancy on the neighbouring farms will transport runners into a wonder world of indigenous forest, mountain fynbos and untouched peaks. Spectacular views over the Little Karoo to the north will stop you in your tracks.

The greater part of the trail network passes through mountain fynbos, remnant forest and rare renosterveld, with a variety of fauna, including, bushbuck, duiker, grysbok, bush pig, porcupine, aardwolf, caracal and a healthy population of Cape leopard. Birders will go 'bos' over nesting Crowned Eagles, elusive Nerina Trogon, Blue Cranes and Secretary Birds strutting their stuff across the veld.

DIRECTIONS Head east past Swellendam along the N2, then turn left onto the R342 after 11km. Drive through Suurbraak on the R322 towards Heidelberg, continuing straight onto the gravel road to Grootvadersbosch (22km from Suurbraak).

ACCOMMODATION Grootvadersbosch is a renowned birding destination and offers hiking and walking holidays as well as mountain bike routes. The closest restaurant or shop is Heidelberg. Check out accommodation at www.grootvadersbosch.co.za or www.honeywoodfarm.co.za

EXPERT'S VIEW

Noel Ernstzen is an ex-adventure racer and mountain biker who has found his true passion in trail running over the past few years. He has competed in more multi-day MTB events, stage races and ultra runs than he cares to remember, often placing on the podium.

My shoe

Brand ~ Inov8

Model ~ X Talon 212

Rating ~ Super-light, very fast and very, very grippy; the most amazing, sure-footed race shoe I have ever worn

FAST FACTS

Grading Difficult
Duration 7–13hrs in total
Configuration Circular route both days
Start point Grootvadersbosch Nature Reserve
GPS co-ordinates 35°59'21.80"S, 20°48'49.49" E
Terrain Mountainous, forest, steep climbs
Map Available from info office
Access requirements Permit required
Trail markings Wooden signs
Facilities Fantastic camp site with good ablutions
Cell reception Mostly
Beware Extreme weather changes on top of mountain
Time of year All year round with appropriate clothing
Local info www.capenature.co.za
More info www.quantumadventures.co.za /Tel (+27 21) 789 0188

THE TRAIL There are a number of well-marked trails in the reserve offering day walks from 2–15km. The Boosmansbos Trail is a two-day, 30km trail that takes you through the wilderness area (it only has a very rudimentary shelter). Tel (+27 28) 722 2412 or gvbosch@telkomsa.net

There is also a three-day walking trail on the neighbouring farm (www.grootvadersbosch.co.za) and a MTB route looping through the reserve and neighbouring farm lands.

THE EVENT Grootvadersbosch is a two-day event, only to be taken on by experienced trail runners. This is not to say that you need to be a racing snake, but just prepare for two tough days on the trail.

Day 1 (30km)

Day one starts with a fantastic gradual contour climb for 12km, in knee-high fynbos of every description, and spectacular views to the east of the Langeberg and wooded kloofs below you. You crest the mountain at 1 257m and the dry northern slope unfolds with endless views of the Karoo. The trail becomes rugged and rocky as you approach the remote huts above the Boosmansbos forest. A 10km decent begins at this point, ending in an awe-inspiring single-track that leads down to the Duiwenhoks River. A final steep climb winds out of the river gorge, and this leads to the jeep track and the last kilometres to the finish in the forest. The only perennial water would be at around 15km and 24km. Never underestimate the weather on this route as it is extremely exposed and can range from hot to freezing conditions and snow.

Day 2 (20km)

This section is not to be presumed easier because of the shorter distance. From the start you plunge into the forest with many short, steep climbs and descents. Pass the giant redwood trees and wind your way through the forest trails to the foothills of the mountain. There are beautiful views of the mountain and the valley towards Suurbraak and the farmlands below. A gentle run through fynbos has you passing the halfway mark, then you descend to Grootvadersbosch Farm. Follow the Grootvadersbosch River, skirting the renosterveld, and then climb back out into the forest and the finish. There are many opportunities to drink, as all running water in this area is potable. There are some seriously steep climbs where you will be forced to walk … take advantage of this to take in your surroundings.

EVENT FACTS

Event name Grootvadersbosch Trail Run
Series name Quantum Country Classics
Venue Grootvadersbosch Nature Reserve
Distances 30km (Day 1), 20km (Day 2)
Time of year July
Enter as Single or relay team
Cut-offs Yes (runners will be briefed at race)
Event organiser Quantum Adventures
Average duration 4hrs (Day 1), 3hrs (Day 2)
Entry info www.quantumadventures.co.za

GRADIENT PROFILES

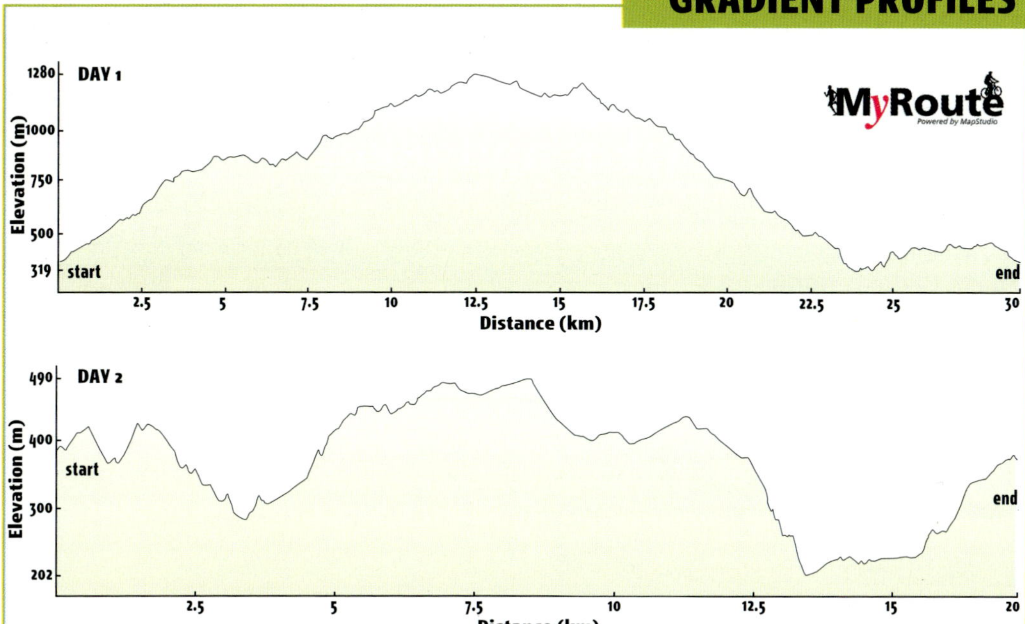

To view maps and gradient profiles go to **www.myroute.co.za**

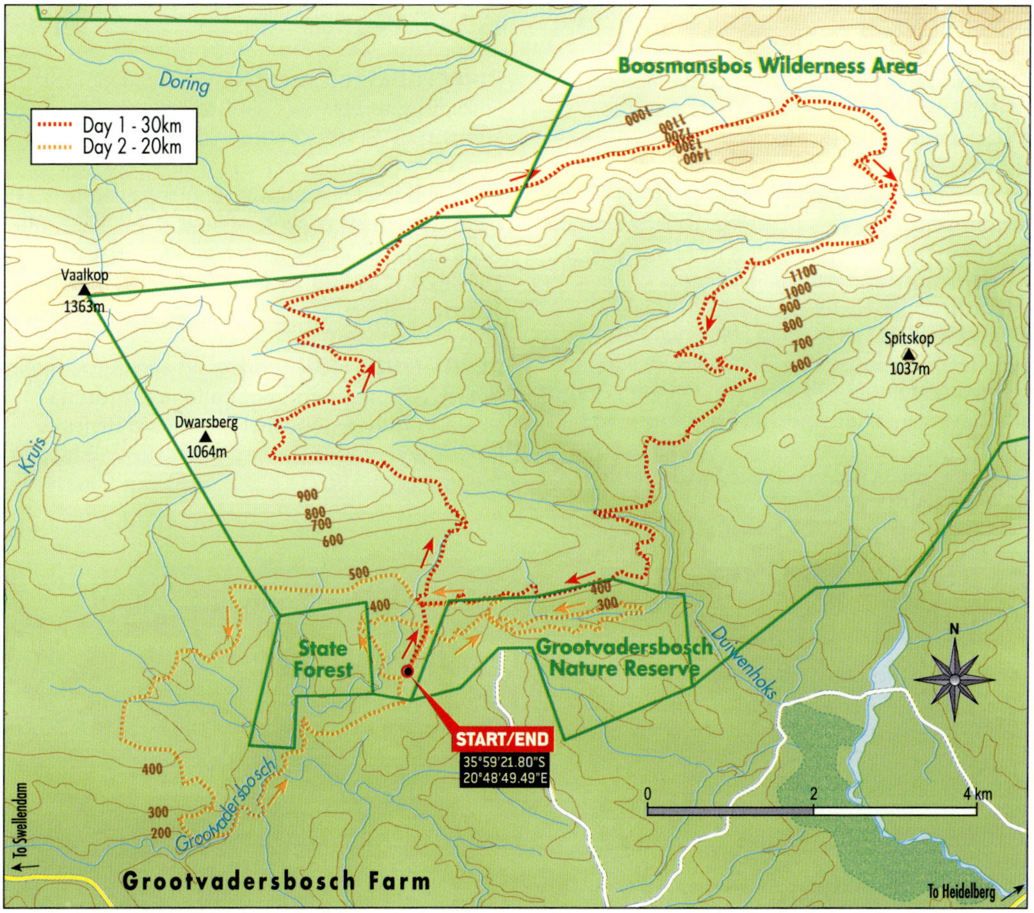

Trail Only

Hedianga Farm

5km, 8km, 12km and 18km

Province Gauteng
Region Gauteng North
Closest town Garsfontein
Trail destination Hedianga Farm
Series N/A
Contributed by Debbie Agenbag (WildTrail)

THE DESTINATION Situated to the east of Pretoria along the Bronberg section of the Magaliesberg ranges, Hedianga Farm promises an exciting trail running, mountain biking, birding and walking experience. The destination encompasses an area of 140ha, mostly along the north-facing slopes of the mountains overlooking Shere and Silverlakes.

THE TERRAIN The trails at Hedianga Farm include lots of loose rock and sand, making the surface technical for novice trail runners. Routes are well maintained, but can be overgrown during the rainy summer season. It is advised to study the maps beforehand to avoid getting lost on the trails.

DIRECTIONS Follow the N1 towards Polokwane onto the Atterbury exit (GPS **25°46′40.9″S, 28°16′16.8″E**) and continue east past Menlyn Shopping Centre. Cross over Hans Strydom Drive and the Olympus Drive four-way stop, then turn left into Ajax Avenue and left again into Achilles Street at the T-junction. Plot 85 (GPS **25°48′24.1″S, E28°21′04.0″E**) is on your right 100m along.

ACCOMMODATION There is no accommodation available on the farm, but options in Pretoria range from guesthouses, hotels and B&Bs to lodges and private game parks – www.tshwanetourism.com

GRADIENT PROFILE

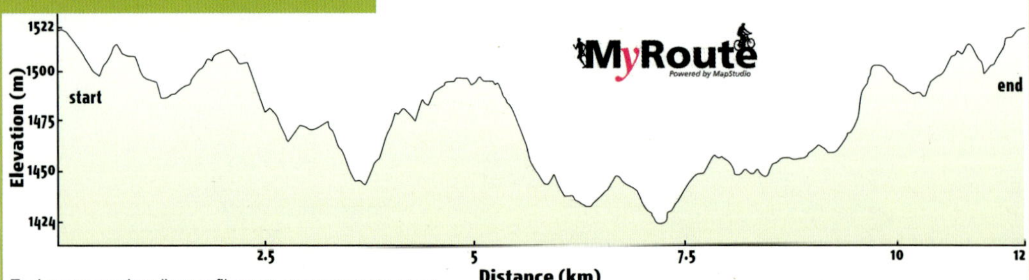

To view maps and gradient profiles go to **www.myroute.co.za**

THE TRAIL There are four primary routes of 5km, 8km, 12km and 18km, all traversing the woodland slopes of the Bronberg Mountains. Trails start off easily along sections of jeep track, but soon morph into the singletrack routes runners have come to expect from Hedianga.

The trail head is situated at the summit of the Bronberg, with views across Pretoria that are sure to leave you breathless before you've even started your run. The vegetation changes as you wind your way through forested kloofs, along steep, rugged ridges and tranquil woodland dells. Once you bottom out at the foot of the range, the hard work starts again as you ascend a good 400m back to the crest.

Take care when negotiating the downhill trails, especially during the early mornings when dew can make the surface exceptionally slippery underfoot. Also avoid heading onto the trail when thunderstorms are threatening. Although the destination is generally safe, it is advisable to run in groups.

Hedianga Farm is all about 'exploration running'; with so many trails crisscrossing each other, it is very much up to you how long and where you run. A high level of fitness is required if you plan to take on the challenging 18–20km route. Hedianga Farm is bordered by several private properties, so keep in mind that if you have to climb through a fence, you are probably trespassing!

FAST FACTS

Grading Intermediate to difficult
Duration 30mins to 2hrs
Configuration Various loops and return options
Start point Hedianga Farm
GPS co-ordinates 25°48'24.1"S, 28°21'04.0"E
Terrain Singletrack and jeep track; loose rocks, sandy sections
Map Available on site
Access requirements Entrance fee, but free on Saturdays
Trail markings Signs and name boards
Facilities Ablutions and water
Cell reception Signal along 80% of route
Beware Technical and slippery surfaces; thunderstorms; snakes and ticks
Time of year Open six days a week; closed on Mondays
Local info www.facebook.com/people/Hedianga-Farm or contact Tel (+27 82) 552 0955
Local info www.wildtrail.co.za / Tel (+27-83) 294 5260

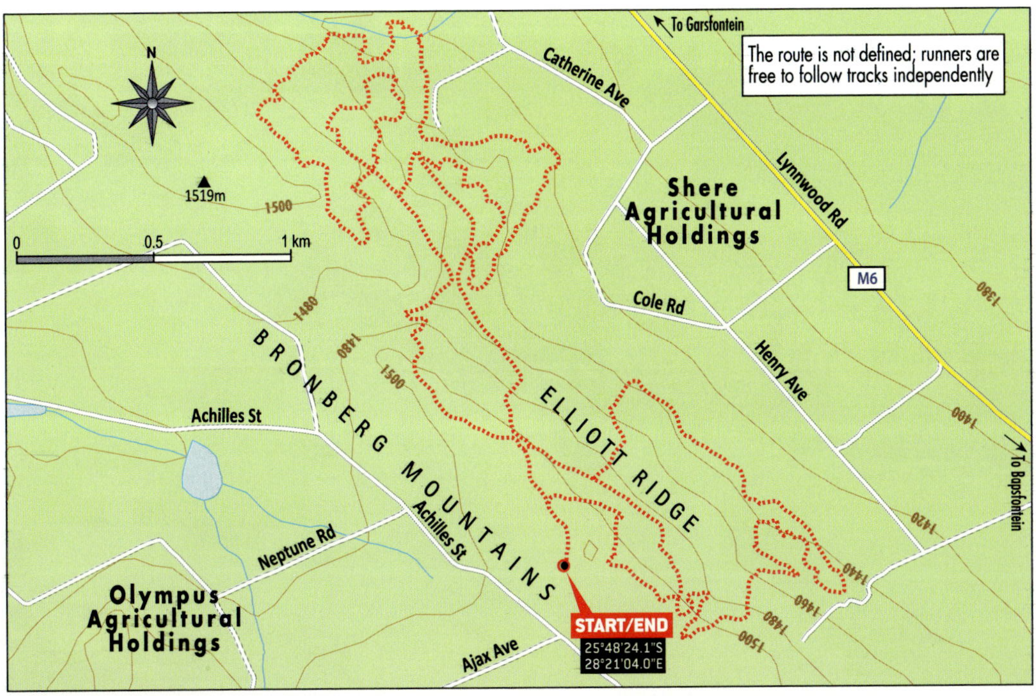

Trail & Event

The Hobbit 100

15km, 38km and 100km (two-day stage race)

Province Eastern Cape
Region Border
Closest town King Williams Town (but Hogsback is the recommended base)
Trail destination Amatola Hiking Trail
Series Mountain Runner Events
Contributed by Tatum Prins and Graham Bird

© KARYN VELLEMAN

THE DESTINATION If you've read *Lord of the Rings* or seen the movie, the fantasy forests encircling the sleepy village of Hogsback will transport you into the very epicentre of modern-day Middle Earth. Hazy pine plantations, serene indigenous woodlands, forested kloofs and sweeping grassland slopes unfold here within the shadow of razorback ridges.

Rambling inns, hideaway cottages and characterful pubs are sure to remind you of Frodo's beloved Shire. Beyond the borders of the sleepy village, cascading waterfalls and tranquil streams will entice you to lose yourself within the surrounding Amatola ranges. Hogsback is named after three ridged summits (reminiscent of bristly-backed wild pigs) and perches upon the western rim of the inland escarpment overlooking the rural valley of Tyume.

THE TERRAIN The region is known for its numerous hikes and a feature of the Amatola Trail is that it generally avoids service roads and plantations. The forest here brims with an abundance of yellowwood trees, while in the drier sections sneezewood and wild olive occur. Rare Cape Parrot and Knysna Turaco can often be spotted, as can Verreaux's (Black) Eagles near Geju Peak.

This latter peak is the highest point along the trail, with the altitude varying from 518m at Maden Dam to 1 850m at Geju. The route can be described as undulating, with some very steep descents, combining indigenous forest trail with technical, mountainous singletrack. Take care through the treacherous boulder garden after Cata Hut and while ascending The Hog (the latter can be very overgrown and is also in the mist belt). Weather conditions can change in an instant and there is a very real danger of getting lost in the mist.

DIRECTIONS Hogsback is 85km from King William's Town (situated on the N2 and R63). Travel west on the R63 towards Alice; after approximately 55km turn right onto the R345, signposted 'Cathcart/Hogsback'. From here it is around 30km to Hogsback. Arranging a transfer to the trail head is recommended as it is in a remote area and vehicles are not secure (chat to the local tourism office).

The trail officially starts at Maden Dam (GPS **32°44'22.5"S, 27°17'51.1"E**). To get here, travel north from King William's Town for 13km along the R346 to Stutterheim. Turn left at the 'Rooikrans/Amatola/Sandile' sign and continue over the Rooikrans Dam wall past the Pirie Trout Hatchery sign.

The trail head is in front of the caretaker's home at Maden Dam, and is very well marked. The total distance is 22km from King William's Town. The trail starts at the information hut, with yellow footprints indicating the route around the picturesque dam and onwards to the banks of the Buffalo River.

ACCOMMODATION Hogsback has a range of excellent accommodation that is provided by several hotels, B&B establishments, self-catering cottages, and backpackers' and camping facilities. Check out www.katleisure.co.za and www.awaywiththefairies.co.za

ACCESS REQUIREMENTS You will require a permit and a map from DWAF (Departments of Water Affairs and Forestry). Phone them on tel (+27 43) 642 2571 or send a fax (+27 43) 604 5529; forget about trying to send emails.

EXPERT'S VIEW

Tatum Prins and Graham Bird are both avid adventure racers, trail runners and mountain bikers. They have competed internationally at expedition events on five continents.

Our shoe

Brand ~ Merrell
Model ~ Seismic
Rating ~ The best balance between foot freedom and surface protection is what you get from the NTR Seismic; this is the perfect shoe for trail runners who love adventure – it's our favourite shoe ever

FAST FACTS

Grading Difficult to extreme
Duration 6–12hrs per day
Configuration Point to point route (100km over two days)
Start point Maden Dam
GPS co-ordinates 32°44'22.5"S, 27°17'51.1"E
Terrain Mountainous; singletrack through forests
Map Available from the Department of Water Affairs and Forestry (DWAF)
Access requirements Permit is required from DWAF
Trail markings 'Yellow feet' marked on trees and stones on hiking trail
Facilities All amenities in Hogsback village; the huts on the trail have toilets, running water and beds with mattresses
Cell reception Minimal coverage along remote sections of trail
Beware Mist on 'The Hog'; snow in winter; trail is slippery when wet
Time of year November, December, March and April
Local info www.hogsback.co.za /Tel (+27 28) 551 1378
More info www.mountainrunner.co.za /Tel (+27 21) 712 8799

THE TRAIL The Hobbit 100 route follows the iconic Amatola Hiking Trail and is run as a two-day staged trail run. Expect magnificent indigenous forests, multiple river crossings, huge waterfalls and a night out in the remote Cata Mountain Hut.

Day 1 starts from Maden Dam and for the first 15km traverses the forest to Gwili-Gwili Hut. The next 18km continues through indigenous woodland, passing numerous waterfalls and rock pools. Along this section, you will descend towards and then follow the cascading Ngobozana stream until you reach Dontsa Hut.

From here, it is a 19km meander up a plantation road to a moss-covered cascade, where you eventually say goodbye to the forest. Ascend along a steep climb, then head west to the distant Hogsback Peak towering above grassland plains. Once you reach Doornkop, descend into the Eseka Valley and onto Cata Hut, your base for the night.

Day 2 will lift your spirits from the word go as you pass two tranquil pools en route to the plateau summit of Geju Peak (1 850m). Enjoy the magnificent views before heading across the scree slope on your descent into the Mnyameni Gorge. Take care on the slippery scree and in the gorge, where the multiple waterfalls are sure to take your breath away.

The trail passes Mnyameni Hut (13km) and crosses the stream before ascending through the forest valley and open veld beyond. At the first of many rock pools, the Zingcuka Loop Trail links with the Amatola Trail; this forms part of the shorter 38km Hobbit Run. Pass by the Wolf River Forest and then negotiate a steep descent into the Schwarzwald section to the Zingcuka Hut.

From here, you are onto the final stretch, including the climb over Hogsback Peak. Take note that a cut-off will be in force here, as the mist on 'The Hog' can be treacherous. The descent down to the Tyume River is steep, but you feel incredible satisfaction with what you have achieved. Follow the road to your right into Hogsback for a fantastic finish.

Solo runners can book to run the trail as they see fit, either staying in all five the mountain huts or just one, depending on their individual level of fitness level and the time available.

THE EVENT The Hobbit 100 two-day event is not recommended if you are a novice off-road runner. Rather start off with one of the other events on the day: either a 15km trail run past the waterfalls surrounding Hogsback, or try the 38km trail run which promises to be a bit more challenging.

EVENT FACTS

Event name The Hobbit 100
Series name Mountain Runner Events
Venue Maden Dam
Distances 15km, 38km, 100km (two-day stage race)
Time of year Mid-October
Enter as Solo
Cut-offs Yes (runners to be briefed before race)
Event organiser Mountain Runner Events
Average duration 1.5–3hrs (15km); 5.5–8hrs (38km); 15–24hrs (100km)
Entry info www.mountainrunner.co.za

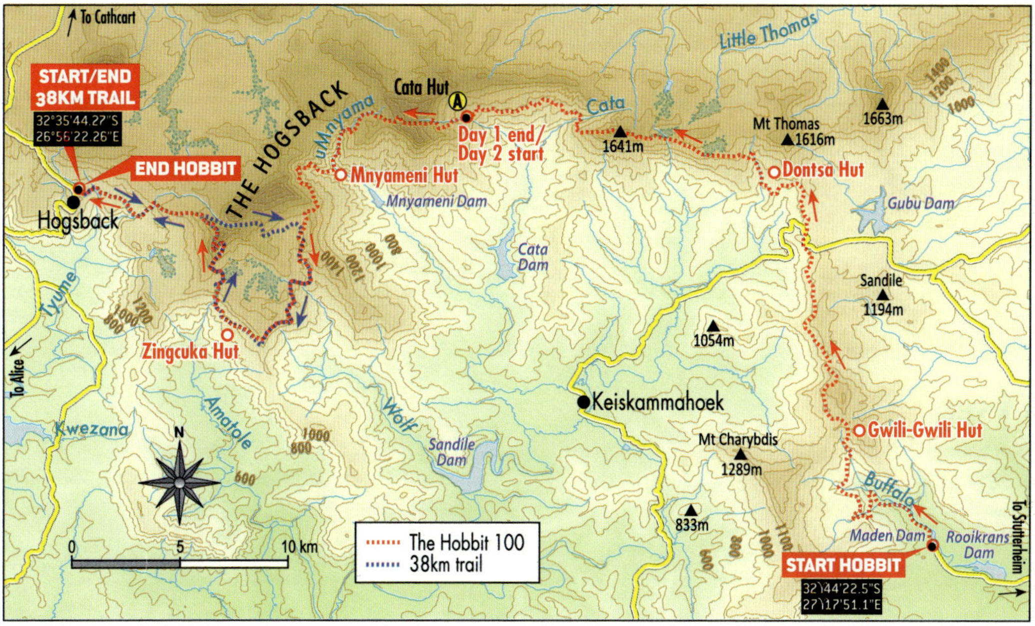

GRADIENT PROFILES

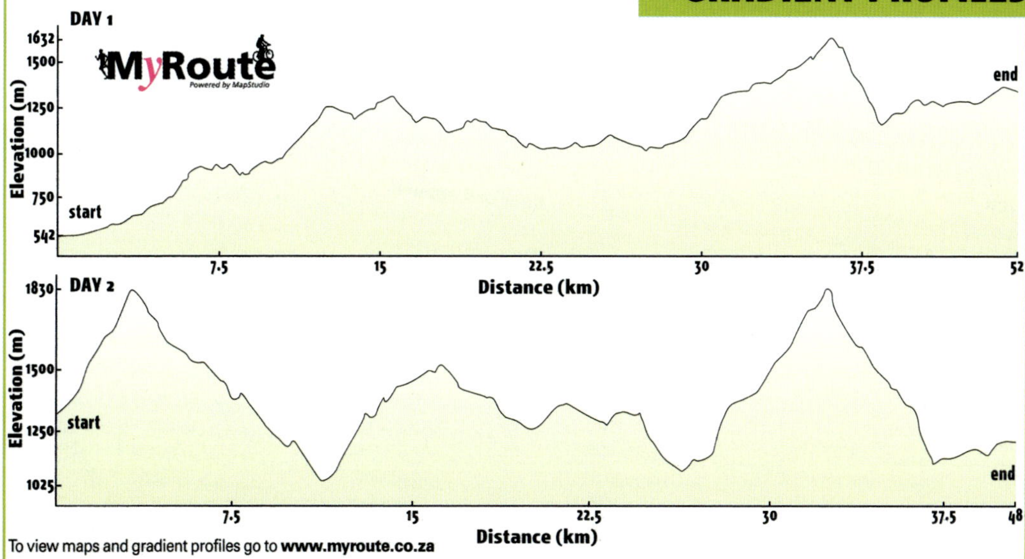

To view maps and gradient profiles go to **www.myroute.co.za**

Trail & Event

Hout Bay Trail Challenge

40km

Province Western Cape
Region Cape Town and Surrounds
Closest town Hout Bay
Trail destination Table Mountain National Park
Series Stand-alone event
Contributed by Claire Ashworth and Allan Benn

EXPERT'S VIEW

Allan Benn is an ex university and provincial cross-country runner. *'Back in the 80s there was no trail running – we ran on the mountains and just called it training.'* He is the 2011 Hout Bay Trail Challenge winner.

My run

'This must be on every trail runner's 'to-do' list – it's one of the toughest and most beautiful trails challenges in South Africa. The 40km route has everything to test a trail runner: a cold start, steep climbs, bush to bash through, technical rocky paths to test your footing, and smooth mountain trails to whizz along. There are some tricky descents and a beautiful finish along the beach.'

My shoe

Brand ~ Nike
Model ~ Pegasus road and trail
Rating ~ Nike introduced this shoe back in the early 80s when I started running at school. It has gone through a number of developments and there is now a trail version. It is still as strong and stable as always.

Insider tips

'Pace judgement is important if you want to do well here. Don't burn out on the first leg to Suikerbossie, and hold back on the early descents. Also, be sure to start drinking early and have enough liquids for the hot and dry section over Vlakkenberg and Constantiaberg.'

Gear and apparel

'I prefer to carry water bottles with wide mouths because these are much easier to fill at rivers along the way than the hydration packs. Fynbos scratches your legs – wear leggings or toughen up.'

Training and pacing

'You'll need strength in the legs for the second half if you're planning on racing the whole way. Put in some distance runs and long climbs in your training. The organisers' map is very good but is only available at registration. Join one of the trail groups to check out the key sections beforehand: the quickest route up to the radar, Llandudno Ridge, behind Hely-Hutchinson Dam and Blackburn ravine.'

THE DESTINATION The route is set in the mountains that surround the village of Hout Bay, approximately 20km from Cape Town. This little town is close to the ocean, wine farms and enclosed by magnificent mountains.

THE TERRAIN The terrain is a mixture of beach, gravel singletrack, jeep track, a little bit of tar and concrete. There are some natural obstacles like rock scrambles, a river crossing on the beach and Leg 1 can be very overgrown in the summer months.

DIRECTIONS Hout Bay has three entry points – via Rhodes Drive, Victoria Road (M6) or the Chapman's Peak Toll Road. The trail starts at the Hout Bay Yacht Club (GPS 34°02'53.1"S, 18°20'51.9"E).

ACCOMMODATION Accommodation options in and around Hout Bay abound. Check the accommodation link on www.houtbaychallenge.co.za or www.fishhoek.com and also check www.houtbayonline.com

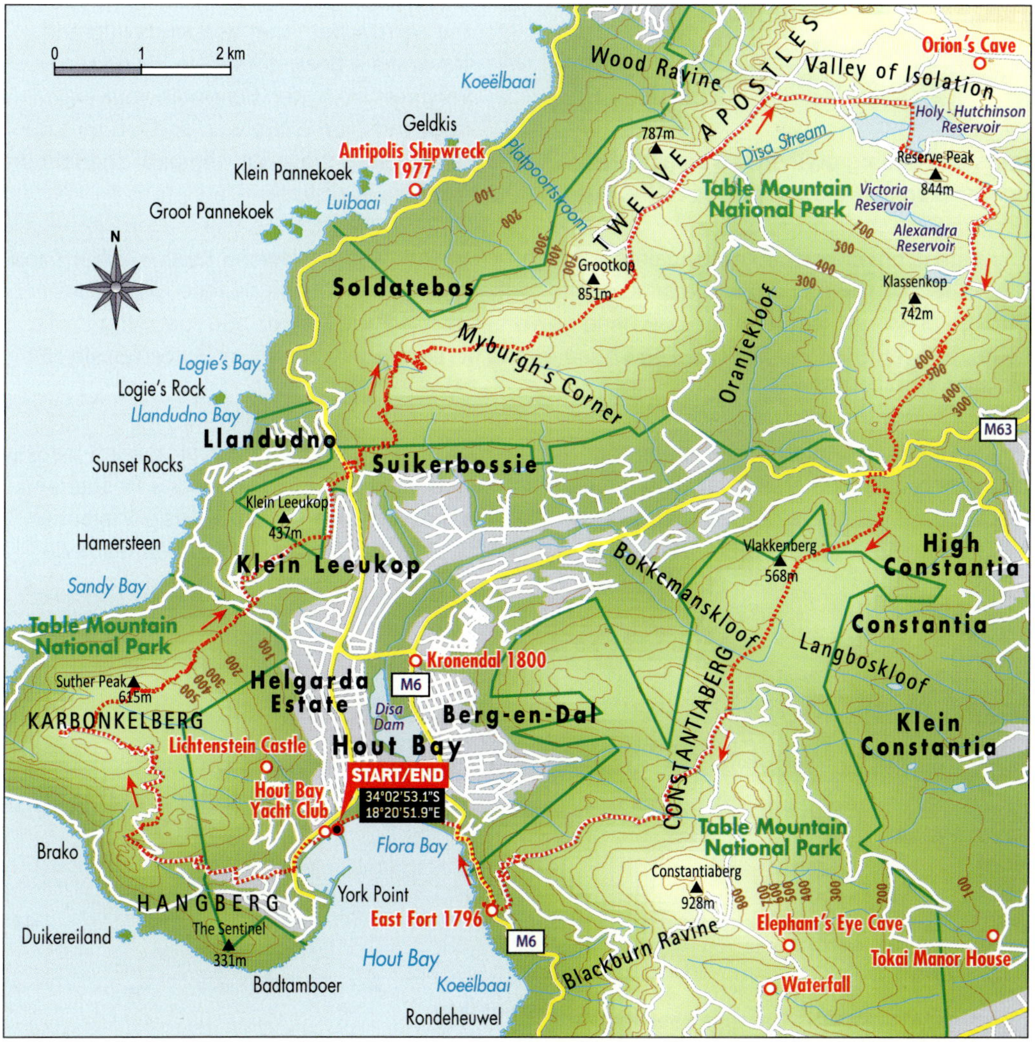

FAST FACTS

Grading Difficult to extreme
Duration 4.5–9hrs
Configuration Circular
Start point Hout Bay
GPS co-ordinates 34°02'53.1"S, 18°20'51.9"E
Terrain Gravel roads, lots of singletrack, technical rocky sections, some scrambling and fynbos 'bashing'
Map Full map and route description given to all runners)
Access requirements Race limited to 250 entries; free access
Trail markings Path only; the route is not marked and has to be self-navigated
Facilities All amenities in Hout Bay
Cell reception Good close to Hout Bay, intermittent en route
Beware Hydration is critical; keep a lookout for snakes (in summer) and mist (in winter)
Time of year July for the race; autumn and spring for the trail
Local info www.houtbay.org
More info wwww.houtbaychallenge.co.za /

THE TRAIL Leg 1 stretches from the Hout Bay Yacht Club to Suikerbossie Restaurant. The route heads west towards Karbonkelberg. From the harbour area, the route heads up to the Table Mountain National Park access gate and onto a jeep track leading to the very summit of Karbonkelberg. It is seriously eroded and full of dongas, levelling off as you near the top of Karbonkelberg. From the radar station at the summit, you'll have to retrace your steps down to the road past the last annexure building on your right in order to find the way to Suther Peak. Approximately 50m beyond this roofless ruin there is an obscure path to your left, marked by a small cairn on each side of the road. This area is not well marked and is fairly overgrown during summer. Follow the narrow path that descends into and traverses a beautiful valley; it's normally very wet in winter. Scramble your way right and then sharply up and left through roots and undergrowth into a small yellowwood forest. Nearing the crest, the path should turn right and around the south side of the peak before dropping in altitude.

The path is not clear, marked by cairns. Head down to the saddle between Karbonkelberg and Klein Leeu Koppie and cross the sand dunes to the brick-paved road. (The race route goes through private property; otherwise head down to Victoria Road.) When you reach the traffic lights, turn left onto Victoria Road and head up the hill commonly known as Suikerbossie Hill to Suikerbossie Restaurant.

Leg 2 runs from Suikerbossie Restaurant to Constantia Nek. There is a track on the left leading to the public parking area from where a path on the left, next to the Suikerbossie Restaurant fence, heads up to the contour paths above the pine forest. Pick a path towards Constantia Nek above the pines until you reach an intersection where a clear path to your left leads directly up to the ridge above you, Hout Bay Corner (300m).

GRADIENT PROFILE

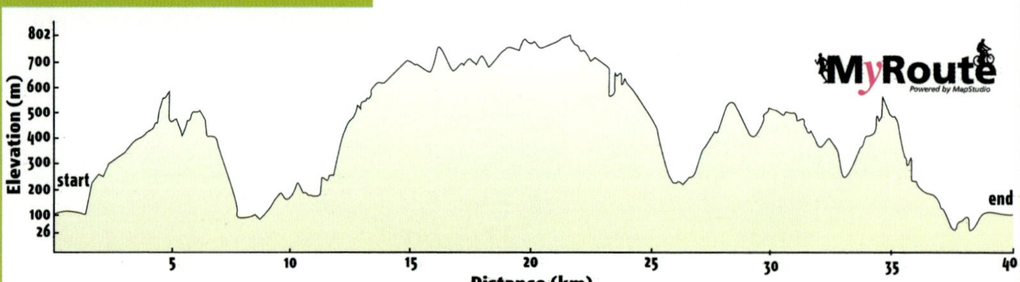

To view maps and gradient profiles go to **www.myroute.co.za**

From Hout Bay Corner the path turns to your right and follows the ridge. Scramble up a few ledges until you are under the cliff face. Head towards the sea and follow the path towards Camps Bay. The path runs below the cliff face and is narrow and sometimes fairly exposed. Keep going until you get to the bottom of Llandudno Ravine. The correct path up the ravine starts at the second stream, which you need to cross carefully. Follow the clear path to green anti-erosion fencing, then take the path that swings off to the left and upwards. It levels off quite quickly, heading northwards over solid rock. The path is initially faint, but well marked with cairns. It swings to the right again and climbs a wide shallow valley. At the top, proceed in the same direction, aiming at a medium-sized boulder, standing alone, from where the path is clear into another broad valley and across to Grootkop.

Climb up a steep, narrow path on Grootkop's right shoulder and down through a tunnel formed by two large overhanging boulders as you descend along a rocky path, which then undulates gently towards the Front Table of Table Mountain. After Slangolie Ravine, keep an eye out for a large cylindrical SANParks 'cairn' with direction markers. Take the path to your right along the 'old railway track' towards Woodhead Dam, looking for a path to the right that leads to the dam wall; run across and turn right onto the concrete jeep track.

Pass Victoria and Alexandra dams on your left and De Villiers Dam on your right. Stay on the road until you come to a hairpin to the right, followed by a tight zigzag. At the next major hairpin to the left, take the 'must-do' shortcut to the right that brings you to the gate at Constantia Nek.

Leg 3 heads from Constantia Nek to the Hout Bay Yacht Club. Run down towards Hout Bay for 100m, turning left just before the Silvermist entrance. Head up the broad path to the left and behind the Constantia Nek Restaurant. After a tortuous climb up some steps, you commence a gentler ascent up and over Vlakkenberg Nek. Drop into another valley where you can see the tar road up to the Constantiaberg Mast on the far side. Ignore any paths off to your left or right. Once on the tar road, turn right and proceed for a short distance. A painted white 'T' indicates the contour path's start on the right. Follow the contour path down left as the correct path to the manganese mines follows the contours of Constantiaberg. After the mines, the path drops more steeply. Make sure you keep dropping towards the jeep track and Chapman's Peak Drive, from where you run down towards Hout Bay Beach and the finish line at Hout Bay Yacht Club.

THE EVENT The Hout Bay Trail Challenge is run the last weekend of July, which is winter in the Cape, meaning cold and wet conditions. Entries are limited to 250 people; you can enter solo or as a relay team of three, each team member doing one leg.

EVENT FACTS

Event name Hout Bay Trail Challenge
Venue Hout Bay Yacht Club
Distance from Cape Town 20km
Time of year End of July
Enter as Solo or team of three
Cut-offs Yes (runners to be briefed at race)
Distance 40km
Average duration 4.5–9hrs
Entry info www.houtbaychallenge.co.za

Trail & Event

The Ilanga Trails
6km, 12km and 20km

Province Mpumalanga
Region Panorama and Lowveld
Closest town Hazyview
Trail destination Sandford Trust
Series Ilanga Trail Series
Contributed by Clive Smart

EVENT FACTS

Event name Horse Whispers 24
Venue Horse Whispers
Distance from Mbombela 62km
Time of year Mid-May
Enter as Solo
Cut-offs 20km only – 2.5hrs at the 10km aid station
Distance 6km, 12km and 20km
Average duration 3–6hrs for the 20km
Entry info www.ilangatrailseries.co.za / www.enteronline.com

THE DESTINATION Described on maps as a holiday village, Hazyview is highly rated as a value-for-money adventure destination, and is actually an unsung adventure mecca. The town boasts more than 30 adventure activities within half an hour of the centre, and stages a number of extreme events annually. The Ilanga Trail Series is just one of them.

THE TERRAIN The trail network predominantly traverses fairly dense bush, occasionally breaking out onto grassy slopes or agricultural lands. A combo of gravel roads and singletrack will allow you to experience the magical Eastern Escarpment of the Drakensberg and some legendary Lowveld venues.

DIRECTIONS Travel to Mbombela and head north on the R40 via White River and on to Hazyview. Horse Whispers (GPS **25°00′38.5″S, 31°06′49.7″E**) is situated to your left, 3.2km north of Hazyview along the R40.

ACCOMMODATION Accommodation in Hazyview and surrounds is plentiful, ranging from clean and neat backpackers and B&Bs to hotels and five-star lodges – www.big5country.co.za or www.krugerinfo.com

GRADIENT PROFILE

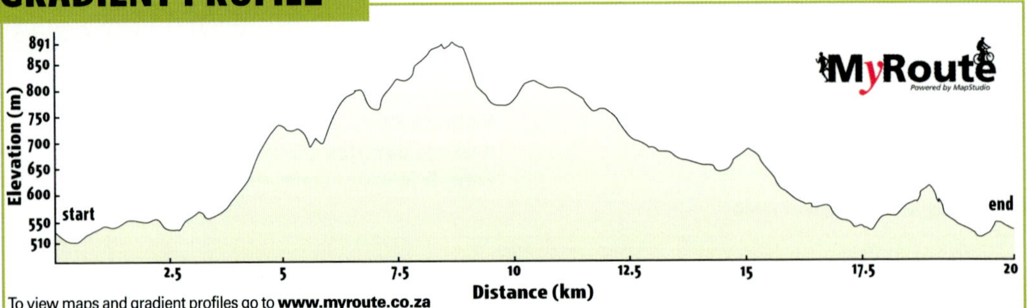

To view maps and gradient profiles go to **www.myroute.co.za**

THE TRAIL The 20km trail boasts that perfect combination of challenging terrain and scenic beauty. Starting in the foothills of Graskop, the trail is rough and ready, cutting through the bush along historical wagon roads dating back to the gold-mining era, or along twisting trails and fence lines bisecting native vegetation, grasslands and stands of wild protea. The elevation gain/loss is about 800m. Please note that the 20km route is not open to the public except on race day.

The 6km and 12km trails run through dense indigenous vegetation, crossing crystal-clear streams and open tracts of grassland. The slopes are not too difficult and most athletes will be comfortable on these routes. Park near the stables and check in; a small fee covers trail maintenance and the upkeep of the conservancy.

FAST FACTS

Grading Intermediate to difficult
Duration 3–6hrs
Configuration Circular
Start point Horse Whispers
GPS co-ordinates 25°00′38.5″S, 31°06′49.7″E
Terrain Mountainous; moderate jeep track and single-track
Map In info pack, e-mailed well before event
Access requirements Race entry fee; trail booking advisable; small conservation fee
Trail markings Metal signs
Facilities Toilets at start/finish, community-run snack stalls on race day
Cell reception Reasonable along most of the route
Beware Usual natural obstacles, hidden rocks, snakes
Time of year Mid-May for race; throughout the year for the trail
Local info www.ilangatrailseries.co.za /Tel (+27 82) 894 0432
More info www.big5country.co.za and www.kruger-info.com

Please note that prior booking, while not essential, is advisable. Make sure that you sign the book and state which trail you are undertaking. The average daytime temperatures in Hazyview range from 17°C in winter to 32°C in summer.

THE EVENT Held every three months – February, May, August and November – the Ilanga Trail Series moves from venue to venue annually. Although walkers are not allowed on the 12km or the 20km runs, the event is aimed at bringing the whole family together for the weekend.

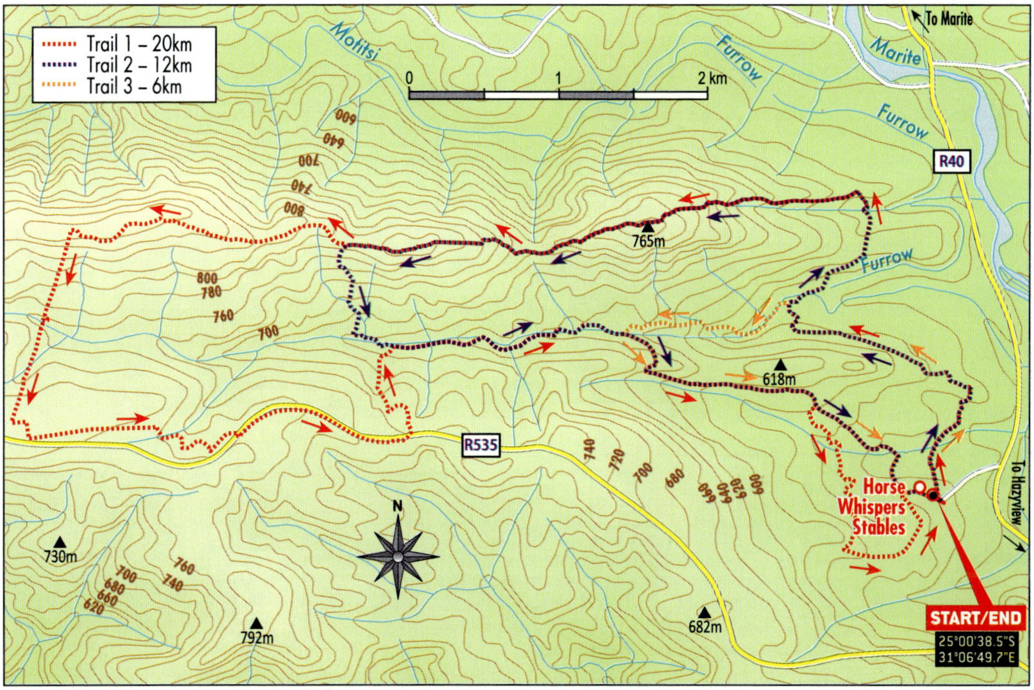

Event Only

Jikeleza

21, 28 and 30km (79km)

Province Eastern Cape
Region Wild Coast
Closest town Mazeppa Bay
Trail destination The Wild Coast between Mazeppa Bay and Cintsa
Series Stand-alone event
Contributed by Sarah Drew and James Hallet

THE DESTINATION The Jikeleza takes place along a picturesque stretch of the lower Wild Coast in the Eastern Cape between Mazeppa Bay and Cintsa. The Wild Coast is typified by steep valleys meandering down to the Indian Ocean, meeting a coastline that varies from golden arcs of solitary beach to treacherously rocky headlands and prominent cliffs.

THE TERRAIN The trail of the Jikeleza links together natural paths, developed by cattle, herdsmen and fishermen over the last hundred years or more, with long stretches of sand and rock beaches, parallel-running footpaths, sand and jeep tracks, and the occasional short section of road. A good 98% of the running takes place in the beach reserve, and there isn't a strictly 'correct' route. The trail can be affected by severe weather conditions – swollen rivers are the primary concern for runners' safety. That said, ferrymen are arranged at all major river crossings.

DIRECTIONS East London is the closest major transport hub to Mazeppa Bay. Coming from Cape Town, Durban or Johannesburg the simplest option is to fly in to East London and travel via shuttle to the start. It is also possible to self-drive: follow the N2 to Butterworth and turn right here at Kentani Road (GPS **32°19'45.0"S, 28°08'59.5"E**). Travel 34km to Kentani, then turn left and continue a further 16km to Mazeppa Bay Road, where you turn right to Mazeppa Bay Hotel (29km, GPS **32°28'40.3"S, 28°39'03.8"E**).

ACCOMMODATION The Mazeppa Bay Hotel is a relaxed three-star family hotel nestled in a beautiful tropical setting above the broad sweep of Mazeppa Bay beach. Options include sea-facing rooms, family rooms and budget bungalows (www.mazeppabay.co.za). Other self-catering options are available on websites such as www.wildcoastholidays.com and www.wildcoast.co.za

EXPERT'S VIEW

James Hallet is an avid trail runner, race director of the Umdoni Park Challenge (UPC) and the Editor of GO TRAIL Magazine, a popular digital trail running magazine.

Insider tips

'When running on a trail with such variable terrain one needs to anticipate what is coming over the next headland or around the next cove and adjust running needs accordingly. When running along the coastline you will often be required to quickly resort to different technical knowledge as the terrain changes so rapidly … the best advice would be to take it slowly on the rock, up the tempo on the runnable tracks (fishermen's and cattle) and then open up a little on the beaches.'

Gear and apparel

'Even though the weather on the Wild Coast is typically mild, for safety reasons you should carry something light that will keep you warm in emergencies. Moisture management is also essential, so wear quick-drying apparel that helps to avoid cramping, chaffing and extra weight. Correct footwear is also important, and your shoes must be comfortable for beach running and uneven terrain and also offer good protection from sharp rocks, etc.'

Training and pacing

Sarah Drew recommends: *'Check out the trail via Google Earth and have a close look at the types of terrain on the trail. By seeing what you need to tackle, it is possible to train in different areas that offer similar types of ground, such as sandy and rocky sections.'*

FAST FACTS

Grading Easy to intermediate
Duration Three days (3–4hrs, 4–5hrs and 4–5.5hrs)
Configuration Point to point
Start point Mazeppa Bay Hotel
GPS co-ordinates 32°28'40.3"S, 28°39'03.8"E
Terrain Beach; organic singletrack on grassy hills/flats; rocky shelves and pebble beach sections
Map Map and race details are included in the price
Access requirements Route restricted to race only, but private tours along this route can be arranged for groups outside of the event – contact Wild Trails
Trail markings None on the ground; a map and directions will be provided, but navigation on this coastal trail is easy and part of the challenge
Facilities No water or food tables on route; runners must be self-sufficient
Cell reception Generally okay; Vodacom have the best signal
Beware Heat, river crossings and slippery rocks
Time of year May – a full moon weekend to coincide with the spring low tides
Local info www.wildtrails.co.za

THE TRAIL The race is staged over three days of trail running, covering a total distance of 79km. The start point on Day One is Mazeppa Bay, with the final day ending at Cintsa.

Day One covers 21km, leaving from Mazeppa Bay. Runners will experience a good mix of Wild Coast territory, getting their bodies and brains in tune with the varied terrain. Sweating up and over grassy knolls, striding wide-open beaches and negotiating uneven rocky headlands – one mustn't forget the numerous river crossings that need to be planned carefully. Getting feet wet can cause havoc with blisters, but removing shoes will slow you down. Runners will skirt sandy bays edged by indigenous forests and *jikeleza* ('jog along') around a number of headlands, passing a few blind estuaries en route. Cebe River Mouth, part of the Cebe Nature Reserve, is a truly magical spot. Day one ends at Wavecrest, a comfortable hotel situated on the beautiful Nxaxo lagoon, with splendid views. Here you can while away the afternoon with a beer and a snooze.

Day Two is a bit more of a push with 28km to tackle. Leaving Wavecrest, runners follow cattle

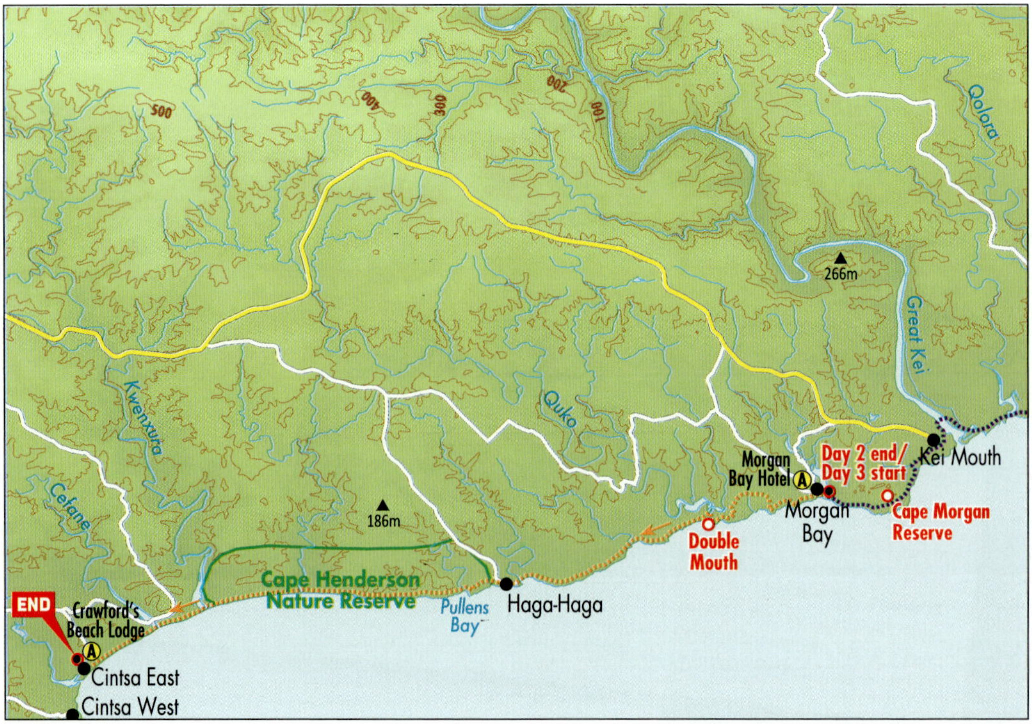

paths to the beach and run over a mix of grass and sand tracks to the first river crossing of the day: the Kobanqaba. If this river is swollen after heavy rains, a ferryman will be waiting, but racing teams may decide to take an early morning plunge. There are many choices in terms of cattle paths and jeep tracks that lead from the river, over which teams can gain or lose advantage, but you don't want to miss the Jacaranda shipwreck as this iconic landmark will hold a compulsory checkpoint. Paying a small fee will get you over the mighty Kei by motorised pontoon; thereafter teams will run through the small fishing village of Kei Mouth, before reaching the Cape Morgan Reserve. Past the old pump house, a final stretch of white sand brings the runners home to the Morgan Bay Hotel and the end of Day Two.

Day Three is the longest, with 30km of wild running terrain to test runners on the final stage of the event. Heading straight up a steep hill, teams find themselves with a bird's-eye view atop the spectacular Morgan Bay cliffs. The track then descends steeply to the beach at Double Mouth with the Quko River providing the first potential ankle-wetting of the day. After this, runners will pick up the organic paths running parallel and just inland of the rocky shore. Passing the abalone farm, you'll know that cold drinks are calling at the nearby Haga Haga Hotel. This also provides a good opportunity to make the next route call: up and over Whale lookout point or scrambling over a rocky shore through to Pullens Bay. The gorgeous Pullens Bay provides an excellent spot to catch a breather, after which runners will know the true meaning of rock-hopping! These boulder-strewn beach sections require a fair degree of balance and concentration to navigate. When you hit the beach again, it should be hard-packed sands flanked by high, vegetated dunes, all the way through to Cintsa. The long beach of Cape Henderson invites a dip in the ocean, while the Chefana Mouth marks the last estuary of the day – the landmark for racing teams to open up the throttle. The last night is spent at the swish Crawford's Beach Lodge.

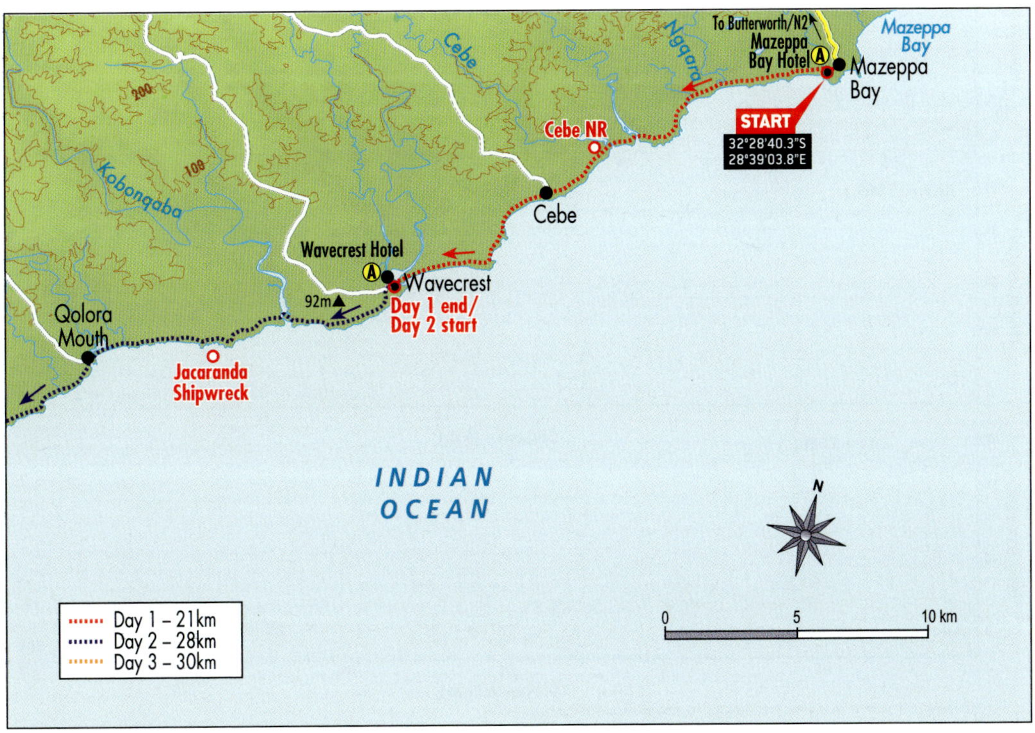

EVENT FACTS

Event name Jikeleza
Venue Southern Wild Coast
Distance from East London 180km
Time of year May
Enter as Teams of two
Cut-offs No, but there are checkpoints along the way
Distances 21, 28 and 30km (79km)
Average duration three days (3–4hrs, 4–5hrs and 4–5.5hrs)
Entry info www.wildtrails.co.za

THE EVENT On the three days (over a full-moon weekend) from Mazeppa Bay to Cintsa, competitors will cover 80km of wild running terrain – an experience not to be missed.

Whilst distances are intended to make racing teams work for their times with a tactical approach, the event will provide a fair but manageable challenge to running rookies. This is the perfect event to cut your teeth on: spectacular terrain, doable distances and a fun vibe; it offers an ample challenge and contest for all.

The aim of the Jikeleza is to provide a fun, challenging and accessible middle-distance trail running event for all levels of runner. However, runners should have a level of fitness appropriate for completing the daily distances.

GRADIENT PROFILES

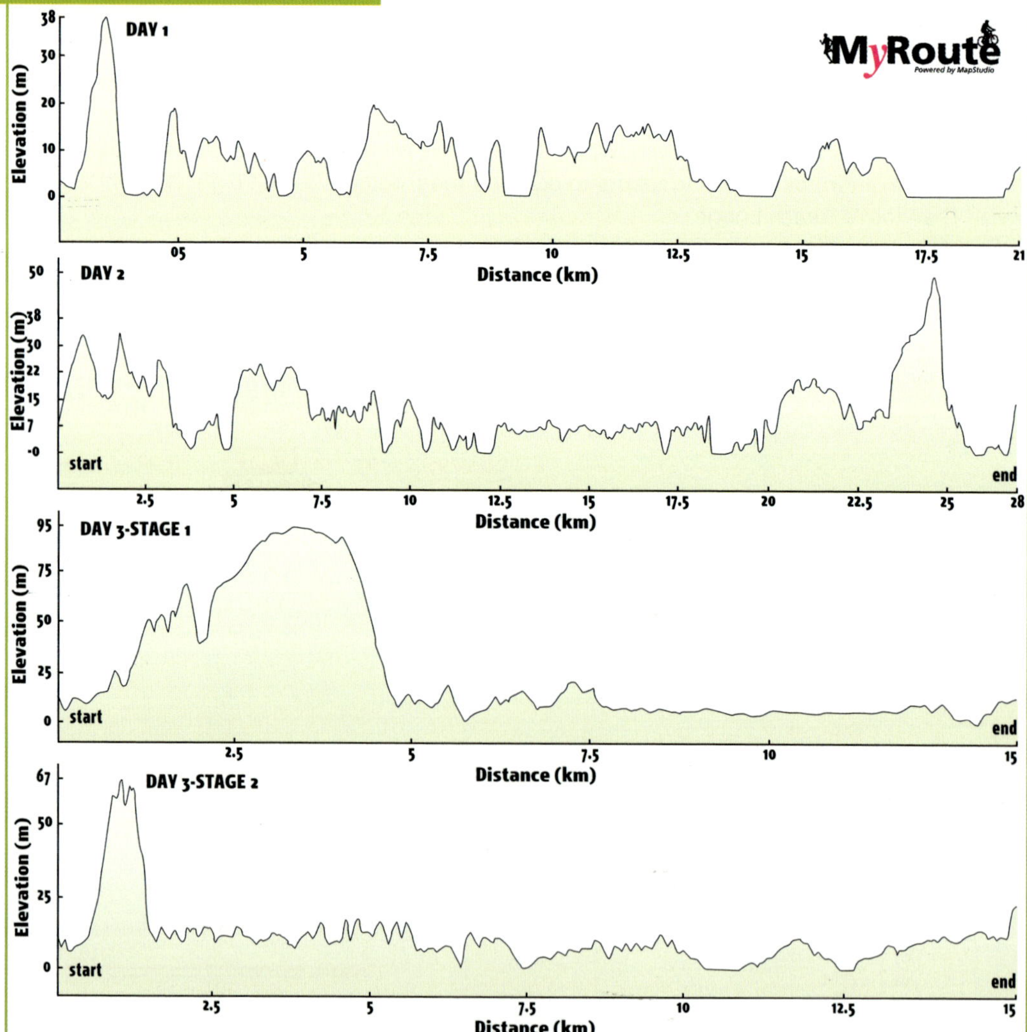

To view maps and gradient profiles go to **www.myroute.co.za**

Kaapsehoop Trail Run 16km

Trail Only

Province Mpumalanga
Region Panorama and Lowveld
Closest town Mbombela
Trail destination Kaapsehoop and surrounding nature reserve
Contributed by Andrew Dollenberg

THE DESTINATION Kaapsehoop is situated just 30km southwest of Mbombela on the edge of the Mpumalanga escarpment. This fairy-tale village is well known for its mist and wild horses that roam free in the area. Weathered sandstone formations, spectacular views, historic sites and pristine nature trails are just a few of the reasons to return here time and again. The most pristine area is the Blue Swallow Conservancy Area. The area to the north and west is dominated by pine plantations belonging to Sappi and Komatieland Forestry.

THE TERRAIN Rock fields cover the plains around the town, with weathered sandstone formations on a bed of quartzite. Boulder hopping along the high, grassy plain is par for the course. A well-marked trail shows the way, though grass and thick vegetation, especially in the summer months, may obscure the track at times. The trail is often slippery due to the constant mist and damp conditions.

DIRECTIONS Follow the Kaapsehoop Road from Mbombela for 30km; it's a winding, steep route. Alternatively, from Gauteng, pass through Machadodorp along the N4, then take the Ngodwana turn-off (GPS **25°34′28.3″S, 30°40′03.8″E**) onto the D799 and continue for 12km to Kaapsehoop (GPS **25°35′31.0″S, 30°45′59.5″E**).

ACCOMMODATION There is plenty of overnight accommodation in Kaapsehoop, ranging from backpackers to luxury suites. Restaurants and eateries dominate the main road of the town.

FAST FACTS

Grading Easy to difficult (depending on route option)
Duration 2hrs to several days
Configuration Return and circular options
Start point Kaapsehoop
GPS co-ordinates 25°35'31.0"S, 30°45'59.5"E
Terrain Singletrack and gravel forestry roads
Map Basic map is available from Komatieland Eco Tourism
Access requirements Paid permit required for overnight trails
Trail markings Painted footprints, wood and metal signs
Facilities Basic huts along trails; water is sparse and shallow streams sometimes silted
Cell reception Good coverage
Beware Loose rocks, slippery surfaces
Time of year All year – summer drizzle and mist; winter clear and dry, but extremely cold
Local info www.kaapsehoop.com
More info www.komatiecotourism.co.za / Tel (+27 13) 754 2724

THE TRAIL This 3 000ha conservancy, including the unspoilt Blue Swallow Natural Heritage Site, provides many options and opportunities for exploring the area. Natural wonders, historical sites, waterfalls and forests all lie in wait. There are many combinations available from the five-day hiking trail loops, which all criss-cross through the town (www.komatiecotourism.co.za). The recommended route described here comprises part of the Florence Hill / Blue Swallow trails. It's an easy to moderate run of 16km and should take you two to three hours to complete.

Follow the Blue Swallow / Florence Hill trails out of town in an easterly direction between the windblown sandstone rock formations towards the edge of the escarpment. The trail is well marked in this part with white painted footprints on the stones and rocks. After 1.5km, there is a short detour to the left to the edge of the escarpment, overlooking Barberton and the Swaziland mountains. This is one of the highest points on the trail, offering magnificent views on a clear day.

Follow the trail along the edge of the escarpment in a southwesterly to southerly direction for a further 5.5km until you reach Adam's Calendar, an arrangement of stone monoliths dating back an estimated 75 000 years, arranged to show the cardinal points, solstices, and Orion's Belt. The

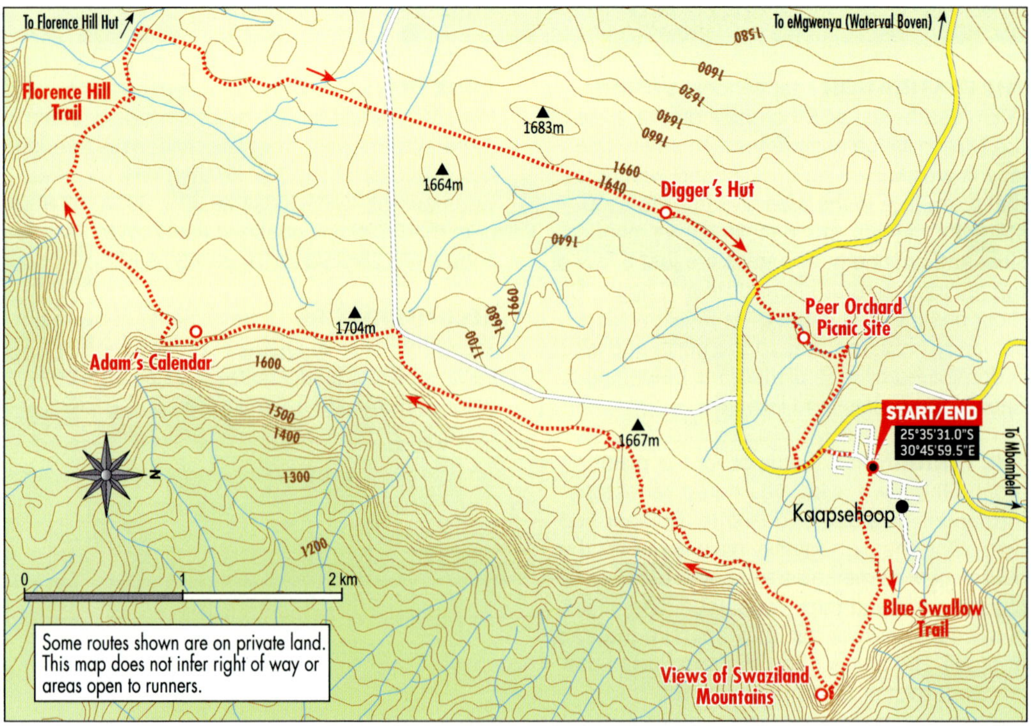

views over the edge of the escarpment on your left as you negotiate this section are breathtaking. Blue swallows are known to nest in this area and you might meet herds of wild horses along these plains. Take care to approach and pass them carefully.

Follow the jeep track just west of Adam's Calendar south for just over 1km; look out for a turn-off to the right. (The Florence Hill hiking hut is straight on.) Head into the forest plantation, cross over a small bridge and follow the path to a gravel forestry road. Turn right and head north, back towards Kaapsehoop. This road emerges from the plantation, and continues with a plantation on your left and open grassy plains on your right. Keep to this road, more of a jeep track now, to the old Digger's Hut overlooking the creek.

Follow the path along the creek to the main road. Cross over the road and head to the picnic site at Peer Orchard where shallow pools offer a refreshing swim. Cross the creek on the weir below the pools, run around the left of a small plantation and follow the river towards a waterfall. Head back towards the main road and Kaapsehoop.

© PETER KIRK

© PETER KIRK

EXPERT'S VIEW

Andrew Dollenberg is a road runner who dabbles in the occasional spot of trail running and mountain biking. He has completed more than 90 marathons and ultras, including 10 Comrades Marathons.

My run

'The misty hills, majestic horses, distant views, tales of gold prospecting and ancient history surrounding this area are astounding. The rocky sandstone formations and the route along the edge of the escarpment call for concentration coupled with sheer enjoyment. This trail can be made longer for the more experienced trail runner, or cut short to be accessible to the amateur'.

Insider tips

'Drinking water is not available along the trail, except at the overnight huts. The trail is well marked, but you may get disoriented in the mist. Pack wet-weather gear, and keep some dry kit for after the run. Speak to any of the locals or contact Enos Zulu, a local birding and tour guide, on Tel (+27 72) 331 1197 for information'.

Training and pacing

'Taking on these trails requires one to be reasonably fit. The altitude and varying weather conditions can put a strain on the body. Going out easy will ensure a pleasant run – the early part of the trail is far more technical and demanding than the return section'.

GRADIENT PROFILE

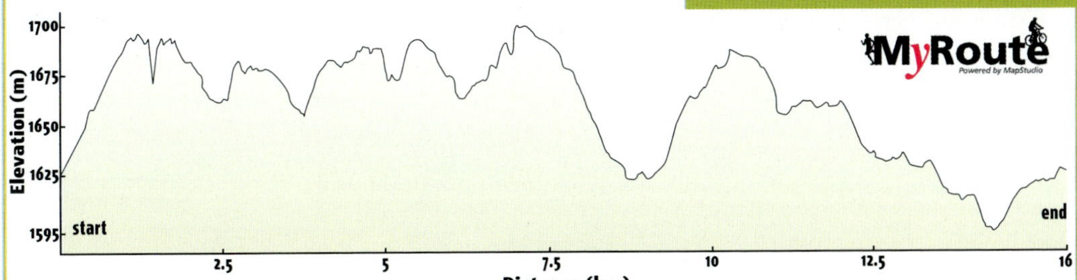

To view maps and gradient profiles go to **www.myroute.co.za**

Event Only

Kalahari Augrabies Extreme Marathon

250km (seven days)

Province Northern Cape
Region The Green Kalahari
Closest town Augrabies
Trail destination Augrabies Falls National Park
Contributed by Laura Forster and Dirk Cloete

© JACQUES MARAIS

THE DESTINATION This is a destination of sunsets, rivers, rocks, sand, wide horizons and endless skies. Presented in a region famous for blistering temperatures, succulent table grapes, and the sixth largest waterfall in the world, the 250km staged, self-sufficient Kalahari Augrabies Extreme Marathon (KAEM) offers runners and walkers a unique way to experience the varied and extreme landscapes of the Green Kalahari. The Augrabies Falls National Park – situated on the southeastern side of the Orange River between Augrabies Falls and Onseepkans – is off limits on foot outside of the actual race.

THE TERRAIN Every year, race director Estienne Arndt devises a new 250km course through the diverse terrain of the arid Kalahari. Athletes run through sandy river beds, across boulder fields, along wide dirt roads, through verdant vineyards, deep within gorges and across never-ending plains to the finish within the Augrabies Falls National Park.

DIRECTIONS Registration for the KAEM is at Augrabies Falls National Park, on the R359, 8km west of Kakamas and approximately 120km from Upington. The race route changes each year: runners are transported to the start from the Augrabies Falls National Park (GPS 28°35'39.3"S, 20°20'16.5"E).

ACCOMMODATION At Race HQ, runners are accommodated in the modern, air-conditioned chalets of the national park. Various packages are offered by the race organisers. Options range from overnight accommodation and transfers from Johannesburg, to pared-down packages where participants make their own way.

FAST FACTS

Grading Extreme
Duration 7-day race (25–70hrs of actual run time), 11-day (day before/after) package
Configuration 250km linear, staged route; self-sufficient; daily distances from 28–80km
Start point Augrabies Falls National Park
GPS co-ordinates 28°35'39.3"S, 20°20'16.5"E
Terrain Varied desert terrain from sand to boulders, flat to steep
Map From race organiser at registration
Access requirements No access outside race
Trail markings Well-marked route with bunting, metal signs, fluorescent orange tabs, LED lights (night stage)
Facilities Before and after the race – full board and accommodation; on the race – checkpoints along route; gazebo-type open shelters at night, with water and cooking fires; carry own food, bedding and kit
Cell reception Variable
Beware Extreme temperatures, dehydration and blisters
Time of year Presented October/November around full moon
Local info www.sanparks.org and www.northerncape.org.za
More info www.extrememarathons.com /Tel (+27 44) 690 3420 or (+27 83) 309 7755

THE TRAIL The Augrabies Falls National Park is accessible only by vehicle and is only open to hikers or runners on some short trails in the vicinity of the falls. As such, the Race Director ensures that full advantage is taken of the range of spectacular route choices available as the race wends its 250km way across the Kalahari. In some places the route emerges from the park and crosses private farms and vineyards. Again, these venues are generally not accessible to the public, and then chiefly by vehicle.

THE EVENT The KAEM spans nine days of racing, offers various packages and is planned around a mid-week full moon. It begins on a Thursday evening with a pre-race dinner, followed by registration and briefing the following day. The race kicks off on Saturday morning and goes through to the following Friday, with one rest day during the week.

Due to the terrain, climate and distance, this gruelling 250k self-sufficient, staged, desert event can only be tackled after a structured period of specific conditioning and training. Participants must carry a pack with every item of food, clothing and kit that they expect to need for a week of running through the desert. Daily distances vary from 25 to 80km, following a fixed, marked route between rest camps, with checkpoints offering water and medical support at around 10km intervals. Temperatures can reach above 40°C and the combination of heat, terrain, and pack weight will challenge even experienced, fit athletes.

Due to the self-sufficient nature of the event, typical pack weights range from 8–12kg, with the bulk of this made up by food and up to 1.5 litres of water. The choice of pack contents is left to the runners, although compulsory items like basic medical supplies and a survival kit are non-negotiable.

EVENT FACTS

Event name Kalahari Augrabies Extreme Marathon
Venue Augrabies Falls National Park and surrounds
Distance from Upington 115km
Time of year October or November, depending on full moon
Enter as Solo
Cut-offs Yes – sunset, other than one long stage including a night run
Distance 250km
Average duration 7 days (25–70hrs of actual run time)
Entry info www.extrememarathons.com

However, none of this precludes the novice, provided that their preparation and conditioning prior to the event has been thorough. For this reason, there is no 'entry requirement' other than a doctor's certificate of a clean bill of health. The event caters for hares and tortoises alike by ensuring that those requiring more time start each day's stage in the cool of the early morning, whilst faster competitors are sent off at later intervals, to provide all athletes with a challenge equal to their ability.

This graded approach is applied particularly to the 70–80km 'long day'. This challenge within a challenge takes place in the first half of the race, when packs are still heavy, and is designed to ensure every runner encounters both the heat of the day and surreal full-moon desert at night. Based on finishing times from the previous 2–3 days, runners are sent off from the overnight camp in small groups from 06:00 to noon on this epic leg, with a rest day to look forward to the following day.

At the regular checkpoints along the marked race route, 1.5 litres of water is available for each runner. Any runner showing signs of injury, ill health, dehydration or heat stress will be assessed, supported and, if necessary, withdrawn from the event.

EXPERT'S VIEW

After sustaining numerous injuries in contact sport, **Dirk Cloete** took up first road running and then off-road endurance racing. Over a running career spanning less than two decades, he has bagged more than 10 silver medals in both the Comrades and Two Oceans marathons and racked up wins in races as diverse as the Washie 100-Miler, Odyssey Stage Race, Kalahari Augrabies Extreme Marathon, Namib Desert Challenge and Gobi Desert Race.

My shoe

Brand ~ Columbia
Model ~ Ravenous
Rating ~ The only trail shoe rugged enough for the roughest of terrain; excellent grip, but still has the cushioning of a road-running shoe; among the lightest shoes in its range

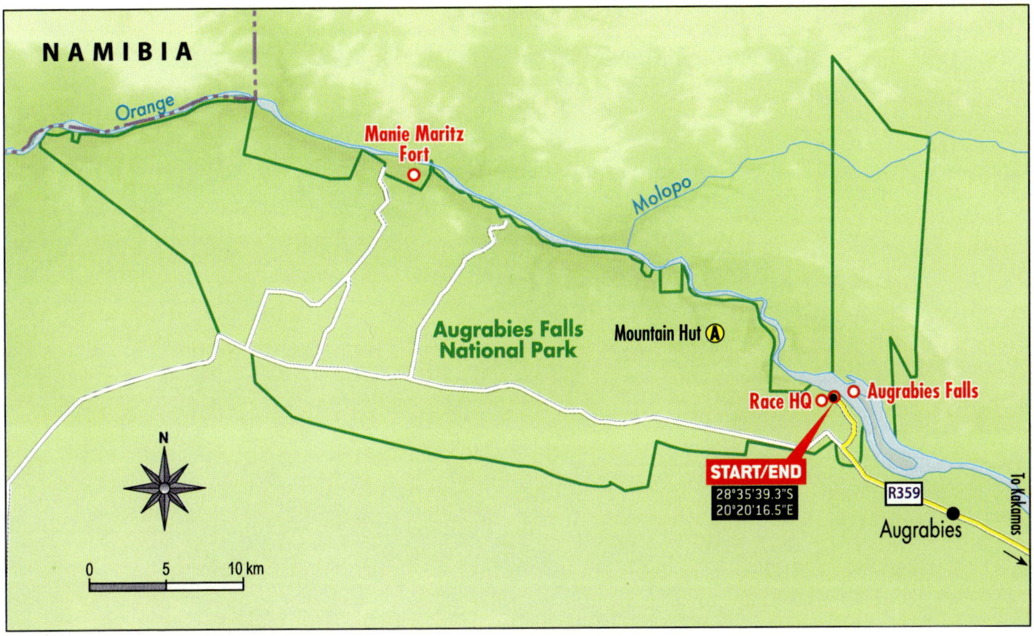

Trail & Event

Katberg Sky Trail

38.3km

Province Eastern Cape
Region Border
Closest town Fort Beaufort
Trail destination Winterberg Mountain Range (Katberg Eco Golf Estate, Hotel & Spa)
Contributed by Liam Victor and Don Simms

© LIAM VICTOR

THE DESTINATION Discover one of the 'Frontier Country's' tourism gems here at the Katberg Eco Golf Estate, Hotel & Spa. Mountains, forested slopes, plantations and grassland plateaus make it a perfect destination for trail runners keen to roam free.

THE TERRAIN Game footpaths, runnable singletrack, logging roads and jeep track combine along a route that will have ultra endurance athletes salivating. Temperate weather prevails for much of the year, but you can expect snowfalls from June through to August.

DIRECTIONS Follow the N6 towards Cathcart and continue onwards to Seymour (you can also approach this little farming town from Fort Beaufort). Look for a gravel road to Balfour, after which you will reach the Katberg Eco Golf Estate, Hotel & Spa. The run starts from the Katberg Manor House on the estate.

ACCOMMODATION The hotel caters for all your needs, from state-of-the-art golf villas and serviced rooms to scenic camping stands with fantastic ablution facilities.

EXPERT'S VIEW

Donovan Simms is an adventure racer with the Merrell Adventure Addicts. He has raced in World Championship events on five continents, and is an avid mountain biker and trail runner.

My shoe

Brand ~ Merrell

Trail Model ~ Seismics

Rating ~ By far the best shoe on the market; neutral and great for anything from slippery rocks to snow

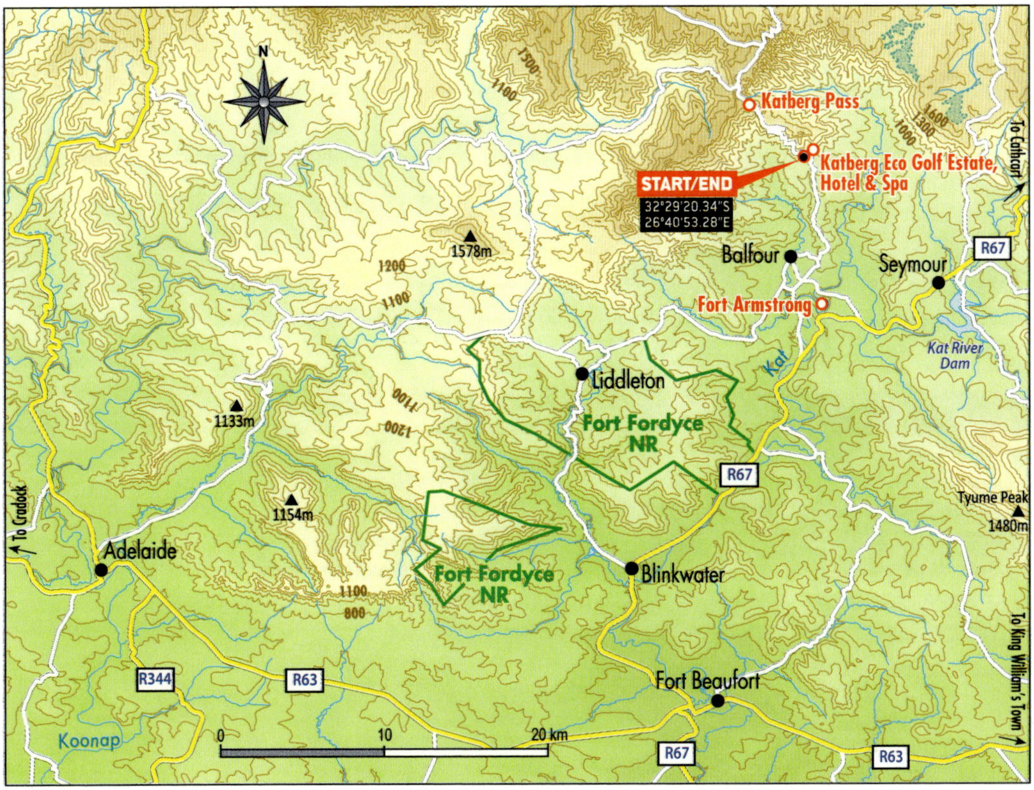

FAST FACTS

Grading Extreme
Duration 4–7hrs
Configuration Circular route (38.3km)
Start point Katberg Halfway House
GPS co-ordinates 32°29'20.34"S, 26°40'53.28"E
Terrain Mountainous singletrack; some gravel road
Map Contact Liam Victor (see below)
Access requirements Only on race day
Trail markings Lumo tape, metal staves and wooden signs
Facilities All amenities at Katberg Eco Golf Estate, Hotel & Spa
Cell reception 100% on most sections of trail
Beware Extreme temperatures; slippery trail surface; fog
Time of year All year long
Local info Liam Victor at liamv@katleisure.co.za / Tel (+27 82) 927 3395
More info www.katleisure.co.za /Tel (+27 43) 706 3000

THE TRAIL The Katberg Sky Trail can only be run in winter, when the route is cut back and cleared for the event.

The initial section of the Sky Trail follows the same route as the Katberg Eco Trail, but there comes a time when you have to truly test your mettle against this mammoth mountain range. Beyond the Katberg Game Reserve, you will begin the first of many a gruelling climb along a steep logging road, with the thin air burning your lungs.

Climb and climb and climb, taking in the views from the 1m-wide trail, until the route gradually flattens out for about 6km at an altitude of 1 600m. When this stretch of heaven ends, you're onto a winding descent along the original road between the Eastern Cape and Gauteng.

Although this is a national road in name, the Katberg Pass has not been maintained in many years, and your foot placement needs to be accurate to avoid loose stones and ruts. Just prior to reaching the base of the mountain, another awesome section of singletrack waits. This trail winds right back onto the Katberg Hotel property, with only the fairways to navigate back to the finish line and the cosy pub.

This is an extreme trail and many finishers may be bleeding from the odd run-in with a 'haak-en-steek' thorn bush. Mud, sweat and tears are soon forgotten, however, when runners plunge into the pool, complete with all their gear. Hot showers, cold beers and a scrumptious meal will have you referring to Katberg as 'Fatberg' in no time at all.

THE EVENT This 38.3km event is not recommended for the faint-hearted; it is run at 1km above sea level for the duration of the trail, with a high point of 1 650m.

EVENT FACTS

Event name Katberg Sky Trail
Venue Katberg Eco Golf Estate, Hotel & Spa
Distance 38.3km
Time of year July
Enter as Solo
Cut-offs Not until dark, depending on weather conditions
Event organiser Kat Leisure Hotel Group
Average duration 4–7hrs
Entry info www.katleisure.co.za

Laborie Paarl Rock Run

10/20km

Trail & Event

Province Western Cape
Region Boland / Winelands
Closest town Paarl
Trail destination Laborie Wine Estate / Paarl Rock Nature Reserve
Series Energy Events
Contributed by Derrick Baard

© JACQUES MARAIS

THE DESTINATION Laborie Wine Estate in Paarl is situated at the foot of the famed Paarl Rock outcrops, and there can be few wine estates where one would rather spend a lazy Saturday morning than this. Manor houses, craft and food markets, quality wines to taste – this is the life.

THE TERRAIN The run commences at the spectacular Laborie Wine Estate situated adjacent to the magnificent Paarl Nature Reserve. Gravel roads, boardwalks, hiking trails and trippy rock-rabbit running all combine for a fantastic day out on the trails.

DIRECTIONS Laborie Wine Estate is set centrally in Paarl; look for the signage to your left about 2km after you've turned into the Main Road off the N1.

FAST FACTS

Grading Intermediate
Duration 2.5–4hrs
Configuration Circular or return
Start point Laborie Wine Estate
GPS co-ordinates 33°45′57.73″S, 18°57′33.22″E
Terrain Farm roads, jeep track, singletrack and rock
Map Available from Paarl Nature Reserve
Access requirements Daily permit must be purchased
Trail markings Painted footprints, wood and metal signs
Facilities Restaurant, shops, market at Laborie; braai facilities, ablutions in reserve
Cell reception Good
Beware Extreme temperatures
Time of year All year round; avoid midday runs in summer
Local info www.paarltourism.co.za

THE TRAIL Start off with a stiff climb right from the gun as you head through the vineyards in order to access the paths and jeep tracks of Paarl Nature Reserve. On the race day, the route is well marked to ensure no-one gets lost, but the many reserve roads and trails make for superb exploration on any given day.

The pleasant surprise of 'discovering' the tiny indigenous forest – tucked away behind the granite inselbergs near the summit – is a major bonus, especially as you could pick up the pace along well-constructed wooden boardwalks.

And then the proverbial cherry on top: the rewarding views and sense of achievement that come with ascending the quad-busting climb along the super-grippy rock surface up the steep summit of Paarl Rock.

From the summit, the 360-degree vista over Paarl and the Winelands adds to the already breathless state of most of the athletes. Enjoy the view, suck in some seriously fresh air and then 'freewheel' your way onto the paths and trails leading back to Laborie Wine Estate.

THE EVENT There are 10km and 20km options, with both routes suited to most levels of athletes. The terrain isn't very technical, but a few short, steep climbs will make you enjoy relaxing on the lawns of the historic Laborie Wine Estate even more.

EVENT FACTS

Event name Laborie Paarl Rock Run
Venue Laborie Wine Estate, Paarl
Distance 10km / 20km
Time of year Mid-October
Enter as Solo
Cut-offs Runners to be briefed at race
Event organiser Energy Events
Average duration 2.5–4hrs
Entry info www.trailrunning.co.za

© JACQUES MARAIS

© JACQUES MARAIS

EXPERT'S VIEW

Derrick Baard is a trail runner and mountain biker sponsored by Hammer Nutrition and Salomon. He has competed in multi-day endurance events such as the 2 300km Freedom Challenge, ABSA Cape Epic, G4 Challenge, Africa X and Dryland Traverse.

My shoe

Brand ~ Salomon

Model ~ SLAB 4

Rating ~ An incredible lightweight all-purpose multi-terrain trail-racing shoe with superior outer sole grip. The SLAB 4's seamless upper lends itself to a very comfortable and snug-fitting shoe that is great on most terrain.

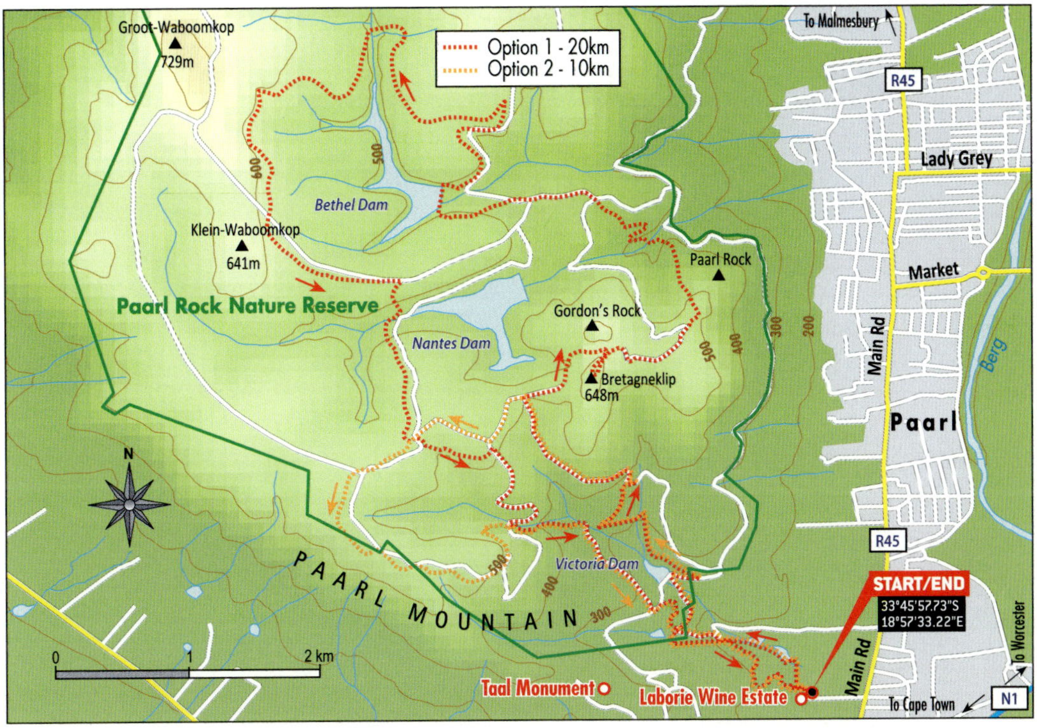

GRADIENT PROFILE

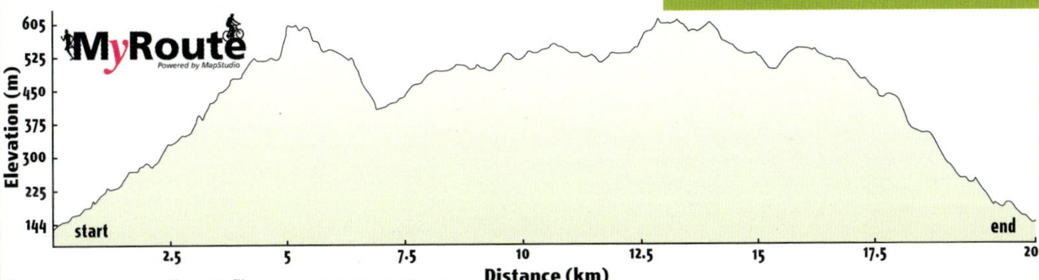

To view maps and gradient profiles go to **www.myroute.co.za**

Trail & Event

Magaliesberg Challenge Trail Run

10 / 20 / 35km

Province Gauteng
Region Magaliesberg / Hartbeespoort
Closest town Hartbeespoort
Trail destination Van Gaalen Cheese Farm
Series Crazy Store Series
Contributed by Grant Ross

© PETER KIRK

THE DESTINATION About 20km west of Hartbeespoort Dam, nestled within mountains more than a million years old, you will find the Van Gaalen Cheese Farm. This is the venue for all three Crazy Store routes on offer. The farm boasts a network of custom-made singletrack of varying difficulty, all starting from a comfortable base camp. A good restaurant, conference centre, children's playground, accommodation and cheese-tasting add to the attraction.

THE TERRAIN The three routes on offer increase in technicality and difficulty with each increment in distance. Expect flowing singletrack along streams, through gullies and dongas, past a scenic Greek Church, and winding through typical Highveld grasslands and rock gardens. A definite highlight would be the challenging sky-running terrain awaiting runners who take on the long route. The terrain caters for runners of all abilities.

DIRECTIONS From Johannesburg, follow the R512 from Randburg all the way to the south side of Hartbeespoort Dam. Continue past Pecanwood Estate and turn left on the R560, then right immediately to Van Gaalen.

The trail head is situated at the base camp on Van Gaalen Cheese Farm. All trails start here and are accessible to the public six days a week (closed on Tuesdays). Park at the restaurant and get your day permits here.

ACCOMMODATION Various accommodation options are available at Van Gaalen. Abundant bird life, a lovely hiking trail, braai facilities and a garden restaurant add to the experience.

FAST FACTS

Grading Easy to difficult
Duration 1–6hrs
Configuration Circular route (10km and 20km), A to B (35km)
Start point Van Gaalen Cheese Farm
GPS co-ordinates 25°47'16.3"S, 27°46'19.6"E
Terrain Gravel roads and technical singletrack
Map Available at venue
Access requirements Open all week, except Tuesdays; day permits available
Trail markings Permanent
Facilities Restaurant and accommodation
Cell reception Intermittent on some sections
Beware Rocky sections and floating bridge; river crossings
Time of year All year round; beware of thunderstorms in summer
Local info www.runtrail.co.za
More info www.trailrunning.co.za

THE TRAIL A range of routes will suit runners of varying abilities; all of these are permanently marked with predetermined distances and difficulty ratings. The Magaliesberg Challenge consists of a 10km river meander, a 20km intermediate route and finally a challenging 30km option to take you beyond your comfort zone.

The 10k route crosses a low river bridge and then meanders along a network of streams for the entire route, so you can expect it to be flat. Entertaining terrain, suitable to any and all runners, traverses riverine forest, reed tunnels, donga trails and a wobbly floating bridge.

The 20km route heads out along the same route, but then climbs away from the river near the 5km mark into the foothills of the Magaliesberg. A gentle ascent takes runners to the quaint Greek Church set within an acacia-thorn thicket, before the route drops down to the valley below toward the finish.

The tough 35km route has a satellite start and competitors are taken by bus to a neighbouring farm. A short burst of gravel road and jeep track quickly morphs into singletrack winding straight to the summit of the Magaliesberg. From here, the route follows a rugged ridge line eastwards along a spectacular divide for a riveting 'sky run'. A technical descent takes you back down to the 20km route into the finish.

THE EVENT The 35km race is not recommended for novices or those with a fear of heights. This is quality technical running for wild-at-heart trail junkies; if this is not your poison, opt for one of the lesser distances. With the Crazy Store as the main sponsor, dressing up is the name of the game, making for a great laugh on the day.

EVENT FACTS

Event name The Crazy Store Magaliesberg Challenge
Series name Crazy Store Series
Venue Van Gaalen Cheese Farm
Distances 10km / 20km / 35km
Time of year Mid-August
Enter as Solo or team
Cut-offs Yes (runners to be briefed at race)
Event organiser Energy Events
Average duration 3–6hrs (35km)
Entry info www.trailrunning.co.za

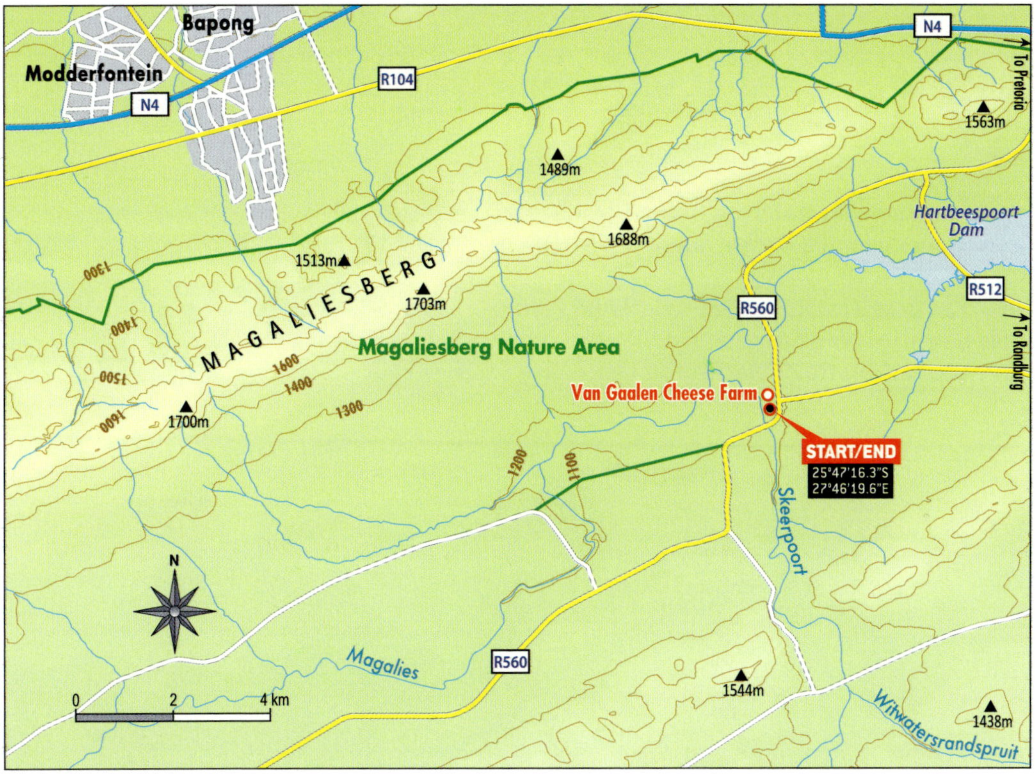
Bapong
Modderfontein
N4
R104
N4
To Pretoria
1563m
1489m
Hartbeespoort Dam
1688m
1513m
MAGALIESBERG
1703m
R560
R512
To Randburg
Magaliesberg Nature Area
Van Gaalen Cheese Farm
START/END
25°47'16.3"S
27°46'19.6"E
1700m
1300
1400
1500
1600
1200
1100
Skeerpoort
N
Magalies
R560
1544m
1438m
Witwatersrandspruit
0
2
4 km

Trail & Event

Mont-aux-Sources Challenge

50km

Province KwaZulu-Natal
Region uKhahlamba-Drakensberg
Closest town Bergville
Trail destination Royal Natal National Park
Series Bonitas Wild Series
Contributed by Heidi Mocke and Lance Chapman

© KELVIN TRAUTMAN

THE DESTINATION The Royal Natal National Park arguably rates as one of the planet's premier hiking destinations, with breathtaking scenery and spectacular natural wonders. The renowned Drakensberg Amphitheatre – a 5km rock wall looming 500m high at the foot of the towering Mont-aux-Sources peaks – is certainly one sight you will never forget. Rivers such as the Orange and Tugela start their meandering journeys to the far-off ocean right here.

THE TERRAIN This is real mountainous terrain with ever-changing weather patterns, from severe summer thunderstorms and swirling mists to snowfalls in winter. The route is a combination of gravel roads and hiking trails, with rocky terrain which can become especially slippery in wet weather. The chain ladders add a challenging dimension to the run and due care should be taken when ascending these at all times.

DIRECTIONS The conventional route is off the N3; turn onto the N11 just past Ladysmith and proceed to Bergville (GPS 28°43′46.5″S, 29°21′05.1″E). The Royal Natal National Park (GPS 28°41′23.2″S, 28°56′46.0″E) is well signposted from here.

ACCOMMODATION The Royal Natal National Park offers several self-catering accommodation options as well as camping at Rugged Glen or Mahai – www.kznwildlife.com

FAST FACTS

Grading Difficult to extreme
Duration 5–10hrs
Configuration Out and back
Start point Royal Natal National Park, Mahai camp site
GPS co-ordinates 28°41′23.2″S, 28°56′46.0″E
Terrain Singletrack, rugged jeep track and chain ladders
Map Available from www.montauxsourceschallenge.co.za
Access requirements The race is by invitation only; email heidim@wildlands.co.za for info; hiking trails open all year
Trail markings Directional arrows and candy tape
Facilities Refreshment tables every 10km
Cell reception None in some of the valleys
Beware Altitude and quick changes in weather; afternoon thunderstorms
Time of year First weekend in September
Local info www.kznwildlife.com
More info www.montauxsourceschallenge.co.za / Tel (+27 33) 343 6380

THE TRAIL Your main reason to visit the Royal Natal National Park is to hike along a network of spectacular hiking trails criss-crossing the park and ascending right to the top of the Drakensberg. A map and booklet are on sale at the Visitor Centre or main entry gate: complete the Mountain Rescue Register and the Berg is your oyster!

THE EVENT There is a reason why the Mont-aux-Sources Challenge rates as one of South Africa's most prestigious trail runs. What more could a runner want than 50km of wild running along the mighty Drakensberg? Pain gives way to magnificent views over the Drakensberg once at the top, but heading down to the finish is when the true battle starts.

Make no mistake: this is a 'toughie'; but it is one of those races that are really worth it. The route follows a hiking path up the Mahai valley and past the Mahai Falls to Witsieshoek Mountain Resort, a climb of some 1 700m over a distance of 9km. From here to Sentinel Car Park (9km) a rough and undulating dirt road climbs a further 300m, with fantastic views all around on a clear day.

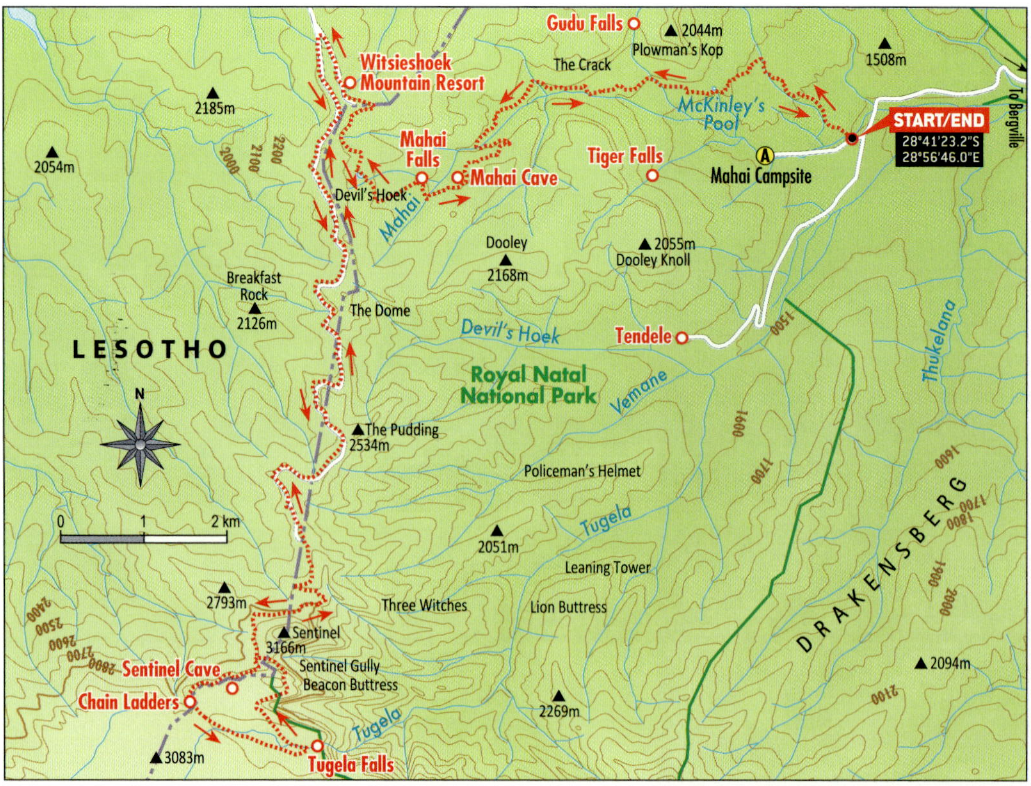

From the Sentinel Car Park to the top and back, water must be carried. Follow a concrete path for a short distance before returning to a zigzag hiking path passing the Witches, Sentinel Peak, Western Buttress and Sentinel Caves until you reach the Chain Ladders (a further climb of 450m). The altitude will be affecting you by this stage, especially if you live and train at sea level.

Everyone wears a safety belt and sliding device attached to fixed ropes alongside the ladders. The Mountain Club of South Africa guides will assist you, and the trick is not to look down. Once you reach the top, a short scramble over rocky terrain leads you over the Tugela River and the welcome run down a gentle slope to the Tugela Falls.

Now the hard part begins up to Sentinel Gully, with the risk of loose rocks being dislodged. Make use of the fixed ropes for stability and to guide you away from unstable sections – proceed cautiously until you reach the bottom. You are now back on the path to the Chain Ladders; just retrace your steps via Sentinel Car Park and Witsieshoek to the finish (there are refreshment points along the dirt road).

All runners have to ascend two chain ladders to reach the summit of the Amphitheatre before running to the lip of the Tugela River. A team from Peak High Mountaineering, a locally based adventure group within the valley, will be manning the top, middle and bottom of the chain ladders, harnessing runners into safety belts and helmets. Runners failing to comply with safety measures will be disqualified from the event.

The start of the event is staggered to relieve congestion on the mountain paths. Each runner is seeded into one of 4 start groups (A, B, C and D) based on their most recent marathon time. You have 10hrs to complete the event.

EVENT FACTS

Event name Bonitas Sunday Tribune Mont-aux-Sources Challenge
Venue Royal Natal National Park
Distance from Harrismith 70km
Time of year Beginning of September
Enter as Solo
Cut-offs 10hrs
Distance 50km
Average duration 4–10hrs
Entry info www.montauxsourceschallenge.co.za

GRADIENT PROFILE

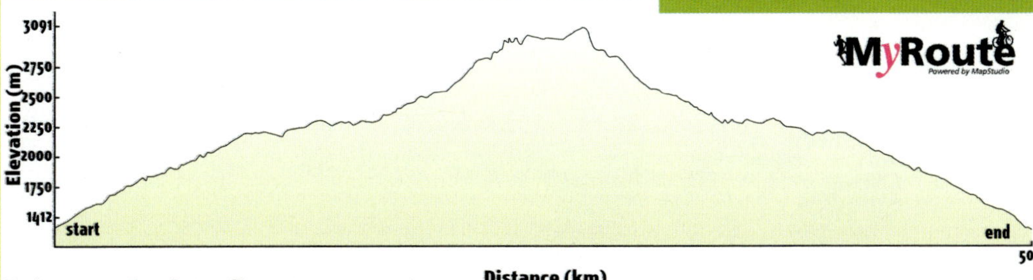

To view maps and gradient profiles go to **www.myroute.co.za**

EXPERT'S VIEW

Lance Chapman has been running competitively since 1991, and has notched up dozens of Comrades, Ironman, Natal Ironman (a combo of Comrades / Dusi / Midmar Mile), SA Triathlon Long Course and other events. He has SA colours and has happily migrated to trail running, with wins in Ultra runs such as Mont-aux-Sources, Rhodes Marathon, 4 Peaks and the Sky Run.

My run

'Start too hard at your peril! No other race I have done climbs to 3 200m as quickly as Monties does. This is not a technical trail run, although you can expect some exciting singletrack on the last 10km decent from Witsieshoek back to the finish at Royal Natal.

'Look around you, not up. You will be running through a World Heritage Park and it's magnificent. On top of the Little Berg is a tough grind up to Witsiehoek and onto the long dirt road up to the Sentinel parking lot. Here it is important to stay relaxed and enjoy the mountain scenery.

'Next up is the Sentinel Gully. The loose rocks and screed are hard on the ankles. Ropes and the Mountain Rescue Club are here to assist you and add a voice of encouragement. The KZN Drakensberg is a place of unique mystery and beauty – we are lucky to live and play here.'

My shoe

Brand ~ Salomon
Model ~ XT Wings SLAB4
Rating ~ A lightweight, technical racing shoe; this shoe keeps me comfortable, stable and protected on any SA trail

Insider tips

'Monties is one of the toughest runs you will ever endure, not just because of the distance but also the terrain and altitude. The best advice would be to take it easy in the first half and make up time in the second.'

Gear and apparel

'Weather can change without warning, therefore it is compulsory to run with a windbreaker and a whistle. A trail shoe with good grip and good support is a must, as is a hydration system.'

Training and pacing

'Your training for the run needs to include hill training and off-road running. Training at altitude will help a great deal and will most certainly contribute to a better run on the day. If you are not used to running at altitude, make sure to take it easy going up the mountain and don't push too hard. Even though most runners are concerned about "running up the mountain," it's the descent that hurts the most. Remember that the last 20km is mostly downhill and will work your legs, impact on your knees and test your core strength.'

© JACQUES MARAIS

Montagu Asics X-Treme Trail Run

4/10/17/20km

Trail & Event

Province Western Cape
Region Boland
Closest town Montagu
Trail destination Montagu Hiking Trails (Nature Reserve)
Contributed by Ilse Esterhuyse and Neil Myburgh

EXPERT'S VIEW

Ilse Esterhuyse is a trail runner, triathlete and mountain biker; she is sponsored by Asics to co-ordinate the Asics X-Treme Trail Run, which takes place during the Montagu Mountain Mania Festival.

© JACQUES MARAIS

THE DESTINATION Montagu is a pretty, rural town set at the foot of some of the most spectacular Cape Fold formations you will ever see in South Africa. It is a soft-fruit farming area, with scenic orchards and vineyards.

THE TERRAIN All hiking trails boast an array of interesting geological features, varying from ravines with mountain streams to craggy cliffs with awe-inspiring rock formations.

DIRECTIONS Follow the R62 past Robertson and Ashton to Montagu, and continue along the Avalon Springs Road to the venue (it is well signposted). A range of accommodation establishments is available in town – see www.mountainmania.net

FAST FACTS

Grading Difficult to extreme (20km)
Duration 2.5–5 hours
Configuration Circular routes
Start point Avalon Springs
GPS co-ordinates 33°45'56.94"S, 20°07'02.76"E
Terrain Mountainous and steep singletrack
Map Available on web
Access requirements Trail fee payable
Trail markings Different-coloured footprints; banner tape on race day
Facilities Avalon Springs Hotel and thermal pools
Cell reception 80% coverage along routes
Beware Steep climbs and descents
Time of year March to November; May for race
Local info www.mountainmania.net / Tel (+27 72) 125 1854 / (+27 23) 614 2880

© JACQUES MARAIS

THE TRAIL A 4km fun trail along the river course leads you to the 17km and 20km trails; these are both along singletrack and for fit, experienced trail runners. Super-steep ascents and dangerous downhills are the name of the game.

The 20km Bloupunt Trail is a beautiful trail for superhero trail runners only. It follows the Bloupunt Hiking Trail, and tops out at a dizzying 1 000m for a breathtaking view across Montagu and the surrounding towns. The trail is marked with white footprints, with a halfway stop where you can fill your water bottles at a stream. The first 4km is along an easy climb, but then it is basically straight up and down for 10km, before the final 3.5km back along the same route to the start.

With less than half the altitude gain of Bloupunt, the 17km Cogmanskloof Trail is way easier, although there are still a few steep climbs and descents. The trail surface is rocky and technical in places, so take care – especially after rain – on this circular loop. The first 3km is flat, after which you climb until you reach the 7km mark before you hit the flats up to 11km. The last 4km is back along the same route as your start; follow the yellow footprints (and blue Asics banner tape on race day).

The 10km Lovers' Trail is an easier trail for less experienced trail runners. The route passes through Badkloof (2.5km), and shares the same start and finish as the Bloupunt and the Cogmanskloof routes, but then heads along 'Lovers' Walk' through town before rejoining the trail to the finish.

EVENT FACTS

Event name Montagu Mountain Mania
Venue Avalon Springs Hotel
Distances 4km, 10km, 17km, 20km; there is also a MTB race on the day
Time of year May
Enter as Solo
Cut-offs Runners to be briefed at race
Average duration 1–1.5hrs (10km); 1.5–2.6hrs (17km); 3–4hrs (20km)
Entry info www.mountainmania.net

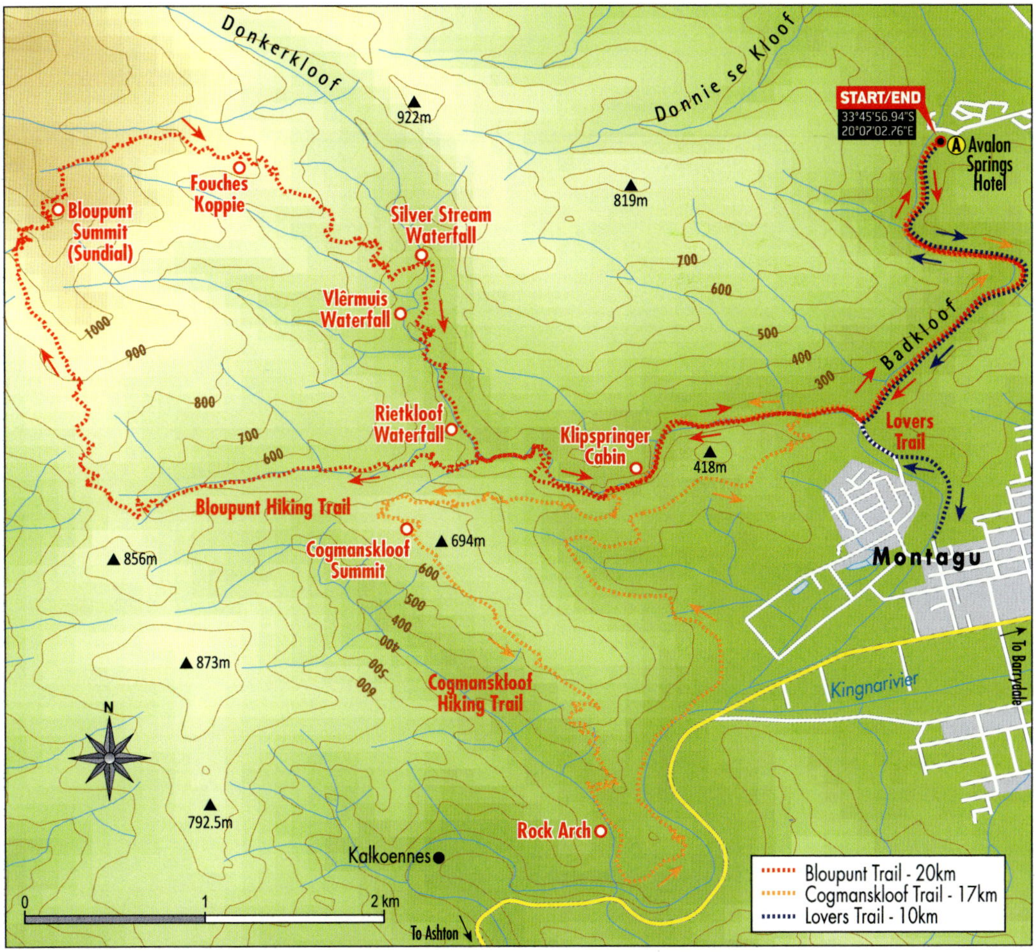

GRADIENT PROFILE

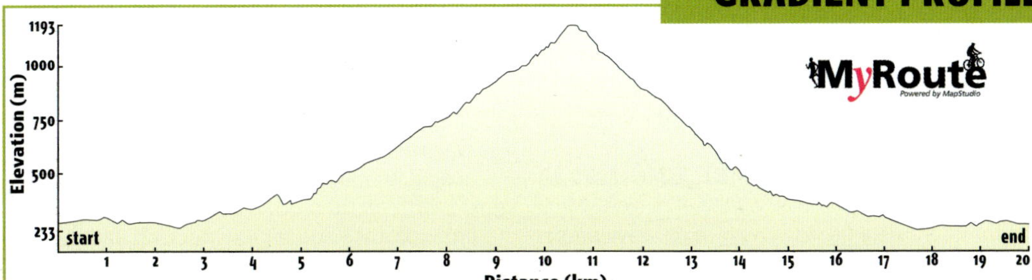

To view maps and gradient profiles go to **www.myroute.co.za**

Trail Only

Mountain Splendour Eco-Resort Trails

30km

Province KwaZulu-Natal
Region uKhahlamba-Drakensberg
Closest town Winterton
Trail destination Mountain Splendour Eco-Resort
Contributed by Iain Don-Wauchope

THE DESTINATION Mountain Splendour Eco-Resort is situated within a forest on a small working farm in the heart of the Central Drakensberg. The resort and trails boast spectacular mountain views directly onto the towering peaks of Cathkin Peak and Champagne Castle, situated within the UNESCO uKhahlamba World Heritage Site.

THE TERRAIN Trails accessible from Mountain Splendour traverse the foothills of the Drakensberg and therefore do not require specialised equipment or super-sized lungs. The terrain along this route is varied and will expose you to most types of trail-running surfaces. Short sections of tar and dirt roads will expose you to pot-holes, rocks and mud, while plantation and 4X4 roads will up the ante further. The latter tend to be softer underfoot, but with more obstacles, such as streams, water, mud, logs, branches and rocks. The singletrack is a mix of smooth African footpaths, soft grassland tracks, and loose rocky sections with some scrambling.

DIRECTIONS From Durban, follow the N3 North and take Exit 179 (Estcourt North). Turn left and go 28km through Loskop and past the iNjasuti turn-off. Turn left onto the R600 to the Central Drakensberg. Drive 12km towards the Champagne Castle Hotel before turning left onto the D19, and travel 1km to Mountain Splendour (GPS 29°00′45.7″S, 29°27′39.5″E).

ACCOMMODATION Mountain Splendour Eco-Resort offers four-star camping and caravanning sites with communal and private ablution facilities. If you don't have your own camping gear, you can hire safari tents equipped with beds, lights, fridges and stoves. There are also a limited number of self-catering units available. The resort is safe and family-friendly, with plenty of activities to keep the kids busy while you are sweating it out on the trails (www.mountainsplendour.co.za).

FAST FACTS

Grading Intermediate to difficult
Duration 1–4hrs
Configuration Circular
Start point Mountain Splendour Eco-Resort
GPS co-ordinates 29°00'45.7"S, 29°27'39.5"E
Terrain Varied: tar, dirt, rocks, mud, footpaths and grassland tracks
Map Yes; provided by owners
Access requirements Resort guests have unlimited free access to the trails; day visitors need to sign an indemnity and pay an entry fee
Trail markings None on 30km route; 10km of Mountain Splendour trails marked
Facilities Runners are expected to be self-sufficient while on the routes
Cell reception 100% coverage
Beware Quick changes in weather; snakes
Time of year Open year-round
Local info www.zulu.org.za
More info www.mountainsplendour.co.za / Tel (+27 36) 468 1172

THE TRAIL The main trail is about 30km long and starts of along a combo of tar and singletrack before you enter Alcatraz Alley. This is a 400m pathway lined by both an electric and razor-wire fence: mid-way there is a wooden pole bridge partially submerged in water. Rocks and logs have been strategically placed, but if your balance is dodgy, opt to get your feet wet rather than losing your footing and stumbling into either fence!

Once you escape from Alcatraz Alley, a whole new world of trail running awaits. Wind your way via plantations of pine and gum trees along a mix of singletrack and narrow back roads, then climb towards a tower on the next ridge line. This section includes a short scramble up a rocky ledge.

Once at the tower, the route follows an old wagon trail along the ridgeline heading south towards iNjasuthi. This is the highlight of the entire route, with eye-popping views over the jagged peaks of the mighty Drakensberg mountain range all the way north to Cathedral Peak. What makes this section even more impressive is that on either side of you, the ridge line plunges steeply into the valleys below. The sensation is one of running 'on top of the world'.

The ridge-line track intersects a rough dirt road mostly used by local Zulu people collecting firewood from the wattle plantations up ahead. Skirt the outside edge of these plantations, then contour around the northern base of Matterhorn Mountain. At this point, you run parallel to the boundary of the uKhahlamba Drakensberg Park. Please note that the park is OUT OF BOUNDS unless you have paid your entry fee at Monk's Cowl.

The final stretch is mostly along a downhill track towards Mountain Splendour, but beware of bone-jarring and very steep S-bends on your return. This is probably the lowlight of the route, especially since it is tarred.

EXPERT'S VIEW

Iain Don-Wauchope is a business owner and father who occasionally trains! He has won numerous trail-running, mountain-biking, multi-sport and AR races.

My Run

'This is one of my favourite training routes because of the spectacular scenery, varied terrain and ease of access. Technically it is not overly difficult, but there are sections where you need to step carefully, so it is sure to improve your balance. There are also enough hills to give you a good workout, especially if you run them hard. It is, however, not a trail for beginners; there are other routes at Mountain Splendour better suited to rookies.'

Insider tips

'Take it easy up the first big climb and save yourself for the rolling hills in the middle sections. When running over rocks and other technical terrain, try to be nimble and lightfooted. Think about floating over the obstacles rather than landing/standing on them.'

Gear and apparel

'Any running shoes will do, even road-running shoes. Trail-running shoes will provide better traction and drainage, but they are not essential. A small backpack with a bladder containing water/juice, some food, cell phone, rain jacket and basic first-aid kit is highly recommended. You are fairly isolated for much of the route, so you will need to be self-sufficient in the event of an accident, snake bite, storm, etc. My First Ascent Apple Jacket is my favourite piece of clothing on this type of run.'

Training and Pacing

'You should be able to run a half-marathon comfortably before attempting this route or any other trail run of this distance. Also start conservatively and save something for the second half. It is not easy negotiating technical terrain when you are tired, and almost impossible once you've blown.'

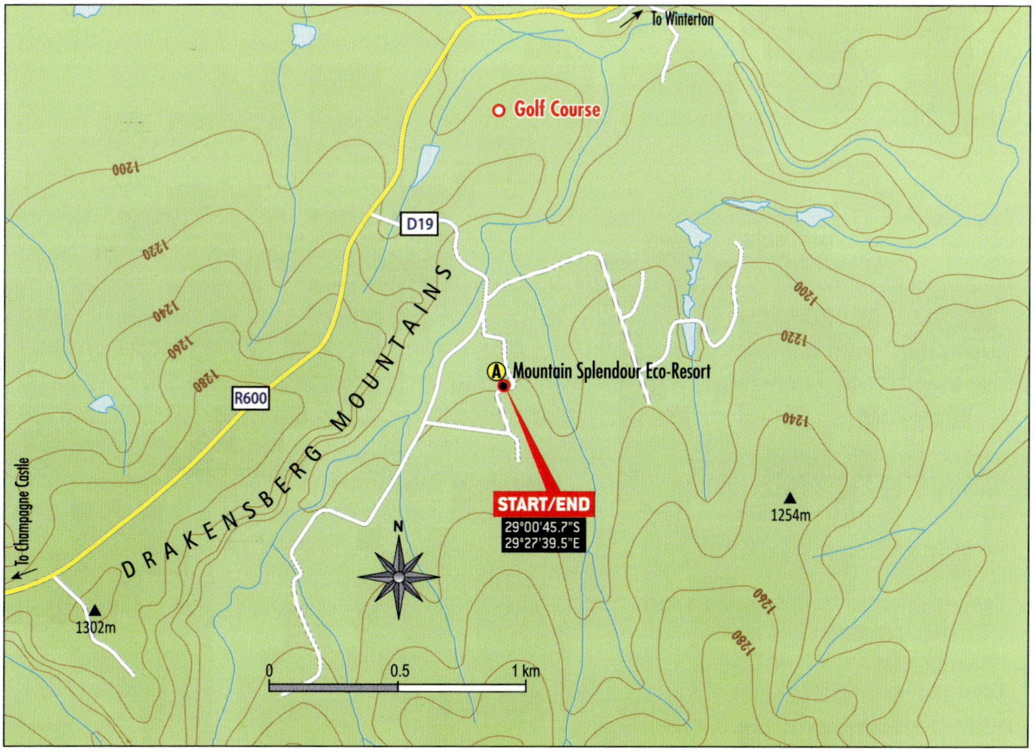

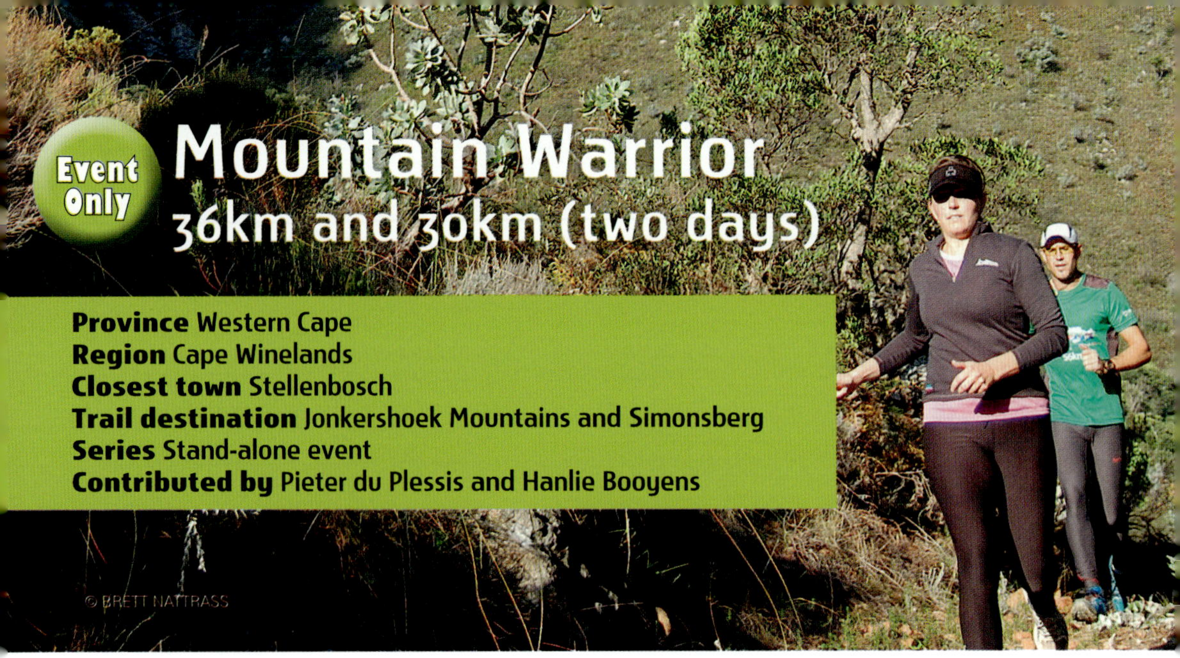

© BRETT NATTRASS

Event Only

Mountain Warrior
36km and 30km (two days)

Province Western Cape
Region Cape Winelands
Closest town Stellenbosch
Trail destination Jonkershoek Mountains and Simonsberg
Series Stand-alone event
Contributed by Pieter du Plessis and Hanlie Booyens

THE DESTINATION Enjoy the unspoilt beauty of one of South Africa's oldest working valleys – filled with scenic vineyards and pristine mountain fynbos – near the historic village of Stellenbosch.

THE TERRAIN The trail starts and ends on jeep tracks, but includes a huge amount of singletrack along ridges, through fynbos, past vineyards and crossing open fields. The trails are at high altitude, so beware changeable weather.

DIRECTIONS Rustenberg Wines (GPS **33°54'40.7"S, 18°53'19.0"E**) is situated on Rustenburg Road, just off the Helshoogte Road (R310) a few kilometres outside Stellenbosch – www.rustenberg.co.za

ACCOMMODATION A range of accommodation is available – www.stellenboschtourism.co.za

THE TRAIL The Mountain Warrior Route follows a network of fantastic trails high up where the Hottentots-Holland and Jonkershoek mountains conjoin, shaping rough peaks and deep ravines, with stunning views over Stellenbosch and Cape Town in the distance.

The long route on Day 1 must rate as one of the most challenging and breathtaking days on any trail in South Africa. Runners will wind their way amid these famous Stellenbosch summits, passing right beneath the iconic Two Peaks and crossing the formidable Botmaskop.

EVENT FACTS

Event name Mountain Warrior Trail Run Festival
Venue Jonkershoek and Rustenberg Wine Estate
Distance from Cape Town 55km
Time of year Early September
Enter as Solo
Cut-offs Yes – runners will be briefed at race
Distances 36km (Day 1) and 30km (Day 2) – Long Course
Average duration 7–13hrs (66km)
Entry info www.4x4teambuilding.com

Day 2 traverses the steep foothills of Simonsberg, winding through many vineyards and fields of fynbos along singletracks in areas only accessible during this event. Expect it to be less technical than Day 1, but your legs will be glad after a huge outing in the mountains the previous day.

THE EVENT This two-day, staged trail run is split into a long and a short course. The long course covers 66km (36km on Day 1 and 30km on Day 2). The short course (30km) covers 15km a day, and is easily runnable for 80% of the run. There is also a 10km night run and 8km fun walk/run.

EXPERT'S VIEW

Pieter du Plessis has completed numerous endurance trail runs, marathons, Ironman events, Xterra triathlons and expedition races. He is Race Director for most Stillwater Sports events.

My shoe

Brand ~ New Balance/Asics
Model ~ 876/Gel Nimbus 13
Rating ~ A great combination for both trail and road running

FAST FACTS

Grading Difficult to extreme
Duration 3–7hrs (per day)
Configuration Point-to-point and circular
Start point Jonkershoek and Rustenberg Wines
GPS co-ordinates 33°54'40.7"S, 18°53'19.0"E
Terrain Mountainous and steep singletrack
Map Refer to website
Access requirements Trails only open on race day, except for hiking trails in Jonkershoek
Trail markings Yellow arrow boards
Facilities Water and refreshment points on race; food and ablutions at finish
Cell reception Minimal coverage along remote sections of the trail
Beware Extreme temperatures
Time of year Early September
Local info www.stellenboschtourism.co.za
Local info www.4x4teambuilding.com / Tel (+27 82) 924 4083

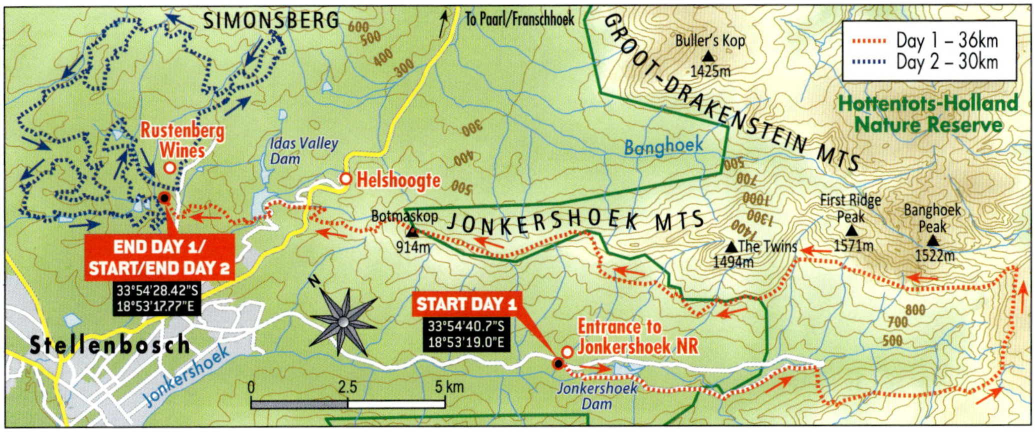

GRADIENT PROFILES

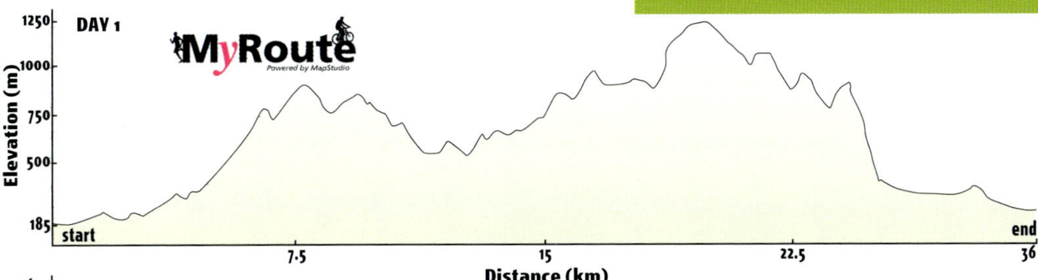

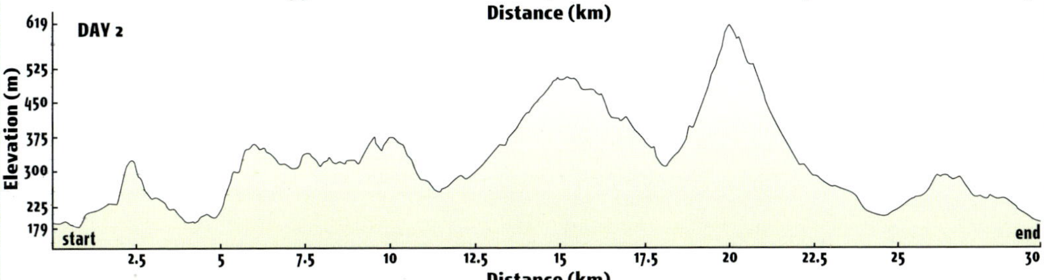

To view maps and gradient profiles go to **www.myroute.co.za**

Mnweni Marathon

42km

Trail & Event

Province KwaZulu-Natal
Region uKhahlamba-Drakensberg
Closest town Bergville
Trail destination Mnweni Cultural Centre
Series Stand-alone event
Contributed by Bruce Arnett

© JACQUES MARAIS

THE DESTINATION The Mnweni area is one of the most remote parts of the KZN Berg, and rated by many as the most dramatically beautiful section of the 'High Berg'. Basalt spires and pinnacles announce your arrival here in the northern section of uKhahlamba, between the Royal Natal National Park and Cathedral Peak reserve area. The Mnweni Cultural Centre, located another 4km from the old police station, serves as the starting point for exploring the area.

THE TERRAIN This is a 'mountain trail run', with all the terrain and weather implications that the term implies. Only the first and last 5km of the route are on jeep track and accessible by vehicle; the remainder of the route is singletrack or off-track. The route is NOT suited to people who are unfamiliar with rugged, singletrack trail running.

DIRECTIONS Take the R74 to Bergville, then turn right onto the Rookdale turn-off (GPS 28°43'50.7"S, 29°20'41.4"E) on entering town. Continue for 16km before turning left to the Mnweni Cultural Centre (signposted, GPS 28°49'12.1"S, 29°06'16.2"E); drive for 1.8km and turn right again. Another 16km on a rough dirt road brings you to the Ntonyelana River and the Mnweni Cultural Centre on your right.

ACCOMMODATION The Mnweni Cultural Centre is the only accommodation available in the Mnweni Valley. It is well run as a community project and they do deserve your custom. Other guesthouses and B&Bs are available further afield. Camping is available at Mnweni and does not have to be booked beforehand, but the comfortable rondavels or dormitory rooms must be booked in advance. SMS Agrippa on Tel (+27 72) 712 2401 and pay in cash upon your arrival.

The entire Berg is a wilderness area and camping is permitted apart from in the immediate vicinity of the entry points and certain caves that contain San art. This is, however, wilderness camping and there are no facilities at all.

EXPERT'S VIEW

Bruce Arnett is the founder of the Mnweni Marathon and is also one of South Africa's original trail-running legends. He has won dozens of extreme events and set many a course record (some stand to this day). Podium places include the Puffer, Four Peaks Challenge, SkyRun (12 wins), Table Mountain Challenge, Addo 100-miler and his own Mnweni Marathon.

My Shoe
Brand ~ Hi-Tec
Model ~ Infinity
Rating ~ lightweight, quick-draining and drying, superb grip, a shoe with an extra top gear

FAST FACTS

Grading Difficult to extreme
Duration 5–12hrs
Configuration Circular
Start point Mnweni Cultural Centre
GPS co-ordinates 28°49'12.1"S, 29°06'16.2"E
Terrain Mountainous, steep singletrack with big climbs; rocky; tall grass
Map You will receive a copy of a 1:50 000 map of the area marked with the route, or get the Peter Slingsby Drakensberg series sheet 1
Access requirements Race limited to 100 entries; entrance fee to the trail payable
Trail markings Path only; the route is not marked and must be self-navigated
Facilities NO refreshment or water stations; carry your own water and food; camping, dorms and self-catering rondavels at Mnweni
Cell reception None, except on the summit
Beware Extreme temperatures and snow; flooding and electrical storms in summer; frequent mist and fog
Time of year Mid-May for the race; May, September and October for the trail
Local info www.drakensberg-tourism.com
More info www.kzntrailrunning.co.za / Bruce Arnett at Tel (+27 83) 564 3750

THE TRAIL The Mnweni Marathon follows the most popular hiking route in this part of the Drakensberg and the trail is open to the public throughout the year. This circular route starts and ends at Mnweni Cultural Centre to wind its way into the Berg alongside the Mnweni River. You follow the Mnweni Valley, ascend Mnweni Pass, cross the source of the Orange River on the plateau and return via the Rockeries Pass and the Ntonyelana Valley.

There is a well-trodden path used by local inhabitants to get to their huts and to travel up Mnweni Pass into Lesotho. The trail often consists of parallel options, but it generally makes its way along the left bank of the Mnweni Valley up to the Shepherd's Cave area.

After about 15km the trail crosses the river for the first time and 1km later winds past Shepherd's Cave, a popular overnight spot for hikers. At this point you have climbed from 1 200m at the start to 1 650m above sea level and are in the remote upper reaches of the Mnweni Valley.

The trail continues for another 5km up the valley, often crossing the river, until you reach the base of Mnweni Pass (2 000m above sea level). Over the next 2.5km you climb almost 1 000m to the summit plateau. A relatively level section of 2km along the plateau follows, where the Orange River is crossed virtually at its source.

The descent is via the aptly named Rockeries Pass and you will pass the imposing Rockeries spires onto the saddle for a bone-jarring 6km descent before the route levels out once more. The last 10km will be faster, as you negotiate the less challenging lower reaches of the Little Berg to the finish along the Ntonyelana River valley.

THE EVENT The Mnweni Marathon was pioneered in the winter of 2000 when trail-running legend Bruce Arnett and friend Mark Tannian scouted the original point-to-point route for the race. The allure of the challenge grew, and the first running of the route as a race happened in 2001. Eleven runners took part in what was to all intents and purposes a gathering of friends. In 2002, the route was changed to the current circular (and less extreme) format due to

EVENT FACTS

Event name Mnweni Marathon
Venue Mnweni Cultural Centre
Distance from Bergville 33km
Time of year Mid-May
Enter as Solo
Cut-offs Yes (11:00 to reach Mnweni Pass, 18:00 for official finishers)
Distance Approximately 42km (off-road)
Average duration 5–12hrs
Entry info arnettbruce@gmail.com

logistical difficulties associated with a linear race. Entries have grown, largely by word of mouth, from approximately 30 in 2006 to the event being fully subscribed with a limit of 100 runners in 2012. Most are now confirmed members of the 'Mnweni family'.

The 42km run ascends from 1 200m to 3 000m on the Berg summit, a gruelling climb of 1 800m. Race start is at 06:00 sharp, with a cut-off for official finishers at 18:00. If you have not begun the ascent of Mnweni Pass by 11:00, you will be accompanied back to the start by a marshal.

© JACQUES MARAIS

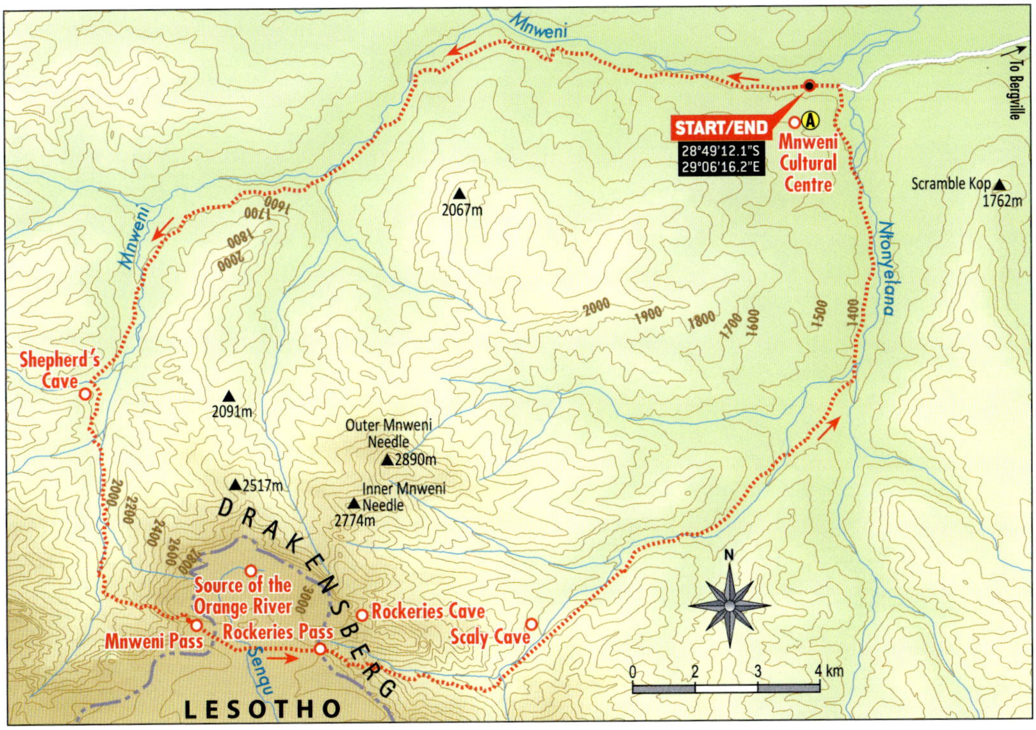

GRADIENT PROFILE

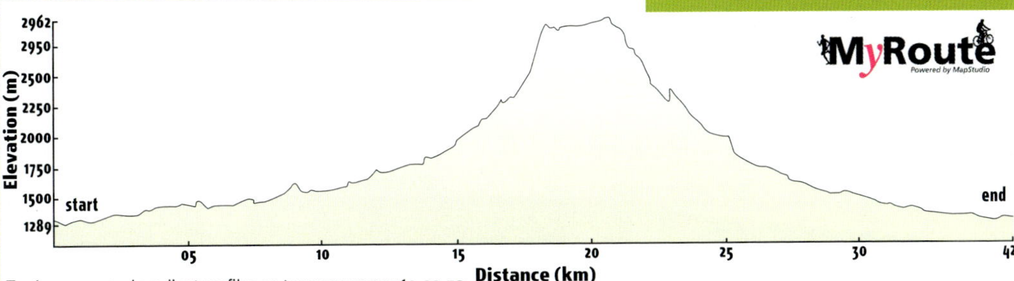

To view maps and gradient profiles go to **www.myroute.co.za**

The Num-Num Trail Challenge

36.5km

Trail & Event

Province Mpumalanga
Region Heartland and Highlands
Closest town Machadodorp (eNtokozweni)
Trail destination The Num-Num Trail Nature Conservancy
Series Stand-alone event
Contributed by Debbie Agenbag (WildTrail)

EXPERT'S VIEW

Debbie Agenbag is a dedicated and enthusiastic trail runner and event organiser. She started the club WildTrails SA and organises a number of popular trail races in Gauteng.

My shoe

Brand ~ New Balance
Model ~ Minimus
Rating ~ Fantastic grip, great protection; a must-have shoe for any trail runner

© PETER KIRK

THE DESTINATION The Emakhazeni district – encompassing Dullstroom, eMakhazeni, eNtokozweni and eMgwenya – is situated an easy three-hour drive from Johannesburg. This is the start of the Drakensberg Escarpment, with a rich Boer War history. You can still see the gun supports carved into rocks by the 'bittereinders' and the well-used bandwagon routes. Don't be fooled by the sleepy old-world atmosphere and mundane grassland views from the N4; there are some stunning adventure options including world-class hiking trails, rock climbing, mountain biking, game viewing and trout fishing.

THE TERRAIN Get ready for a diverse and stunning range of landscapes, from sandstone labyrinths to grassland biomes, gorges, cascading waterfalls and pristine indigenous forest. Num-Num is rated as one of the most technically challenging trails in the Mpumalanga / Gauteng area; anything goes, from loose rocks to testing descents and ascents into the Schoonspruit and Bankspruit Gorges, ladders and swing bridges. There are very few flat and straight sections to the standard trail, and at 1 800m this is a great high-altitude training site.

DIRECTIONS The Num-Num Trail starts at Pongola Express Camp (GPS **25°47'49.3"S, 30°22'25.2"E**), 22km south of eNtokozweni and just off the R541.

ACCOMMODATION There are five unique and comfortable camps on The Num-Num Trail, with a range of accommodation options in the area. Check out www.emakhazenitourism.com

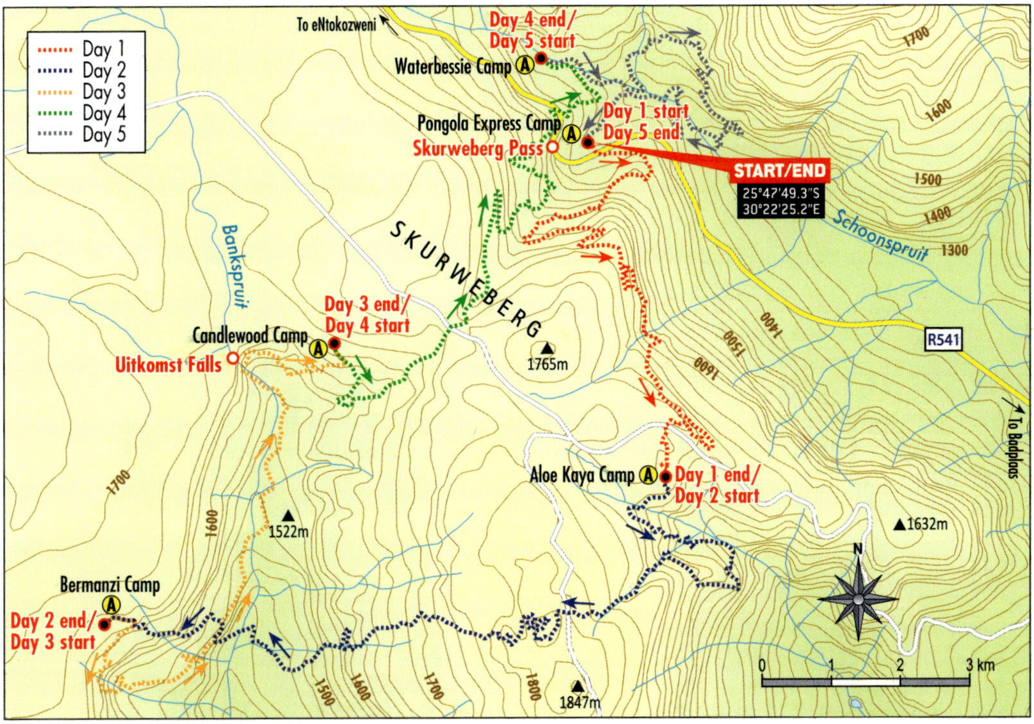

FAST FACTS

Grading Difficult to extreme
Duration 5–10hrs (36.5km)
Configuration Circular
Start point Pongola Express Camp
GPS co-ordinates 25°47'49.3"S, 30°22'25.2"E
Terrain Kloofs, gorges, open grasslands and sandstone labyrinths
Map Available at www.thenum-numtrail.co.za/download_maps.html
Access requirements Race limited to 100 entries; trail must be pre-booked
Trail markings Brown leaf signs with Num-Num Day Trail markings
Facilities Slack-packing, equipped kitchens and hot showers
Cell reception Intermittent
Beware Loose rocks, flooding, veld fires (May–Aug)
Time of year July for the race; throughout the year for the trail
Local info www.emakhazenitourism.com
More info www.thenum-numtrail.co.za / Tel (+27 72) 889 9284

THE TRAIL The Num-Num Trail is a 36.5km self-guided, five-day hiking trail. Though open throughout the year, you have to pre-book to get onto the trail, and the organisers will plan a trail-running route for you.

Start off with a 400m climb up a hill through gullies of indigenous forests and spectacular red stone cliffs along the driest part of the trail. After Aloe Kaya Camp you briefly go into Hell's Kloof with its beautiful ironwood trees before hitting an open climb into the moonscape sandstone labyrinth; the trail here is tricky as it goes up and over the rock formations.

You then descend into the beautiful Bankspruit Gorge before the 1.5km climb to Bermanzi. Superb views across the Komati Gorge are worth the climb, and afterwards a 2km downhill awaits back into the Bankspruit Gorge. Meander up the gorge to Uitkomst Falls (the second highest in Mpumalanga), criss-crossing the river along convenient swing bridges.

A 1km climb from Uitkomst Falls takes you to Candlewood Camp, from where the trail winds down to the R541 and the banks of the Schoonspruit River. Some tricky ladders into Waterbessie Camp lie ahead before the trail detours to Wathaba Rainbow Falls for a classic 'under the waterfall' swim. The next 4km along the Schoonspruit gets tough once you ascend halfway up Skurweberg, but the views across the Maputo Corridor will keep you going. The trail finally descends back into the Schoonspruit Gorge and past the tranquil Mac Falls to loop back to Pongola Express Camp.

Winter months are dry and temperatures can drop to near freezing in the evenings. There is a stunning display of aloe flowers. Chances of rain, thunderstorms and high temperatures in the summer are high. October and November bring milder weather conditions and wild flowers.

THE EVENT The annual Num-Num Trail Challenge is a small event packing a huge punch, combining awesome racing with generous dollops of country hospitality. The 36.5km is not recommended if you are a rookie trail runner, so rather start yourself off on the 15km. Entries are limited to 100 runners.

EVENT FACTS

Event name The Num-Num Trail Challenge
Venue The Num-Num Trail Nature Conservancy
Distance from Pretoria 240km
Time of year July
Enter as Solo
Cut-offs Yes – runners will be briefed at race
Distances 15km and 36.5km
Average duration 2–4hrs (15km) or 5–10hrs (36.5km)
Entry info info@thenum-numtrail.co.za

Old Fisherman's Challenge 22km

Trail & Event

Province Western Cape
Region Cape Town and Surrounds
Closest town Fish Hoek or Hout Bay
Trail destination Silvermine Nature Reserve
Series Stand-alone event
Contributed by Claire Ashworth and Michelle Lombardi

© JACQUES MARAIS

THE DESTINATION You do not have to go far to get yourself onto a mountain in Cape Town; the area is truly blessed with any number of stunning trails right at any runner's fingertips. The Old Fisherman's route encompasses many of these trails and thus allows runners to run from Fish Hoek to Hout Bay.

THE TERRAIN The trails offer a mix of beach, gravel roads, boardwalks and singletrack. Very little scrambling is required, except down Blackburn Ravine, but this will be over before you even realise it. There is one river crossing on the beach; at low tide this is ankle deep, but during spring highs you might want to head onto the road.

DIRECTIONS The race starts from Fish Hoek or Hout Bay. Hout Bay has three entry points via Rhodes Drive, Victoria Road (M6) or the Chapman's Peak Toll Road. Fish Hoek can be reached by following the M4 from Muizenberg to Simon's Town. GPS co-ordinates are as follows:

Olympia Café, Kalk Bay 34°07'40.9"S, 18°26'51.3"E
Fish Hoek Beach 34°08'17.6"S, 18°26'00.8"E
Hout Bay Yacht Club 34°02'45.6"S, 18°20'58.3"E

ACCOMMODATION Accommodation options in the South Peninsula can be found at www.capepointroute.co.za

FAST FACTS

Grading Intermediate to difficult
Duration 2–6hrs
Configuration Point to point
Start point Fish Hoek or Hout Bay
GPS co-ordinates 34°08'17.6"S, 18°26'00.8"E (Fish Hoek); 34°02'45.6"S, 18°20'58.3"E (Hout Bay)
Terrain Gravel roads, singletrack, some beach and scrambling over rocks
Map Full map and route description is given to all the runners
Access requirements Race limited to 100 entries; entrance fee to Silvermine payable
Trail markings Path only; the route is not marked and has to be self-navigated
Facilities Basic ablutions in Silvermine
Cell reception None within Silvermine; good close to Hout Bay and Fish Hoek
Beware Hydration is critical; beware of snakes (summer) and mist (winter)
Time of year June for the race; autumn and spring for the trail
Local info www.houtbay.org
More info www.fishermanschallenge.co.za / Tel (+27 82) 553 3833

THE TRAIL Start from Olympia Café in Kalk Bay and head up Clairvaux Road onto Boyes Drive where the trail head starts at the steps going up to 'Weary Willy's Wait'. Keep right on the path to Spes Bona Forest, ignoring any smaller paths leading back to Boyes Drive on your right. Keep going in a northeasterly direction until you reach the crossroad at Nellie's Pool. Turn left here and proceed along the jeep track towards Gate 2 of Silvermine East.

Take care as you cross the busy Ou Kaapseweg tar road onto a narrow footpath into Silvermine West. Follow this path through some scrub until you reach the Silvermine River Walk for a lovely run up to the dam wall. Pass Silvermine Dam (to the right past the ablution block) and continue onto the dual concrete tracks ascending towards Elephant's Eye Cave.

Ignore the various footpaths to the cave as you thump your way to the top of Blackburn Ravine. Kick into high alert as you hit the 'stone highway' with bits of boardwalk, passing the wooden lookout deck above Hout Bay before bombing onto the Blackburn Ravine footpath.

This section of the route is extremely steep and should be approached with caution. Always keep left, zigzagging down to the stream and aiming for Chapman's Peak Drive far below. Turn right onto the tar here and slog 1km across Hout Bay Beach to finish at the Yacht Club for a cold beer.

THE EVENT Every year the race director alternates the direction of the trail run to create the Up Run (Fish Hoek to Hout Bay) and the Down Run (Hout Bay to Fish Hoek).

EXPERT'S VIEW

Michelle Lombardi is a trail runner, mountain biker and multi-sport athlete sponsored by Salomon, Giant and GU energy products. She has graced the podium in expedition races, stage runs and Xterra triathlons around the world.

My run
Fishermans Trail Challenge is my favourite medium-distance trail run. Although only 22km, it offers runners a mix of wonderful technical terrain, climbing, amazing views and enough fast running to keep the adrenalin flowing'.

My shoe
Brand ~ Salomon
Model ~ Salomon S-Labs
Rating ~ Lightweight

Insider tips
Never look at the distance of a trail run and compare it to a road run. You can at least double the distance or even more on very technical runs. Train on the route if you can.'

Gear and apparel
'I would go with Salomon S-Labs as these are lighter and do not need to be quite as tough and hardy as for the Hout Bay Challenge. Clothing needs to be light, comfortable and quick drying. A raincoat is essential, as is a backpack or waist-belt for carrying food, drinks and that raincoat.'

EVENT FACTS

Event name Old Fisherman's Trail Challenge
Venue Hout Bay Yacht Club or Fish Hoek
Distance from Cape Town 20km or 32km
Time of year June
Enter as Solo

Cut-offs Yes (runners to be briefed at race)
Distance 22km
Average duration 3–5hrs
Entry info www.fishermanschallenge.co.za

GRADIENT PROFILE

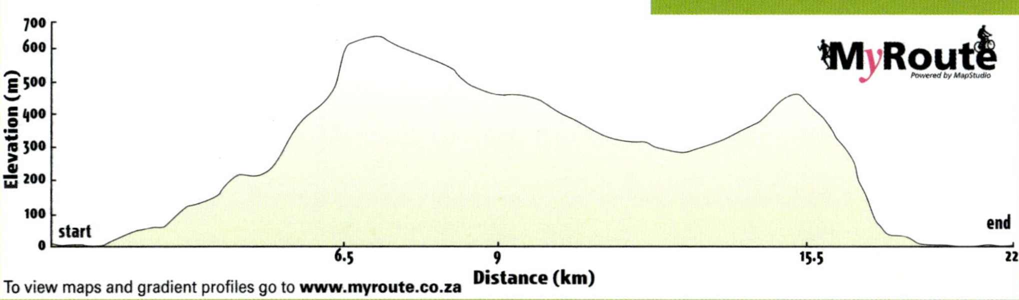

To view maps and gradient profiles go to **www.myroute.co.za**

Event & Trail

Oorlogskloof Mountain Trail Run

18km / 42km

Province Northern Cape
Region Namaqualand
Closest town Nieuwoudtville
Trail destination Oorlogskloof Nature Reserve
Series Quantum Country Classics
Contributed by Ugene Nel

THE DESTINATION Tog up and trip northwards beyond Nieuwoudtville into the uppermost reaches of the gorgeous Cederberg Mountains. Here, within the dramatic splendour of the Oorlogskloof Nature Reserve, a true trail runners' paradise awaits you. The reserve encompasses the craggy 'War Gorge' canyon, and as a destination it rates right up there with the most spectacular outdoor running arenas in South Africa.

THE TERRAIN The Oorlogskloof River describes a deep, spectacular gorge of approximately 500m wide through a thin layer of Table Mountain Sandstone and quartzite, thus exposing softer floor formations such as limestone, shale and frit below. The rugged landscape is criss-crossed by an extensive network of gravel roads and hiking trails tailor-made for serious mountain running.

DIRECTIONS The turn-off to Oorlogskloof is 6km east of Nieuwoudtville along the R27 to Vanrhynsdorp, and not far from Calvinia, the capital of the scenic Hantam region. Look out for a sign (GPS **31°22'17.13"S, 19°02'27.73"E**) to Oorlogskloof and turn left here. Negotiate a rough jeep track southwards for around 10km (passing through a gate) until you reach the reserve entrance gate at Groot Tuin.

ACCOMMODATION This is an extremely remote nature reserve, so don't expect the perfect cappuccino or a salmon, rocket and cream cheese ciabatta. Snack on a pack of trail mix, then hightail it back onto the R27 to the delectable culinary delights of Hantam Huis in Calvinia. Or check out www.papkuilsfontein.co.za

EXPERT'S VIEW

Ugene Nel is an adventure racer, trail runner, mountain biker and event organiser, sponsored by First Ascent (www.firstascent.co.za), Spur (www.spur.co.za) and Vibram. He has competed in multi-day expedition races around the world, and has completed the gruelling, 2400km 'Freedom Challenge MTB Race across South Africa' three times.

My run

'Negotiating the rock-strewn routes meandering through Oorlogskloof is incredible, but you had better be ready for extreme technical running along the thumping, cliff-top trails. Slippery rocks, fynbos singletrack, river crossings and vertiginous drops make for an exhilarating nature run, made all the more breathtaking by the endless vistas towards the Knersvlakte shimmering far below.'

Insider tips

'Drinking water can be obtained from the Oorlogskloof River, with several springs along its course – there may also be seasonal water in rock pools on the mountain during rainy seasons. All trails are marked through clay tiles or wooden signs, or demarcated with cairns along some stretches.'

Gear and apparel

'Sturdy trail shoes are an absolute must as you will be carrying a pack with emergency clothing and provisions. I personally prefer my old Salomon Raids, but any shoe with good underfoot grip and protection will ensure solid traction on the rocks. Do not even think of entering this event without a fully rainproof jacket, extra dry clothing and a first-aid kit.'

My shoe

Brand ~ Salomon

Model ~ Raid

Rating ~ Fantastic underfoot protection; heavier than new range, but still my favourite shoe ever

Training and pacing

'The 42km trail run is in effect equal to a 150km road run, so don't think you can take this one on if you've previously finished a tarmac marathon. Even elite athletes can expect to be out in the elements for seven hours or more, so make sure you are 100% fit and injury-free before you venture out into the Oorlogskloof wilderness.'

FAST FACTS

Grading Difficult to extreme, depending on the temperature and distance of your run
Duration Anything from two hours to seven days (the latter at hiking pace)
Configuration Various return or circular options (5.2km to 52.4km)
Start point Groot Tuin Entrance Gate
GPS co-ordinates 31°26'38.07"S, 19°04'13.68"E
Terrain Gravel road and lots of singletrack
Map Basic map from Conservation Office
Access requirements Paid permit from Conservation Office in Nieuwoudtville before you set off
Trail markings Clay tiles, wooden signs, or stone cairns
Facilities Basic huts and tents along trails; water is available in the river year-round
Cell reception No coverage
Beware Hydration is critical, and keep a look-out for snakes and loose rocks
Time of year Typical Mediterranean weather, with winter rains and searing, dry summers
Local info www.northerncape.org.za / Tel (+27 27) 218 1159 / or 218 1010
More info www.quantumadventures.co.za / Tel (+27 82) 658 3078

THE TRAIL At nearly 5 000ha, Oorlogskloof demands more than one day of exploration. There are three one-day hikes to choose from, plus various combos of the seven-day multi-day routes. The Rock Pigeon Trail (Kransduifroete) covers 52km over 4–5 days, and running this will be way more strenuous than doing the Otter African Trail Run. The official hiking trails are as follows:

One-day circular routes
Leopard Trap Day Hike – 15.5km (6–9hrs)
Revile Day Hike – 17.9km (7–10hrs)
Sailor Day Hike – 5.2km (2–3hrs)

4–7-day circular routes
Rock Pigeon Route – 52.2km (4–5 days)
Rameron Pigeon Route – 52.4km (4–7 days)

How does one even begin to describe this natural wonder? Deep gorges, cliffs, plateaus covered in stands of Cape suikerbos and giant Waboom proteas ... contorted rock pillars, arches, caverns and lunar-like craters as old as the planet itself, with ancient rock art that is sure to blow your mind ... it's all there.

The Oorlogskloof Mountain Run starts and finishes at Groot Tuin, the reserve entrance 16km from the village of Nieuwoudtville. The 42km route follows a combination of various hiking trails, meandering between rock formations toward the edge of Saaikloof before descending and then almost immediately ascending toward Spelonkkop.

Approximately 4km after the start you reach Brakwater where you can find fresh water; the track then crosses the Oorlogskloof River and for the next 3km follows a contour route below the cliffs before dropping down to the river. The normal hiking trail on the left bank carries on toward Eland se Kliphuis, but the runners cross the river at this point: look for a cairn on a rock bank and continue through reeds on the opposite bank.

The trail now veers in the opposite direction for less than 2km before swinging to the left into the Rietvlei Valley. Here the route twists and turns along the valley floor, onto plateaus and escarpments, through numerous arches, squeezing through narrow cracks in rocks and cliffs. Small wonder then that the trail seemingly just bumps into natural wonders and numerous ancient rock art sites. Names like Draaikraal, Granaatdraai, Donkiestasie, Arrie se Punt, Pramkoppie and others mark areas of significance (including an ancient burial site near Suikerbosfontein). There are many natural rock shelters along the route, as well as five locations where three-man tents are erected for people doing the hiking trails. This option is purely in case of emergency, injury or freak weather, as cellphone reception is sketchy and mainly only available along the south and east side of Oorlogskloof (from around the halfway mark to the finish) and only on higher-lying landforms.

If you plan to go and run outside the event, a map with detailed info is supplied when you obtain your permit from Nature Conservation in Goedehoop Street, Nieuwoudtville. A maximum group size of 30 hikers (or a minimum of three adults) is enforced for your own safety.

EVENT FACTS

Event name Oorlogskloof Mountain Trail Run
Series name Quantum Country Classics
Venue Oorlogskloof Nature Reserve (Groot Tuin Gate)
Distance from Cape Town 349km
Time of year End of May
Enter as Teams of two
Cut-offs Will be enforced – runners will be briefed at race
Distances 18km / 42km
Average duration 3hrs / 8hrs
Entry info www.quantumadventures.co.za

THE EVENT The Oorlogskloof Mountain Trail Run is the second event in the Quantum Country Classics series – options include 18km or 42km mountain runs during the event scheduled for the end of May. Due to the route being remote and in a wilderness area, the event is entered as a team of two, meaning two people must run as a unit from start to finish. The area is described and listed as 'pristine', and runners will – in every sense – experience a unique adventure.

The 42km run is not recommended if you are a novice trail runner, and proof of previous trail event finishes may be required. Rather opt for the 18km run presented on the same weekend.

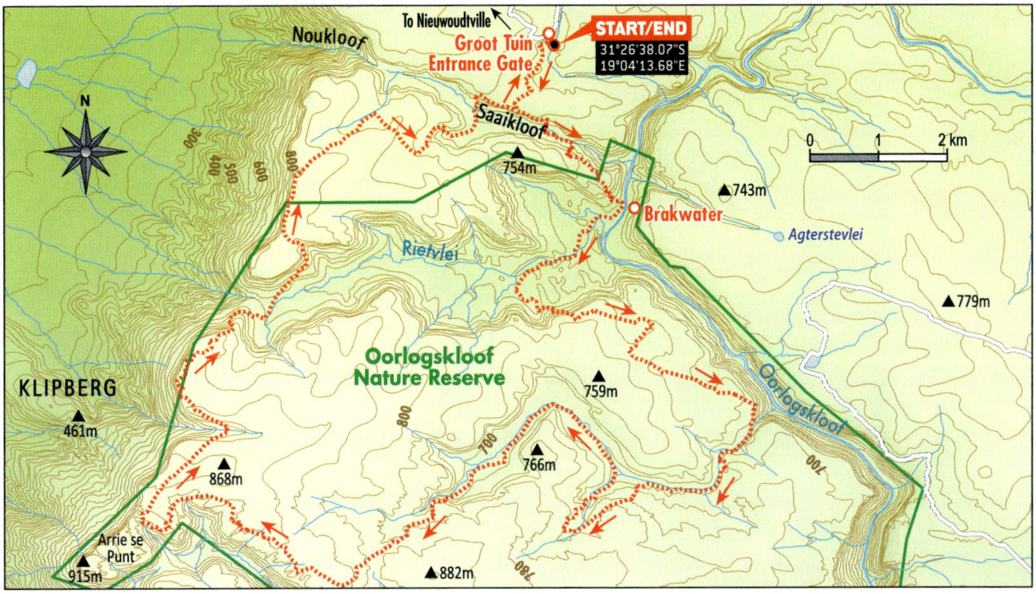

GRADIENT PROFILE

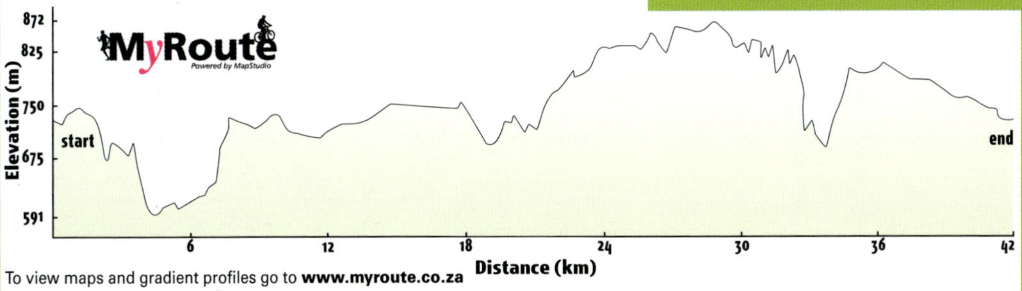

To view maps and gradient profiles go to **www.myroute.co.za**

Otter African Trail Run

4.8km and 42km

Event Only

Province Eastern Cape and Western Cape
Region Tsitsikamma and Garden Route
Closest town Storms River Village
Trail destination Tsitsikamma National Park
Series Stand-alone event
Contributed by Mark Collins and Ryan Sandes

THE DESTINATION Trip into the Tsitsikamma trance zone and discover a secret world where the deep-forest delights of indigenous woodland unfold along the so-called 'Garden of the Garden Route'. This land lies between the sea and the Tsitsikamma Mountains and stretches from the Bloukrans River in the west to Eerste Rivier in the east. Take time out and escape into what the Khoisan called the 'Place of abundant or sparkling waters' and reclaim some much-needed soul space.

The Otter Trail is South Africa's iconic and internationally renowned five-day hiking trail, traversing a spectacular and pristine section of the continent's southern coast within the Tsitsikamma National Park. Known for its lush green forests, deep gorges and towering cliffs overlooking the Indian Ocean, the Tsitsikamma is Africa's oldest and biggest marine reserve. Visitors to the park are often treated to the sight of whales, dolphins and otters from the shoreline. Less frequently sighted but also inhabiting the reserve are the apex predators – sharks and leopards.

THE TERRAIN The Otter is on the upper end of the difficulty scale in terms of the technical nature of the trail and this is sustained with multiple climbs in and out of the many river valleys. In a word, participants describe it as relentless. The trail includes steep-stepped inclines and descents, rutted and root-lined coastal trails, jagged rocks, sand and pebbled beaches, open trails and boulder fields. No fewer than 16 streams and rivers are traversed, four of which may require swimming. The Bloukrans River is an infamous crossing and may only safely be attempted around low tide.

DIRECTIONS The Tsitsikamma National Park is in the heart of the Garden Route stretching along the coast between the holiday village of Nature's Valley in the west and Storms River in the east. The nearest airports are Port Elizabeth and George, each being about two hours' drive from the park.

The main park entrance is on the Storms River side and can be accessed off the N2. Coming from Port Elizabeth, turn left approximately 8.5km after crossing the Storms River Bridge. From Cape Town, turn right off the N2 18km after crossing the Bloukrans Bridge. GPS co-ordinates are as follows:

N2 turn-off 33°58′16.2″S, 23°50′23.3″E
Storms River 34°01′15.6″S, 23°52′48.7″E
Nature's Valley 33°58′14.6″S, 23°33′45.6″E

ACCOMMODATION The Tsitsikamma National Park, one of the Garden Route's most popular tourist attractions, offers chalet, cabin and camping accommodation, an informative visitor's centre, a shop and an excellent restaurant. The de Vasselot Camp Site near Nature's Valley is less often visited but just as beautiful, with rustic log cabins and camping under giant yellowwood trees on the lagoon banks (www.sanparks.org).

FAST FACTS

Grading Extreme
Duration 5–11hrs
Configuration Point to point
Start point Nature's Valley or Storms River Rest Camp, depending on year
GPS co-ordinates 34°01'15.6"S, 23°52'48.7"E (Storms River) and 33°58'14.6"S, 23°33'45.6"E (Nature's Valley)
Terrain Rugged singletrack, coastal rock shelves, pebbled beaches and deep river crossings
Map Available at www.theotter.co.za
Access requirements Route restricted to race only
Trail markings Directional arrows
Facilities Refreshment table at 20km and finish line
Cell reception 30% of route
Beware High seas and flooding rivers
Time of year Last two weeks of September to first two weeks of October; date dependent on tide
Local info www.naturesvalleytrust.co.za

THE TRAIL Dubbed the 'Grail of Trail' by participants, the Otter African Trail Run is regarded by many as the 42km trail-running yardstick. This challenging event demands that participants negotiate the beautiful but brutal five-day Otter Hiking Trail in just a few hours. The allure of the Otter Run, however, not only lies in it being considered a true test of trail-running ability over the marathon distance, but perhaps also in the knowledge that the trail is off limits to all trail runners outside of this event, leading some to label it the 'Forbidden Run'.

The Otter Hiking Trail itself starts at the gate on the Storms River side of the Tsitsikamma National Park and follows the protected coastline for 38km westwards to reach the seaside village of Nature's Valley on the reserve's western boundary. Hikers, who have to book months in advance, are limited to groups of 12 people and stay in the four overnight huts along the route. The hike is acclaimed as one of Africa's premier wilderness experiences.

Trail running on the actual Otter Trail outside of the organised event is strictly forbidden, although the day hiking trails on both sides of the trail offer magnificent trail-running opportunities ranging in distances from 4–16km.

THE EVENT The Otter Run / Challenge is a two-day event with a 4.8km prologue race on the first 'registration' day and the feature 42km race on the second day. The event also sets off in two departures with the Otter Run (8hr cut-off) and the Otter Challenge (11hr cut-off). The events run consecutively, with each event limited to 200 athletes. The event is run in different directions in alternating years. The Otter Run is the east-to-west running of the trail, whereas the Retto* Run starts on the Nature's Valley side and follows the trail in reverse, thus finishing at Storms River. (*Retto is Otter backwards.)

The 4.8km Prologue Route The prologue races for the Otter Run / Challenge take place on the trails on either side of the Otter Trail (dependent on the direction of the run for that year), with the splendid 4.8km Salt River Prologue in the west leaving from Nature's Valley, and the 5km Storm Run Prologue in the east leaving from the Storms River Rest Camp in Tsitsikamma. Participants may run the prologue at any time between 11:00 and 17:00 on the registration day of the event. The prologue routes may also be run at any time of the year outside of the event.

GRADIENT PROFILE

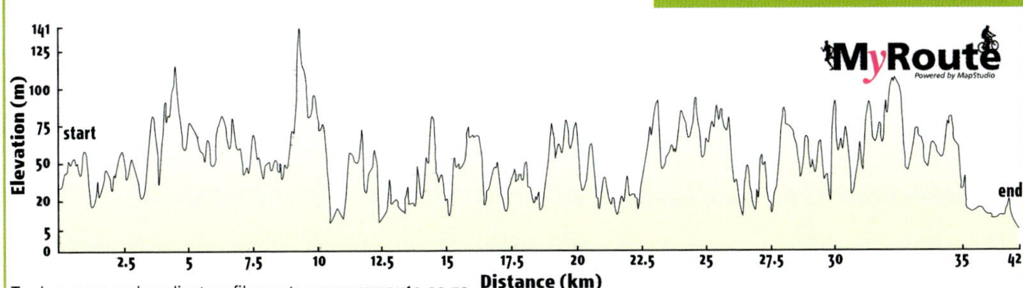

To view maps and gradient profiles go to **www.myroute.co.za**

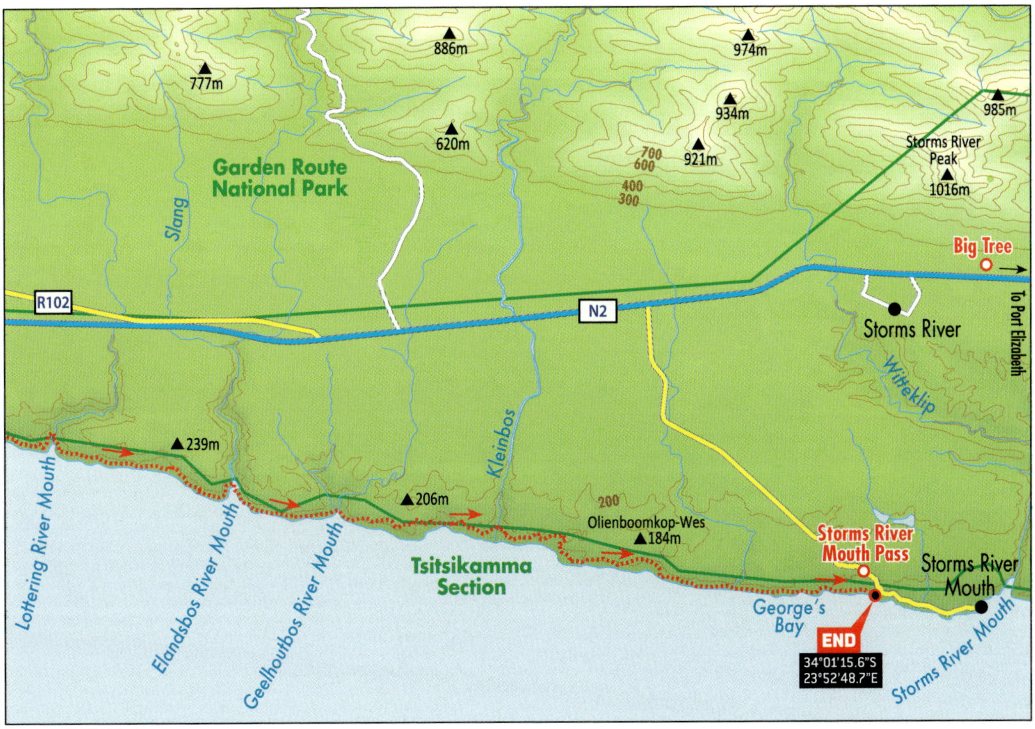

The 42km Race Route followed by the Otter / Retto Run / Challenge traverses the Otter Trail plus a bit extra on either side of the trail to make up the 42km.

The Otter Run and the Otter Challenge events are identical but for their different cut-off times. Both events are two days in duration, with a short prologue route on the first day and the main race on the second day. Participating in the Prologue is obligatory and the results from this race serve the purpose of seeding the participants for the main race, where the runners are set off in staggered intervals according to their seeding. The cut-offs are strictly enforced at checkpoints along the route, and participants failing to pass these checkpoints in the maximum allocated time are removed from the course for safety reasons.
The Abangeni Places on the Otter Run podium may only be contested by runners who finish the Prologue Race in a time ranking among the top 10%. These participants are set off in one esteemed group known as *The Abangeni* ('The Challengers' in Xhosa).

Participants must be over 18 years of age and have completed events of a similar nature. The scheduling of the Otter Run is determined by Mother Nature – organisers set the date around the most favourable low tides between 15 September and 15 October.

EVENT FACTS

Event name Otter African Trail Run
Venue Tsitsikamma National Park
Distance from Port Elizabeth 180km
Time of year Last two weeks of September to first two weeks of October – date dependent on the tide
Enter as Solo
Cut-offs 8hrs for the Otter Run and 11hrs for the Otter Challenge
Distances 4.8km and 42km
Average duration 5–11hrs
Entry info www.theotter.co.za

EXPERT'S VIEW

Ryan Sandes is South Africa's most accomplished trail runner, recording wins in major races on every continent, including Antarctica, and in environments ranging from deserts to jungles to snow-capped mountains. Ryan's many extraordinary accomplishments have been well documented and the extensive acclaim has seen him become a household name in South Africa. Despite his fame, Ryan remains humble and grounded, earning him the respect of his fellow elite competitors. He rates the Otter as trails' 42km yardstick. He is the winner of the Otter Run 2011 and the current record holder at 04:40:15.

My run
'The Otter Trail is really beautiful, with loads of breathtaking views, but at the same time the route is incredibly challenging. The Otter Trail is a true test of your athletic ability with over 2 800m of climbing over the 42km distance. It is arguably the toughest marathon distance trail run in South Africa and definitely the most beautiful. The Otter Trail has a bit of everything in it: steep climbs, technical descents, never-ending singletrack, river crossings and constantly changing terrain, giving you the ultimate trail experience.'

Insider tips
'Most participants do not remove their shoes for the river crossings. Being immersed in the cold water during the river crossing can be quite a shock to the body and it is a good idea to take stock of your condition immediately after the swim before continuing. Even the best runners walk the big climbs. Expend your energy wisely.'

Gear and apparel
'Participants are required to carry a certain amount of compulsory gear determined by the Weather Alert Level. A full list of the compulsory and recommended gear is on the event website.'

Training and pacing
'Training for the Otter Run should include preparing for seriously technical terrain and for more than 2 400m of vertical ascent. Preparations should embrace steep ascents and descents while focusing on the anticipated duration of the event rather than the distance. The average participant takes double their best road marathon time to complete The Otter. On the actual event the most experienced participants' advice is to run well within oneself for the first half of the race as the effects of the trail are cumulative and the consequences of starting out too hard can result in the feared and fabled "Otter Bite".'

Outeniqua Traverse

10, 25 and 38km

Trail & Event

Province Western Cape
Region Garden Route
Closest town George
Trail destination Wittefontein Nature Reserve
Series Mountain Runner Events
Contributed by Tatum Prins

THE DESTINATION The Outeniqua Mountains, towering above George, are covered in diverse vegetation – the moist southern slopes are predominantly clad in mountain fynbos while the northern slopes are much drier, with hardy, drought-resistant Karoo veld. A variety of animal species finds shelter here, including the klipspringer, grey rhebuck, numerous small rodents and the elusive leopard. Birds include large raptors such as the Verreaux's (Black) Eagle, as well as smaller typical fynbos birds like the Cape Sugarbird.

THE TERRAIN The trail is predominately a well-maintained hiking trail. The surface is mostly gravel with the odd rocky section. There are some tricky sections on the northern slopes where the trail climbs back over the mountain before descending to Tierkop Hut. Depending on the rainfall, the trail in the natural forest regions on the southern slopes can be waterlogged.

DIRECTIONS All the trails start at the George Botanical Gardens (GPS 33°56'44.0"S, 22°27'53.0"E) in Caledon Street, at the foot of the Outeniqua Mountains.

ACCOMMODATION A wide range of accommodation options is available in and around George (www.visitgeorge.co.za and www.georgetourism.org.za).

FAST FACTS

Grading Intermediate to difficult
Duration 4.5–9hrs (38km)
Configuration Circular
Start point George Botanical Gardens
GPS co-ordinates 33°56′44.0″S, 22°27′53.0″E
Terrain Mountainous and technical singletrack
Map Available at www.mountainrunner.co.za
Access requirements Race entry fee upon registration; free entrance
Trail markings Arrows and bunting tape
Facilities Parking and all amenities in the Botanical Gardens
Cell reception Good coverage along most sections
Beware Steep switchbacks between North Station and Tierkop
Time of year August for the race; year-round for the trail
Local info www.visitgeorge.co.za and www.georgetourism.org.za
More info www.mountainrunner.co.za / Tel (+27 21) 712 8799

THE TRAIL The 38km route starts with a 5km run along forest tracks at the base of the Outeniqua Mountains towering above George, before turning onto the hiking trail traversing along the face of the range. It then ascends a huge 700m over the next 6km, to eventually provide competitors a spectacular view of the surrounding area. From there the trail descends behind the George Peak, before climbing back over the ridge to once again drop down into the forested foothills. The final few kilometres of the trail meander through a spectacular section of natural forest, finishing back at the George Botanical Gardens. This is a tough, but achievable run, with a total ascent of 2 000m. (The trail forms part of the Cape Nature Wittefontein Nature Reserve).

The 25km trail starts along the trails and paths running next to the railway line at the base of the Outeniqua Mountains, looping into the upper reaches in the vicinity of the George Dam. From here, the route climbs up to Tierkop Hut before turning west and joining the 38km route for a final 12km of spectacular forest running. Prepare yourself for 25km of pure joy, along trails with great views and a total ascent of 700m.

Finally, the 10km route is for anyone new to trail running. This easy route winds along the various forest jeep tracks and singletracks above the botanical gardens – it is a fun run with a great atmosphere and around 200m of ascent.

EXPERT'S VIEW

Tatum Prins and Graham Bird are both avid adventure racers, trail runners and mountain bikers. They have competed at expedition events on five continents.

The shoe

Brand ~ Merrell
Model ~ Seismic
Rating ~ The best balance between foot freedom and surface protection is what you get from the NTR Seismic – it's is the perfect shoe for trail runners who love adventure

© JACQUES MARAIS

THE EVENT Imagine ridge lines, fynbos, flowing trails and magnificent views of the Outeniqua Mountains. The Outeniqua Traverse is raw, real and brings out the best in every trail runner, from the novice to the experienced. The beauty of this event is that there is something for everyone, including a wonderful tea garden at the start and finish in the gardens.

EVENT FACTS

Event name Outeniqua Traverse
Venue George Botanical Gardens
Distance from Cape Town 435km
Time of year Beginning of August
Enter as Solo
Cut-offs Yes – runners to be briefed at race
Distances 10km, 25km and 38km
Average duration 1hr, 2.5–5hrs and 4.5–9hrs
Entry info www.mountainrunner.co.za

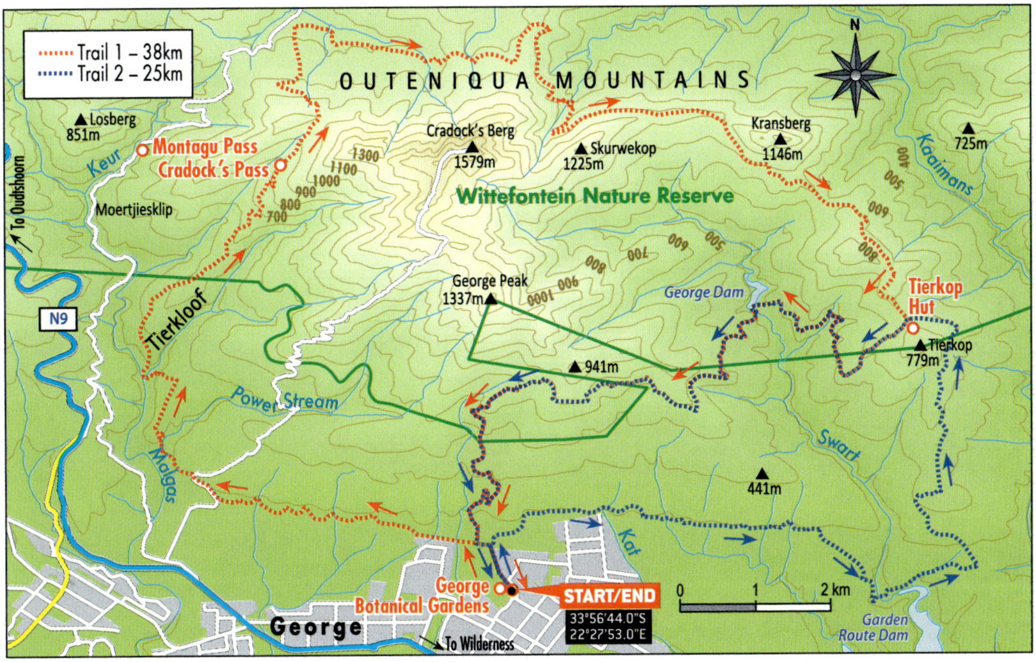

GRADIENT PROFILE

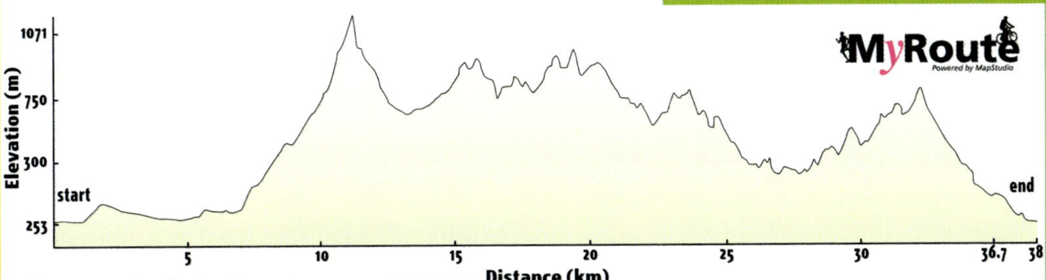

To view maps and gradient profiles go to **www.myroute.co.za**

Trail & Event

Owl's Nest Pure Trail

7, 12 and 21km

Province Gauteng
Region Gauteng North
Closest town Pretoria
Trail destination Owl's Nest Wedding and Conference Venue
Contributed by Debbie Agenbag (WildTrail)

© NICKY SWANEVELDER

THE DESTINATION The serene Owl's Nest, situated a mere 20km east of Pretoria, is one of the region's best-known wedding and conference venues. Few people realize that it is also a trail-running paradise, with a range of stunning routes traversing the foothills of the magnificent Magaliesberg range. Tog up and trip into the African bush here, and it will feel as if you're a thousand miles away from the urban jungle.

THE TERRAIN Owl's Nest's trail network winds through diverse terrain varying from typical Highveld thicket to more open vegetation. Tree-lined jeep track along the valley floor gives way to rugged singletrack once you ascend the eastern mountain slopes.

With its natural obstacles and stream crossings the mountain section will test runners, so chances are you will get wet and muddy. Conditions during late summer usually go hand in hand with mild weather, perfect for running, with spectacular 360-degree views from the higher ground.

DIRECTIONS Events start and finish in the lovely Owl's Nest gardens in front of the restaurant. To get to the venue, follow the N4 east onto the Boschkop / Donkerhoek off-ramp. Turn left after the toll-gate and left again at the four-way stop, then right onto the Old Bronkhorstspruit Road (R104) at the T-junction. Follow this road through a mountain cutting and turn left as you summit to Owl's Nest – venue markers will lead you to your destination.

ACCOMMODATION Each of the 11 separate double rooms and chalets are set within indigenous bush, featuring en-suite bathrooms, dressing rooms and separate toilets. The sounds of nature are sure to lull you into a tranquil mood, especially around the sparkling swimming pool set amidst bushveld trees.

THE TRAIL The well-established Owl's Nest MTB and running trails serve as the routes of all three runs during the event. From the start, the route descends along undulating singletrack into the valley. After just on 5km, runners climb back up from the valley floor to join a gravel road behind the venue, allowing the 7km runners to finish their short stint on the trail.

The 12km and 21km runners continue towards the mountain (still along the gravel road) for 1km, resting their legs before they reach the game farm gate where a punishing, steep and rocky uphill awaits. The 12km runners turn for home here, along the stream course.

FAST FACTS

Grading Easy to intermediate
Duration 1–3hrs
Configuration Circular route
Start point Start by the braai / picnic area at Owl's Nest
GPS co-ordinates 25°46'4.56"S, 28°29'2.27"E
Terrain Jeep track and singletrack
Map Available at www.runtrail.co.za
Access requirements Free entrance
Trail markings Wooden signs
Facilities Braai / picnic area, swimming pool, toilets
Cell reception Good cell reception
Beware Snakes, ticks and dehydration
Time of year Summer and winter
Local info www.owlsnest.co.za
Local info www.wildtrail.co.za /Tel (+27 83) 294 5260

The long route climb will require major effort and stamina, but the incredible panorama which will greet you at the summit will make it so worthwhile. This is Pretoria's own 'Little Serengeti', with zebra, giraffe, kudu and many more mammal species dotting the plains below. Follow the technical jeep track along the escarpment before dipping into the gorge below for a muddy stream crossing.

From here you are into the home stretch, tramping along the valley and across a few earthen dam walls on a comfortable run to the welcoming gardens of Owl's Nest.

THE EVENT The 7km route constitutes an easy and well-kept singletrack suited to the whole family and runners of any level. The 12km route incorporates a section through beautiful riverine forest and offers more of a challenge, while the 21km route is reserved for experienced runners.

EVENT FACTS

Event name Owl's Nest Pure Trail
Venue Owl's Nest Wedding and Conference Venue
Distances 7km, 12km and 21km
Time of year End of March
Enter as Solo
Cut-offs Yes – runners will be briefed at race
Event organiser WildTrail SA
Average duration 30–90min (7km), 1–3hrs (12km) and 2–6hrs (21km)
Entry info www.wildtrail.co.za

EXPERT'S VIEW

Thanbang Madiba is a trail runner and duathlete sponsored by Nissan South Africa and New Balance Gauteng. He has won the Hi-Tec Mystic Sable 50km Stage Run and The Crazy Store Magaliesberg Challenge, and has also competed in the ITU World Duathlon Championships.

My shoe
Brand ~ New Balance
Model ~ MT100
Rating ~ Low-profile trail-running shoe for fast, minimalist trail running

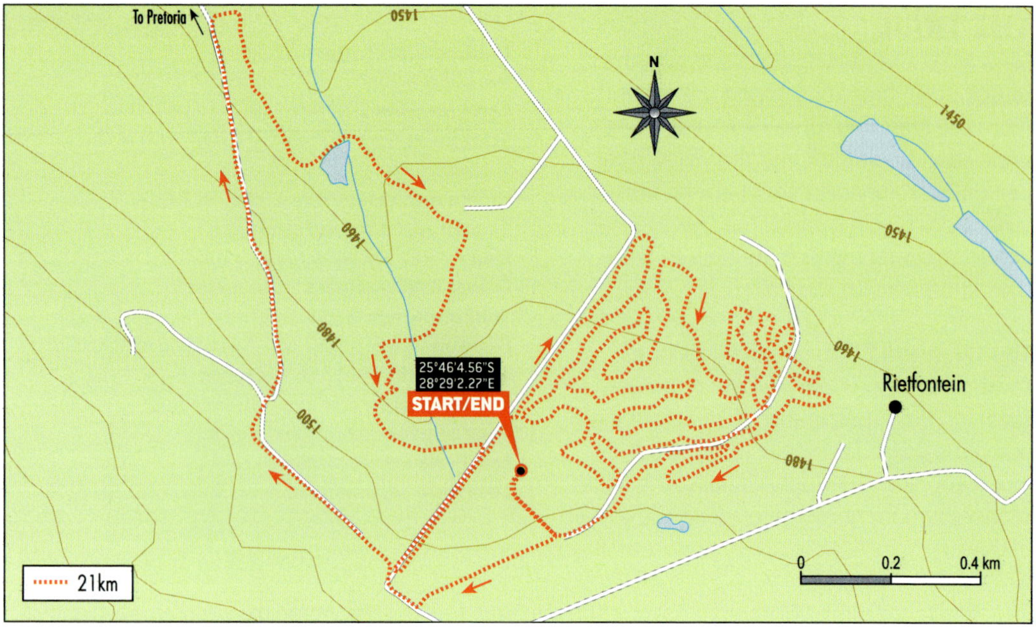

GRADIENT PROFILE

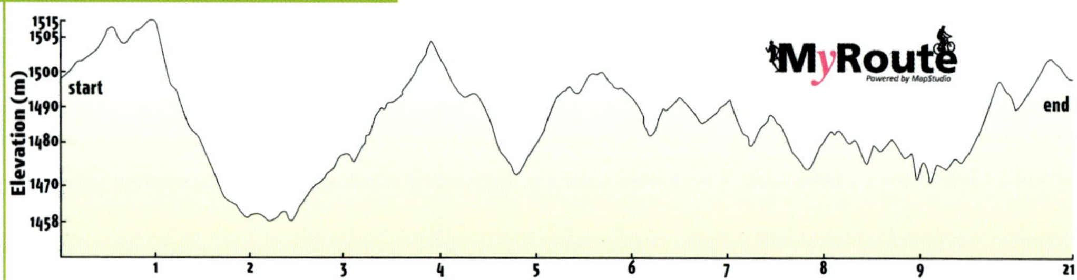

To view maps and gradient profiles go to **www.myroute.co.za**

© NICKY SWANEVELDER

Puffer
73km

Trail & Event

Province Western Cape
Region Peninsula
Closest town Cape Town
Trail destination Table Mountain
Series Stand-alone event
Contributed by Karoline Hanks

THE DESTINATION Adventure awaits at the southwestern tip of the African continent. Here, along a narrow spit of land known as the Cape of Storms, is a historic city where the cosmopolitan spirit of Europe rushes headlong into traditional African culture. Once you've had your urban fix, head beyond the funky Cape Town streets to where the legendary Table Mountain National Park unfolds along the rugged peninsula spine.

THE TERRAIN Although you may grumble at the initial 20km of tar, you will sample the exquisite fynbos singletrack and gravelly/ sandy jeep track traversing an unspoilt fynbos paradise. Steep climbs along the Old Wagon Trail and towards Elephant's Eye, stream crossings, zigzag descents and stacks of technical singletrack will transport you onto another plane as you pass through indigenous Afromontane forest and endless fields of fynbos.

The section up to the highest point of the whole route – Maclear's Beacon (at 1 088m) – is always tough and more of a scramble than a run, but soon the steep climbing gives way to some faster rock hopping along the 'table'. On top it can get very soggy in August, so expect to get your shoes wet. Platteklip Gorge is a nemesis for many a Puffer runner, but the eye-popping beauty should take your mind off the knee-jarring steps!

DIRECTIONS From Cape Town city, head south via Simon's Town or Scarborough along the Peninsula – Cape Point is well signposted and easy to find. Turn south into the entrance gate around 12km from Simon's Town.

ACCOMMODATION Overnight accommodation is available in the national park itself, but it is quite expensive – go to www.sanparks.org.za for info.

FAST FACTS

Grading Difficult to extreme
Duration Anything from 7 hours to 14.5 hours
Configuration Point to point: Cape Point to V&A Waterfront
Start point Cape Point car park
GPS co-ordinates 34°21'2.25"S, 18°29'3.11"E
Terrain Tar, gravel and sand jeep track, singletrack
Map Supplied to runners
Access requirements Park entry fees apply; most of route is accessible to the public outside race day
Trail markings Cairns in some sections; some park signage
Facilities Water and food tables only during race
Cell reception Coverage sporadic, none in places on Table Mountain
Beware Criminal elements have been seen on Table Mountain stretch, so be aware
Time of year Typical Mediterranean weather, with winter rains and searing, dry summers
Local info www.puffer.fishhoekac.com
More info www.capepoint.co.za /Tel (+27 21) 780 9010

THE TRAIL At 05:30 you and 119 other runners set out from the very tip of Cape Point. A much needed head torch will be a boon along the 13km or so of tarmac to the reserve gate, from where you stick to the tar towards Red Hill for another 8km. At the top, you finally hit the trails and jeep track for a while as you meander past the dams towards Glencairn Expressway.

Once you hit the bottom of the Old Wagon Trail, you can finally whip your trail shoes on, then start the long slog up the rocky jeep track (about 5km) as you head up into Silvermine Nature Reserve. Pass the dam en route to Elephant's Eye and continue along the rather rough and ready trail until you pop out onto the Level 5 road in Tokai Forest.

Keep climbing until you reach the tar road to the Sentech Mast, but veer right here towards Vlakkenburg, crossing a little wooden bridge to the top, and then all the way down the other side to Constantia Nek. This is a seconding and re-supply point (as well as a cut-off), so grab your kit bag and head onto either the Bridle Path or new steps (it makes little difference time-wise). Ascend to De Villiers Dam and pass the Hoerikwaggo Trail Hut onto a really gorgeous section of singletrack for more than an hour.

Smuts Track is up next: keep going past Skeleton Gorge junction, heading north towards Maclear's Beacon on a path that is in great condition, with steps and well-maintained wooden walkways and bridges. Now set course for the Aerial Cableway station, all the while keeping your eyes peeled for the sign to Platteklip.

EXPERT'S VIEW

Karoline Hanks has been a competitive trail runner for six years. She prefers longer-distance events, and has run Puffer four times and won it twice. She has a Hout Bay Trail Challenge win under her belt, as well as the 2008 Odyssey Ladies' Team win with partner Linda Doke.

My run
*'Winning Puffer is, in my view, 99.9% mental. When you hit the Old Wagon Trail and your body is screaming at you, you have to negotiate with those pesky voices in your head all the way up. Once you reach the 56k mark at Constantia Nek, any pain there is (and there will be!) has to be set aside and you just have to focus on those relentless steps that go up into the mountain. Platties is always a rush (physically and mentally), no matter how bad the pain. The last stretch of Signal Hill tar is a b*tch, for sure, but it goes by so quickly as by then you can smell the V&A and hear the sirens and you just cannot wait to hear the sweet sound of your feet slapping that flat Portswood Road stretch!'*

Insider tips
'Good nutrition is essential and you need to ensure you are feeding your body (with adequate protein) during training and (if possible) while you are running. Ideally one should be refuelling hourly, but this is easier said than done and so often on these ultra runs your body rejects food. It goes without saying you need to keep well hydrated throughout. I also swear by fairly regular Vitamin B jabs in the weeks prior to Puffer.'

Training and pacing
'For both my Puffer wins, I had a pace chart strapped to my wrist. It is a huge boost when you are at certain points along the way and you glance down and see that you are bang on schedule. It is an interesting run in that you can be cruising at 4.45mins/km in some sections and, when the going gets tough, you're climbing rocky sections up to Maclear's Beacon at an exceedingly slow 12–13mins/km.'

EVENT FACTS

Event name Peninsula Ultra Fun Run
Series name Stand-alone event
Venue Cape Point Nature Reserve (start), Mitchell's Brewery (finish)
Time of year August
Enter as Individual
Cut-offs Enforced at Constantia Nek – 13:30
Distance 73km
Average duration 9–10hrs
Entry info www.puffer.fishhoekac.com

This is an extremely steep downhill – with many loose rocks, big steps and wire-clad gabions – and must not be rushed. Look out for the contour path (about 100m above Tafelberg Road) where you turn left to pass below the cableway. Now it is very much tar all the way onto Signal Hill road before you hit the final descent to the V&A Waterfront past the Noon Gun. You've done it!

THE EVENT The Peninsula Ultra Fun Run (PUFFER) is organised by Fish Hoek Athletic Club and sponsored by Hi-Tec – entries are limited to 120 runners. This 73km run has been dubbed 'The Big Daddy' of trail running; it is not recommended for novice trail runners, and at least an ultra-marathon is required to qualify.

GRADIENT PROFILE

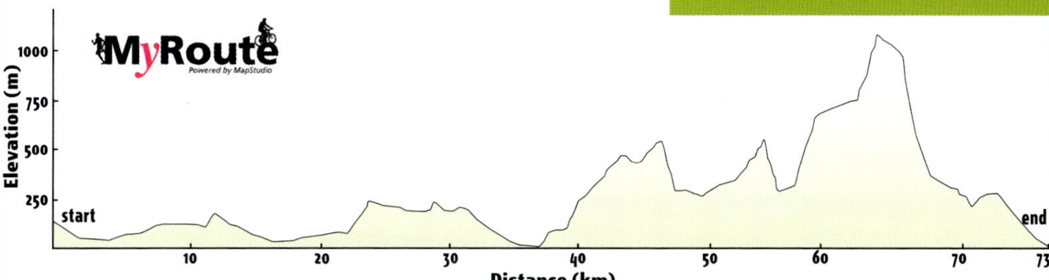

To view maps and gradient profiles go to **www.myroute.co.za**

Event & Trail

Rhodes Trail Run

52km

Province Eastern Cape
Region Friendly N6
Closest town Rhodes
Trail destination Southern Drakensberg around Rhodes
Series Stand-alone event
Contributed by Tammy Kelly

© JACQUES MARAIS

EXPERT'S VIEW

Tammy Kelly has completed seven Rhodes Trail Runs, and is the only five-time winner.

My run

'My first run was the best. I never pace myself, ever. I run from the heart and how I am feeling at the moment. I don't like to run in a crowd, so the Rhodes run is ideal because you are never in a crowd unless you get caught up in the kloof behind the people who walk. I find that in the kloof you must not think. Just run. Mavis Bank is a mental challenge. I don't think anyone can run up it. I put my head down and power walk up it, focusing on the top marker.

'The cold at the start may be a bit daunting for a first-timer, but a kilometre into the run you are warm and it just adds to the spirit. It's not an easy run at all. And every year the weather is different and it has different challenges. So in the seven years I have run it I have had a different run each year.'

My shoe

Brand ~ Asics

THE DESTINATION The historic Victorian-era village of Rhodes, established in 1891 and named after Cecil John Rhodes, was proclaimed a conservation area in 1997 (conferring National Monument status) to preserve its 'olde-worlde' character and charm. It is tucked away in the Eastern Cape Highlands, near the escarpment and right on the southernmost end of the mighty Drakensberg. Set at 1 832m above sea level, it is only 16km due south of the Mountain Kingdom of Lesotho. The village is surrounded by the towns of Maclear, Ugie and Elliot below the escarpment and Barkly East above this barrier.

Rhodes village exudes a timeless charm and beauty and is surrounded by pristine rivers and magnificent mountains. It's the ideal getaway for adventure lovers and for those seeking a break from the stresses of big-city life.

THE TERRAIN The terrain is rugged at over 2 500m above sea level, with numerous mountain streams that drain into sizeable rivers. The Kraai River flows from the junction of the Sterkspruit and the Bell River at Moshesh's Ford, which is 1 724m above sea level, to eventually enter the Atlantic more than 1 000km downstream at Oranjemund.

Above the escarpment, narrow streams meander across remote plateaus and tumble down waterfalls and rapids. They gradually descend into more readily accessible valleys. This remote corner of the Drakensberg boasts a unique South African experience, including subalpine mountains, handsome Victorian villages and diverse nature reserves.

DIRECTIONS Getting to Rhodes Village (the race starts at GPS **30°47'46.0"S, 27°57'58.0"E**) is half the fun. The trick is to find your way to Barkly East and then take the R396 gravel road (a good 60km) through the mountains. Rhodes is at least an hour's drive from Barkly East, which is the closest town, on a poorly maintained gravel road that is narrow, winding and must be driven with care.

ACCOMMODATION Limited accommodation is available in Rhodes and at guest farms in the vicinity of Rhodes. It is advisable to book accommodation early. Those unable to stay in Rhodes must note that high-speed travelling is not possible on the dirt roads, and entrants must give themselves adequate time to reach the start.

The Rhodes Hotel (www.rhodeshotel.co.za) and Walkerbouts Inn (www.walkerbouts.co.za) are in town, and there are several guesthouses and guest farms in the area (www.rhodesvillage.co.za).

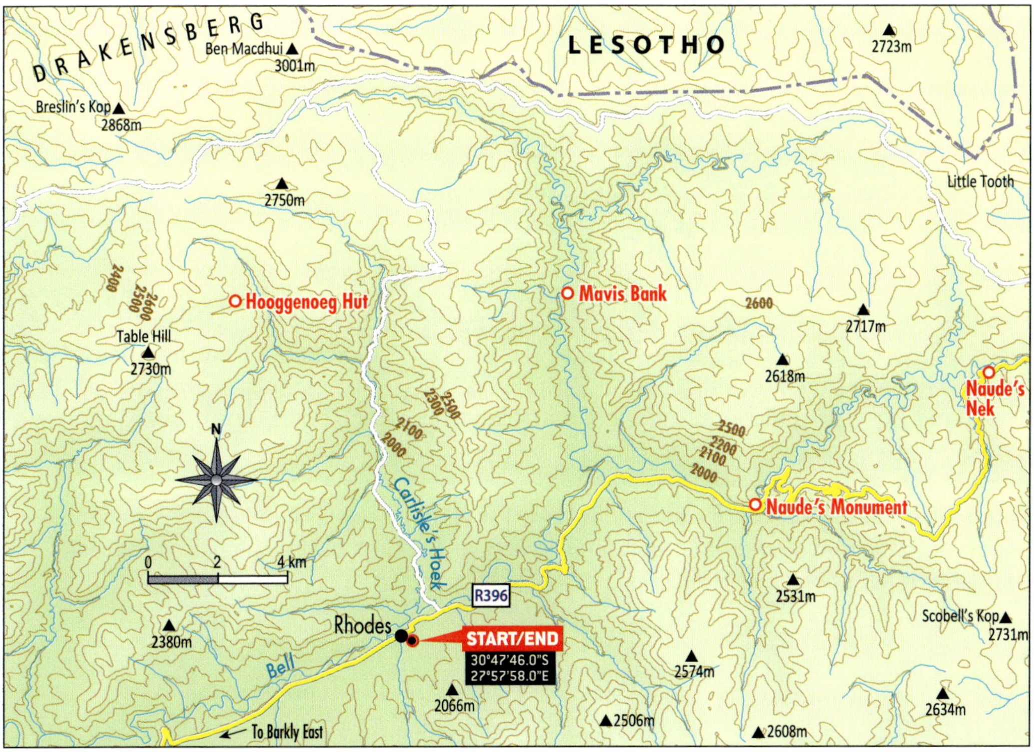

FAST FACTS

Grading Intermediate to extreme
Duration 5–9 hours (52km)
Configuration Circular
Start point Rhodes village
GPS co-ordinates 30°47'46.0"S, 27°57'58.0"E
Terrain Gravel roads, footpaths, cattle and sheep trails, river crossings, rough, uneven terrain, snow and mud
Map Available at www.rhodesrun.za.net
Access requirements Route restricted to race
Trail markings Flags
Facilities Feeding stations can, depending on weather conditions, be up to 10km apart
Cell reception None
Beware Extreme conditions and altitude could accelerate dehydration; you may have to contend with snow, icy conditions, wet roads and strong wind
Time of year Mid-July
Local info www.rhodesvillage.co.za

THE TRAIL The Rhodes Trail Run, South Africa's iconic trail run, takes runners into the southern Drakensberg on the Lesotho border in the remote and rugged far northeastern Cape. Sections of the route are through private property and there is no access outside of race day. The trail starts at 1 800m, reaches its highest point at 2 680m and has an average 'on top' of 2 560m.

The first stage takes runners from the start in Rhodes along the Bell River and into the Kloppershoek Valley. The road crosses the Bell River several times via causeways and low-level bridges before the second stage: an off-road section of approximately 8km from Mavis Bank to the Lesotho border checkpoint. You'll be running along footpaths and cattle and sheep trails and through river crossings marked by means of flags. There is a very steep ascent (1:3) from the valley to the Lesotho border checkpoint.

Before reaching 'the top', runners make their way up Mavis Bank, which is either an easy walk or a lung-searing clamber. Mavis Bank has been described as '...nothing more than a steep, grassy slope', 'die slegte vrou', '...made me forget how challenging it is, especially that lady Mavis Bank', '...I was suffering from a headache, nausea, dizziness, fatigue and shortness of breath'. Being the lady she is, her temperament changes from year to year. She can be miserable and very cold. Sometimes she's rather windy and white on top; always a bit of a 'conversation stopper', and her vertical climb is somewhat more than the height of Johannesburg's Sentech Tower.

The third stage follows the Lesotho border through the Ben MacDhui snowfields. Runners reach the highest point of the route on this section when they pass Lesotho View at 2 680m. Snow, mud and strong head-winds may be encountered.

The fourth stage is another off-road section of 9km from the Quarry checkpoint to the Hooggenoeg Hikers' Hut, along Hooggenoeg Ridge via Hooggenoeg Point. There are no footpaths on this section and competitors follow the ridge line south to the next checkpoint. Here you'll be running along the ridge. Extreme caution is required as the route covers terrain that is extremely uneven and rough underfoot with hidden rocks and holes. Again, snow, mud and strong wind may be encountered.

Along the final stage of 12km a steep descent (1:3.4) drops the runners from the mountain plateau into the Carlisleshoek Valley (dropping several hundred metres per kilometre) and thereafter the route follows the Carlisleshoek Valley back to the finish in Rhodes.

THE EVENT The idea of the race came up during a discussion between Rhodes property owners over a couple of drinks one night in 1986. The intention was to put Rhodes back on the map before it followed the same fate as other small platteland villages, which faded into obscurity. This vision led to the birth of a unique event on the South African sports calendar; 2012 will see the 24th Rhodes Trail Run.

The atmosphere, before and after the race, is always extremely festive. It is common for the temperature at the start to be below zero, usually around -10 degrees Celsius.

The race is not recommended for unfit runners or for those who are not prepared to cover rough terrain. Competitors must expect to walk through snowmelt-fed mountain streams and may have to contend with snow, icy conditions, wet roads and strong wind. Severe wind-chill conditions must also be anticipated.

The distance is 52km but will vary from year to year as the route will depend on prevailing conditions. There is a cut-off at the Mavis Bank checkpoint (approximately 21km into the race) of 4.5 hours, and an overall time limit of 9 hours to qualify as a finisher.

The race has a limited field of about 300 runners. Entry is by invitation only, with an effective substitution facility. The popularity of the Rhodes Trail Run has meant that there is at least an eight-year waiting list for the highly valued invitations, but this is offset by the very efficient invitation substitution system.

In the true spirit of trail running there are no lucky draw, spot, position or financial prizes and, other than a few floating trophies, all runners are treated equally with the same pre- and post-race hand-outs.

EVENT FACTS

Event name Rhodes Trail Run
Series name Southern Drakensberg around Rhodes
Distance from Aliwal North 175km
Time of year Mid-July
Enter as Solo
Cut-offs At Mavis Bank (21km) 4.5hrs; 9hrs to qualify as a finisher
Distance 52km
Average duration 5–9hrs
Entry info www.rhodesrun.za.net

GRADIENT PROFILE

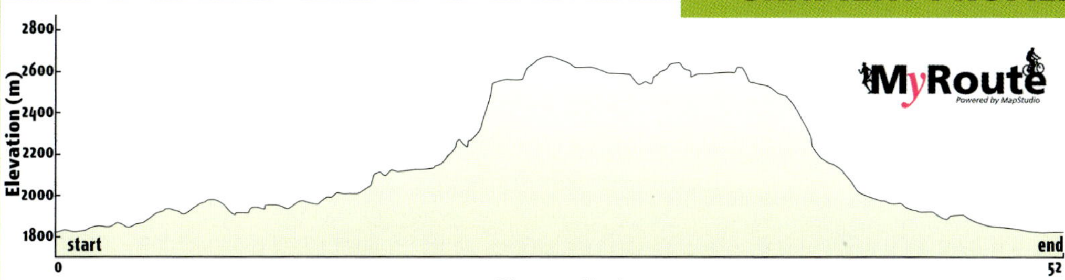

To view maps and gradient profiles go to **www.myroute.co.za**

Trail & Event

Robberg Run and Robberg Express
5km and 8km

Province Western Cape
Region Garden Route
Closest town Plettenberg Bay
Trail destination Robberg Nature Reserve
Series Stand-alone event
Contributed by Mark Collins

EXPERT'S VIEW

Mark Collins has competed as an international adventure racer with three top-five finishes in Adventure Racing World Championships. His passion is sport in the wilderness, and he spends all his free time exploring the wilder regions of the Southern Cape. Mark regards Robberg as the centre of his universe.

Insider tips

'As Robberg is frequented by hikers, trail running is best done early in the morning and out of peak season when you can have the mountain all to yourself. As anywhere, encounters with hikers should always be conducted courteously: warn them of your approach to avoid alarming them and offer them right of way.'

My shoe

Brand ~ Salomon
Model ~ SLAB
Rating ~ Lightweight performance trail shoe that balances excellent durability and protection

THE DESTINATION Robberg – and its surrounding waters – is a protected reserve managed by CapeNature and, apart from everything else, it is a geological, anthropological, historical and botanical treasure. It is a South African National Monument and rightly so. Named after the Cape fur seals (*rob* being the Afrikaans word for seal) that colonise a ledge on the base of the cliffs on the northern shoreline, this finger of rock juts proudly 4km out into the Indian Ocean forming the headland of the beautiful Plettenberg Bay.

THE TERRAIN At least two of the three rock systems from which the mountain is moulded are immediately and delightfully apparent in any exposed crag. At the bottom of the strata lies the older Table Mountain quartzite, visible on the lower bands and protruding through the beach sands, with the intriguing and attractive-looking rock conglomerate formed above it. The higher regions are capped by the more horizontal sandstone layers. Runners will become familiar with the different trail surfaces these formations produce and the unique footwork challenges each type poses.

DIRECTIONS Robberg is a prominent and defining landmark visible from any sea view out of Plettenberg Bay. It is the mountainous peninsula defining the southern part of the bay and hard to miss although there is no direct road access along the beachfront. The road to the Robberg Nature Reserve is well signposted, leading off the airport road which leaves the town on the 'inland' side. The trail starts at the Robberg Nature Reserve car park (GPS 34°06'02.2"S, 23°22'39.1"E).

ACCOMMODATION Plettenberg Bay is a renowned holiday destination offering a wide choice of accommodation and entertainment options (www.plettenbergbay.co.za).

FAST FACTS

Grading Intermediate to difficult
Duration 45–90mins
Configuration Circular
Start point Robberg Nature Reserve car park
GPS co-ordinates 34°06'02.2"S, 23°22'39.1"E
Terrain Rugged singletrack, coastal rock shelves and beaches
Map Available from www.magneticsouth.co.za
Access requirements Entry permits at reserve gate
Trail markings Directional arrows
Facilities Finish-line refreshments
Cell reception 60% of route
Beware High seas, sharp drop-offs and freak waves
Time of year April
Local info www.capenature.co.za and www.plettenbergbay.co.za

THE TRAIL Metre for trail metre, the Robberg Run is one of the finest trail running experiences on the planet. It's hard to imagine a comparable trail that includes as much diversity of scenery, spectacular views and trail types all packed into one short but enchanting 8km loop as does the route around the Robberg Peninsula. This trail is nothing short of breathtaking, in every sense of the word.

Despite it being a popular tourist hiking attraction and drawing hikers of all aptitudes, actual trail running on Robberg is neither for beginners nor for those with an aversion to technical running. This trail is as technical as it is diverse, and many sections veer dangerously close to the top of some big vertical drop-offs. A rookie mistake on many parts could easily result in a serious injury or worse. The standard run follows the hiking trail, starting and finishing in the parking lot, and makes a clockwise circumnavigation of the mountain. The trail starts immediately with a rocky path and runners will negotiate heaps of this trail type together with steep climbs, sandy dunes, coastal forest trails, rock shelves, boulder gardens, a stretch of open beach and even a few wooden walkways in the loop.

The standard route is exceptionally challenging for a run of only 8km, but it can be lengthened by including a lap of the island on the southern side which will add an additional 900m of blissful trail. Other variations include cutting down the climbing dune which will halve the distance of the run, an option for the less energetic, and many runners do the run in figure-of-eight variations of the regular route. Some hardy souls have even been known to do multiple laps of the mountain.

Dangerous and out-of-bounds sections: All hikers and runners are required to stay strictly on the trail. As with all coastal runs, it is a good idea to keep one wary eye on the sea when negotiating the shoreline sections. Freak waves are not as infrequent as might be thought and have been known to reach high above the high-water marks. Just after leaving The Gap, the route cuts below an overhang and trail runners should take care not to gash their heads on the low overhanging rock. They won't be the first.

The entrance to the Robberg Nature Reserve is access controlled and and entry fee is payable at the gate. Wild Cards are accepted. Safe parking with ablutions, an info centre and picnic decks are just inside the reserve. The picnic decks have braai facilities and this is a lovely place for runners to regroup after the run.

THE EVENT The Robberg Express is the organised race around the Robberg Nature Reserve and is named after a 7m great white shark that is frequently sighted in the bay. The run was originally part of a multi-sport race including mountain biking and paddling, but with many athletes preferring just to do the run, organisers have made the trail run the feature of the event.

EVENT FACTS

Event name Robberg Express
Venue Robberg Nature Reserve
Distance from George 70km
Time of year April
Enter as Solo
Cut-offs None
Distances 5km and 8km
Average duration 45–90mins
Entry info www.magneticsouth.net

GRADIENT PROFILE

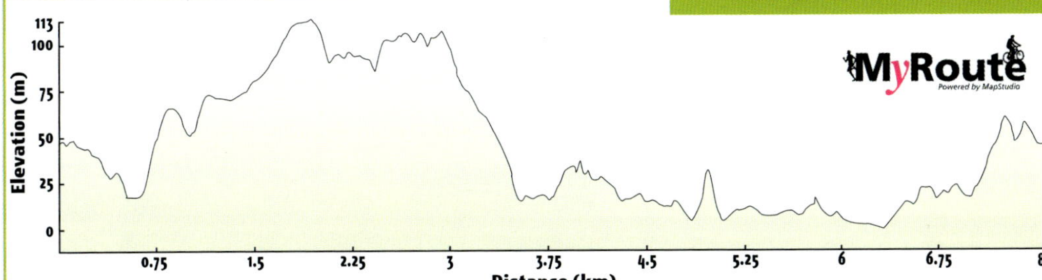

To view maps and gradient profiles go to **www.myroute.co.za**

Event Only

Sky Run
65km and 100km

Province Eastern Cape
Region uKhahlamba
Closest town Lady Grey
Trail destination Wartrail Country Club
Series Pure Adventures
Contributed by Linda Doke and Michael de Haast

EVENT FACTS

Event name Salomon Sky Run
Venue Lady Grey
Distances 65km and 100km
Time of year Early November
Enter as Individuals
Cut-offs Will be enforced – runners will be briefed at the race
Average duration 16/30hrs
Entry info www.pureadventures.co.za

© JACQUES MARAIS

THE DESTINATION Dominated by the towering buttresses and spurs of the Witteberg ranges, this northerly corner of the Eastern Cape nestles up against the majestic mountain kingdom of Lesotho. Lady Grey is a considerable trek from just about any major urban centre, but visitors who commit to the gravel road trip will be utterly charmed by the laid-back lifestyle of this rural hamlet.

The highest Witteberg peaks skyline at a dizzying 2 408m, stretching along the horizon for about 60km from Lundin's Nek in the east to Lady Grey in the west. Lady Grey languishes within the shadows of these rugged ranges, and denotes the trail head for the annual Salomon Sky Run, unarguably one of South Africa's premier trail-running events. The tiny village is also famous for its annual nativity play, and its quaint houses, incredible scenery, San rock art and endless list of outdoor activities make it well worth a visit.

THE TERRAIN The Salomon Sky Run epitomises true mountain running, with varying terrain along the network of jeep tracks, hiking paths and off-track scrambling making up the 100km route. If you have never done this race, familiarise yourself with the terms 'self-supported' and 'route navigation', as this will very much be in the hands of individual competitors.

Then there is the landscape here in the Wartrail / New England area – it is harsh to say the least, and very high too (1 900m in the valleys, and touching 3 000m along some of the peaks). The landscape is windswept and baked by harsh sun in the day, and icy conditions occur at night, with the cracked and brittle rocks underfoot telling a story of the extremes experienced throughout any given year. The region gets four or five heavy snowfalls between May and August, and the highest peaks are usually snow-capped throughout winter.

Once you have stepped beyond the town limits of Lady Grey, it is not uncommon to run much of the race without encountering any real traces of human civilization, except for the occasional support point or fellow racer. An impressive list of fauna and flora – including over 650 plant and 80 animal species – will enhance a true lifetime event here within the incredible uKhahlamba region.

DIRECTIONS Lady Grey (GPS **30°42′48.60″S, 27°13′6.96″E**) can be accessed via regional tarmac networks in South Africa. The town is situated approximately three hours from Bloemfontein, six hours from Durban, seven hours from Johannesburg and just on 10 hours from Cape Town by car.

To reach the Wartrail Country Club (the finish), continue from Lady Grey on the R58 towards Barkly East. About 48km along this road, turn left at the New England turn-off onto a gravel road. After 7km the road forks. Keep right following the signs to Tiffendel / Lundin's Nek. Drive for 8.5km to the Wartrail / Barkly East fork and then keep left towards Wartrail / Tiffendell. Drive for 15km and, at the next New England / Wartrail junction, turn right towards Wartrail / Lundin's Nek. Drive for 2km, and at the Tiffendell / Lundin's Nek fork keep left towards Lundin's Nek. You'll see the Wartrail Country Club on your right.

ACCOMMODATION Lady Grey itself boasts a number of accommodation options (for a list of establishments visit www.ladygreytourism.co.za). The only seconding point along the route is Balloch Caves, where athletes descend into the valley before hitting the dreaded Balloch Wall. Balloch boasts a few chalets as well as one of the most beautiful camping sites on Planet Earth – www.ballochcottages.co.za (and don't miss out on Margy Frost's legendary food at this stopover).

FAST FACTS

Grading Very difficult to extreme, depending on the temperature and weather
Duration Anything from 17hrs to 36hrs
Configuration Start in Lady Grey and traverse the Witteberg Mountain to Wartrail Country Club
Start point Lady Grey
GPS co-ordinates 30°42'48.60"S, 27°13'6.96"E
Terrain Cattle paths; off-track navigation by GPS
Entries Limited to 200
Map Basic map provided
Trail markings None; must navigate – GPS units are available on loan
Facilities Camping, B&Bs, lodges and farm-stays in the area
Cell reception Minimal coverage in valleys; mountain coverage
Beware Hydration is critical; keep a look-out for snakes and loose rocks
Time of year November
Local info www.ladygreytourism.co.za
More info www.pureadventures.co.za / Tel (+27 82) 655 6558

THE TRAIL Both the Salomon Sky Run and Sky Run Lite are unique in that they are completely self-supported and self-navigational races. Athletes tackle the remote terrain of the Witteberg ranges with a map, compass or GPS unit, and a backpack containing all the food and water they require. A list of compulsory equipment will be supplied, and it is stressed during the race briefing that these items may be the only differentiating factor between life and death when racing within a harsh environment at an average altitude of between 2200m and 2500m.

The events set off from Lady Grey, and the first 65km of the route is the same for both races. A compulsory stop and medical check at Balloch will determine whether the Sky Runners can continue, while this is the end of the line for the Sky Run Lite competitors.

From the start, the route climbs sharply out of Lady Grey to the first checkpoint at the Tower (12km) along a combo of hiking trails and cattle tracks. Majestic views unfold below you as dawn colours the eastern skyline, while inquisitive cows track your progress along the steep, grassy ridges. Follow the fence line from here to the second checkpoint at Olympus (22km), traversing terrain devoid of paths or trails, and basically leaving you to decide on the best route along the grassy ridges.

A quick breather at Olympus will set you down on a faint trail leading to Snowden, the third checkpoint at approximately 33km. Look out for the natural spring just past Snowden and top up your water bottles and bladder – note the supply is dependent on rainfall though – before slogging up Avoca Peak, the highest point on the course at 2 756m. The ascent up Avoca is challenging, and the steep gradient and uneven terrain are sure to take their toll on your feet after a few hours.

Sky Runners are tough buggers though, and will persevere along the testing 'Dragon's Back' ridge line lying in wait. This 3m-wide crest plummets steeply on either side, with fantastical rock formations stacking up into infinity and beyond on a clear day. Fortunately the route flattens out after this as you move towards checkpoint 6 at Skidor, a leg of about 10km. Prepare for a technical descent into the valley, then follow the river course channelling you into the compulsory stop at Balloch Caves (65km).

Once cleared by the medical team, it is time to tackle the intimidating and near-vertical ascent up the Balloch Wall. You will climb more than 500m over a matter of 3km, hauling yourself up boulders and through sharp-edged tufts of chest-high spear grass. If you make it to the top, helter-skelter down the opposite side to checkpoint 8 at Edgehill Farm. The majority of athletes will now be well into the dark zone, a blessing after 12 hours in the harsh African sun.

Navigate your way through the Bridal Pass from Edgehill and back onto the ridge line, following a scramble along a pine-ridged spur to the left of the river course. (The Bridal Pass has now been included as a waypoint en route to assist athletes in negotiating this rather tricky entry point.) A steady climb to the top will take you onto the ridge line and a further checkpoint at The Turn, from where you double back to Wartrail Country Club via Halston Peak (the final checkpoint along the route).

Athletes should take care on the rugged descent from Halston Peak, as fatigue from nearly a 100km of mountain running will by now be seeping into their very bones. The fact that you may be doing this in the dark further contributes to the challenge, but the knowledge of the finish line within your grasp is sure to buoy you on to the welcoming Wartrail Country Club.

© JACQUES MARAIS

GRADIENT PROFILE

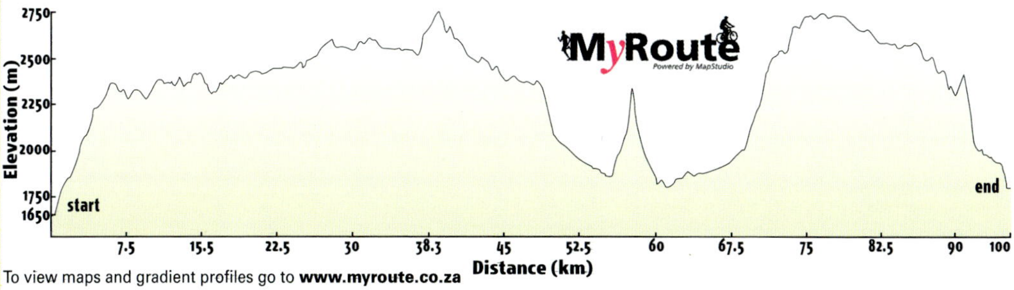

To view maps and gradient profiles go to **www.myroute.co.za**

THE EVENT The **Salomon Sky Run** is an Epic Mountain Run of 100km, and is rated by many athletes as the toughest trail run in South Africa. The event is made up of two options: the **Sky Run Lite** (a 65km one-day run) or the 'Big Daddy' **100km Sky Run**. The event takes place in November and is unique in that it is self-supported, with all athletes expected to navigate themselves along the route.

The event is for serious and experienced trail runners only, with entries limited to 200 athletes for both race options. The 100km run is not recommended if you are a novice trail runner, and proof of previous trail event finishes may be required. Rather opt for the 65km run presented on the same weekend.

EXPERT'S VIEW

Linda Doke is an ultra-distance trail runner, sponsored by Salomon (www.salomon.com/za), PeptoSport/PeptoPro (www.peptopro.com) and Garmin (www.garmin.co.za). She has competed in numerous ultras and multi-day stage races, both locally and around the world, and has completed Sky Run three times, the third time (2011) securing first position in the ladies and tied third overall.

My run

'For me Sky Run is not just about the race and the competition. It's about the incredible feeling of running alone in a remote expanse, far from anywhere, and feeling very small amid the power of nature. The night section is even more special – being in such an isolated region means there's no light pollution, and the black night sky is studded with more stars than you can ever imagine. It's also very much about challenging yourself – whether you're racing this event or you're there "just" to complete it, you have to dig deep within yourself to see it through. You're definitely a bigger soul by the time you cross this finish line.'

Insider tips

'There's very little water along the Sky Run route, so plan your refilling carefully. The event is long and the checkpoints do not stock food, so carry all you need to get to Balloch, where you can get supplies from your pre-arranged drop-bag or your seconds.'

Gear and apparel

'Sturdy trail shoes with good grip are essential. Temperatures can bake in the daytime and drop dramatically at night, so plan accordingly. You're following a ridge line for much of this race, so you're high up. November is the start of the rainy season in the New England region, so be prepared for pelting thunderstorms. The strict kit list is there for a reason – respect it!'

Training and pacing

'Stamina and endurance are what completing Sky Run is all about. Train hard for this one and you'll have good memories of the race. Practise technical running and long runs, strengthen your legs and core, and learn to run on tired legs. Do not underestimate the importance of solid preparation – there are no shortcuts.'

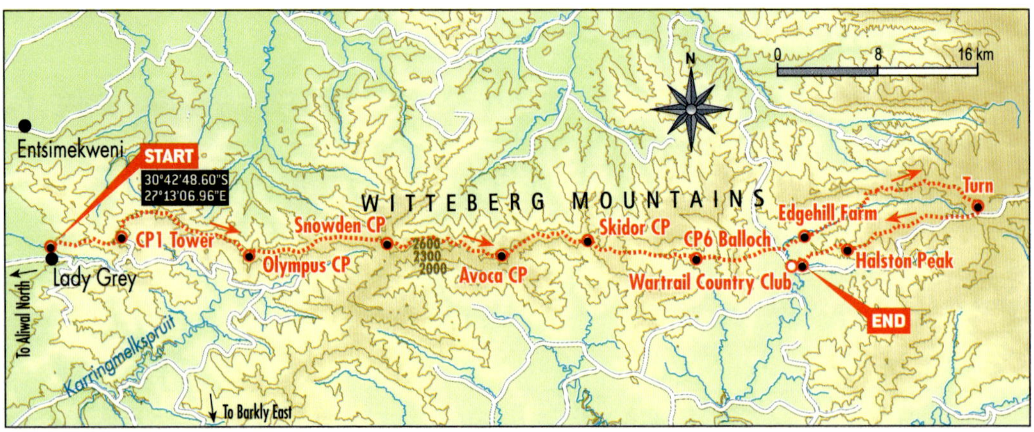

Southern Cross Three-day Trail Run

Trail & Event

25km, 30km, 20km

Province Western Cape
Region Garden Route
Closest town Sedgefield
Trail destination Goukamma, Outeniqua Mountain and Garden Route Coastal Hiking Trails
Series Southern Cross Adventures
Contributed by Hano Otto

JACQUES MARAIS

THE DESTINATION The 38 000ha Outeniqua Nature Reserve is fragmented over a series of rugged mountain ranges which lie parallel to the coast, while the Goukamma Nature Reserve comprises an area of about 2 500ha, with a coastline of 14km.

THE TERRAIN Experience the untouched beauty of the Garden Route. The trails covered by the Southern Cross Trail Run will take you through lush indigenous forests, up challenging mountain climbs and along an unforgettable trail along the stunning coastline.

DIRECTIONS Pine Lake Marina resort is next to the N2 highway between Wilderness and Sedgefield. It is situated on the Swartvlei Lake. Follow the N2 from Wilderness to Sedgefield for approximately 35km until you see the Swartvlei turn-off on your left. Turn left here and travel for 1km on the tarred road to the Pine Lake Marina gates on your right (GPS **34°00'12.7"S, 22°44'38.2"E**).

ACCOMMODATION You can stay at Pine Lake Marina (www.pinelakemarina.co.za). They have very comfortable and affordable accommodation and can sleep 800 people. Or go to www.visitsedgefield.co.za for other options such as B&B, camping, etc. in Sedgefield. The Gericke's Point camping ground is about 5km from Pine Lake Marina.

FAST FACTS

Grading Intermediate to difficult
Duration 4–8hrs per day
Configuration Circular and point to point
Start point Pine Lake Marina
GPS co-ordinates 34°00'12.7"S, 22°44'38.2"E
Terrain Singletracks, jeep tracks, kloofing sections, rocky sections and sandy sections
Map Maps available at the start and posted on the website
Access requirements Can be run on race day only; if you want to do some of the hiking routes on your own, a day fee needs to be paid to SanParks and/or CapeNature
Trail markings The race will be marked with arrows, marshals and bright orange ribbon
Facilities Toilets and restaurant at the Marina; none en route
Cell reception Minimal coverage along remote sections of trail
Beware Extreme temperatures; flooding streams and rivers
Time of year April for the race; year-round for the trails
Local info www.visitsedgefield.co.za, www.sanparks.org and www.capenature.co.za
More info www.southerncrossadventure.co.za / Tel (+27 82) 579 7595

THE TRAIL There are various scenic hiking routes accessible from the Sedgefield, Wilderness or Knysna areas. Maps and more information are available from the local Tourism Information Office in Sedgefield or at the SanParks office in Wilderness.

Day 1 of the Southern Cross Race is a challenging 25km route into the Outeniqua Mountains. It kicks off on short sections of jeep track leading to hiking trails and mountain singletracks; the latter are 80% runnable for a relatively fit trail runner. The highest peak will be 1 600m.

Day 2 covers 30km of spectacular trails through the beautiful indigenous forests of the Garden Route. The coast can be seen every now and again when cresting a hill or coming out of a kloofing section.

Day 3 ends with a 20km trail along the coast in the Goukamma Nature Reserve. The trail follows the escarpment of the coastline with only a few kilometres on the beach. There are several sections where you run on the cliffs and have the sea on one side and the mountain range on the other side.

THE EVENT The three-day Southern Cross Trail Run ensures that each day will be a unique experience, running through the beautiful Garden Route area over berg, through bush and on the beach. The race takes place towards the end of April, is run in pairs and entries are limited to 300 teams.

EVENT FACTS

Event name Southern Cross Three-day Trail Run
Venue Pine Lake Marina
Distance from George 31km
Time of year End of April
Enter as Team of two
Cut-offs Yes; 16:00
Distances 25km, 30km and 20km
Average duration 4–8hrs per day
Entry info www.southerncrossadventure.co.za

EXPERT'S VIEW

Hano Otto is an event organiser, adventure racer, trail runner and mountain biker sponsored by Sports Centre, Penny Pinchers, Innov-8 and Pine Lake Marina. He has competed in many multi-day expedition races around the world, and he completed the gruelling Borneo Eco Challenge in 2000 with his wife, Sonja Terblanche-Otto.

My shoe

Brand ~ Innov-8
Model ~ Roclite 315
Rating ~ The most durable shoe in the range with a dual layer mesh upper and protective rand; provides sufficient cushioning and comfort for ultra-distance trail racing and everyday training

© ERIK VERMEULEN

Trail Only

St Blaize Trail
13km

Province Western Cape
Region Garden Route
Closest town Mossel Bay
Trail destination St Blaize Trail ending in Dana Bay
Contributed by Erik Vermeulen

THE DESTINATION Just off the N2 and an easy four-hour drive from Cape Town, you will find Mossel Bay and, quite surprisingly, one of the most scenic trails in South Africa. The drive through town to the Cape St Blaize lighthouse is blatantly uninspiring, but maybe that is purely to keep this beautiful trail a secret for a while longer.

THE TERRAIN Stretching along sea cliffs from the Cape St Blaize Lighthouse, the trail winds its way for more than 13km to the small coastal town of Dana Bay. For the most part, the trail follows the 30m contour, so you can be assured of a relatively flat run for most of the way. The path itself is very runnable throughout, probably due to the many hikers frequenting the route.

DIRECTIONS The trail starts below Cape St Blaize Lighthouse (GPS 34°11′09″S, 22°09′27″E). Take the Mossel Bay off-ramp from the N2 and drive through town following the tourism signs to The Point.

There is ample parking at The Point. From there, head to the small car park adjacent to the cave below the lighthouse. The trail begins in front of the cave. You do not require a permit to run the trail, but remember to sign in at the security hut and make arrangements to be collected at the finish in Dana Bay (34°12′12″S, 22°03′22″E).

ACCOMMODATION There is a great caravan park (Punt Karavaanpark) adjacent to the start if you're on a budget. Otherwise, call Mossel Bay Tourism on Tel (+27 44) 691 2202.

GRADIENT PROFILE

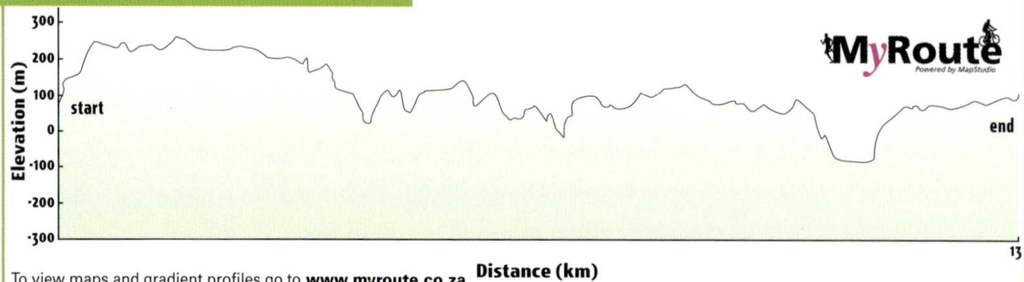

To view maps and gradient profiles go to **www.myroute.co.za**

THE TRAIL The trail winds its way from the Cape St Blaize Lighthouse almost due west for 13km. A quick 30m climb takes you to the contour path, but then you're onto an easy, 7km run boasting breathtaking views.

Take care around the 4km mark (loose rocks) and keep an eye out for whales, schools of dolphins and amazing ocean vistas. The majority of the route is run along singletrack, but for 4km you will traverse the Pinnacle Point Golf Estate, passing close to the fairways and greens – keep your eyes open for misdirected golf balls.

This is not a trail to race, and the run should rather be enjoyed at a leisurely pace with some friends. Secluded beaches and massive caves may entice you off the trail before you hit the last 3km as you descend to sea level and the finish at Dana Bay.

FAST FACTS

Grading Easy
Duration 1.5–2hrs
Configuration One way
Start point Cape St Blaize Lighthouse
GPS co-ordinates 34°11′09″S, 22°09′27″E
Finish point Dana Bay
GPS co-ordinates 34°12′12″S, 22°03′22″E
Terrain Relatively flat cliff-top singletrack
Map GPS Track download at http://connect.garmin.com/activity/142292772
Access requirements No fee; arrive and run
Trail markings Painted birds on rocks
Facilities Public amenities at start
Cell reception Coverage most of the way (both MTN and Vodacom)
Beware High cliffs for most of the trail; slippery in wet weather; golf balls
Time of year All year round; cold and wet in winter
Local info Mossel Bay Tourism on Tel (+27 44) 691 2202

EXPERT'S VIEW

Erik Vermeulen is a motivational speaker and business consultant with a love for the great outdoors, adventure and photography. Constant travel makes training and racing difficult, but he nevertheless hits the trails whenever he can – www.erikvermeulen.com

My shoe
Brand ~ Salomon
Model ~ Crossmax
Rating ~ Comfortable with plenty of cushioning and support

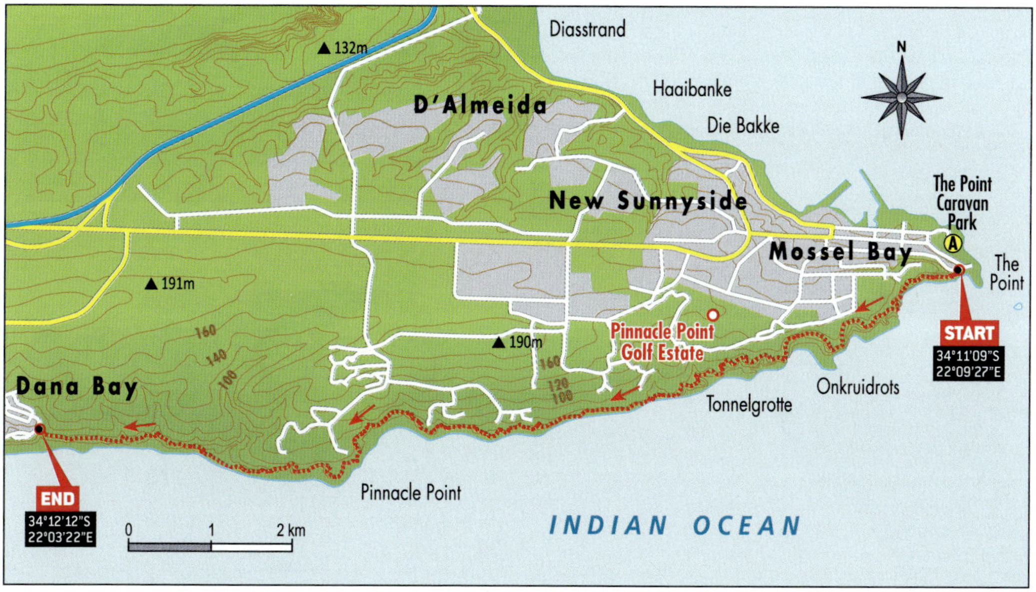

Stanley's Mountain Run
13km and 24km

Trail & Event

Province Western Cape
Region Western Cape
Closest town Ladismith
Trail destination Ladismith Hiking Trails Nature Reserve
Series Quantum Country Classics
Contributed by Ugene Nel

THE DESTINATION Travel east through the gorgeous Hoeko Valley, or navigate the rugged sweep of the Seweweekspoort gorge, revelling in the spectacular rock formations en route to the laid-back town of Ladismith. Picturesque valleys, fruit orchards, vineyards and old farmhouses line the back roads, with the impressive Towerkop (2 198m) looming high above the town.

Legend has it that a witch passing overhead found the peak obstructing her route, and she struck it in anger with her wand to cleave a deep gash into the granite massif. Halfway up Elandsberg (2 128m), you'll notice a famous local landmark – Stanley's Light (1 500m). It was installed in 1963 by Oom Stanley de Wit, and consisted of a bicycle lamp and dynamo which, when powered by the mountain stream, gave an indication of the availability of water for the surrounding farms and the town itself.

THE TERRAIN A short section of jeep track leads you onto the hiking route, a mountain singletrack which is 80% runnable for any relatively fit trail runner. This is by no means a walk in the park, but the indescribable vistas will make it worth your while!

Higher up in the mountain, the conditions and temperatures are generally much colder and can change in an instant. Black ice is prevalent on rocks during cold spells, and cascading stream levels in some of the ravines will make for interesting water crossings! Snow does fall here regularly, though with the run scheduled for the end of April, chances are good you'll be enjoying mild weather.

DIRECTIONS The run starts at the Ladismith School sports fields (GPS 33°29′21.18″S, 21°16′6.41″E) in the centre of the little town nestling at the foot of the Klein Swartberg Mountains. Situated on Route 62, Ladismith is linked by main roads to all major centres, including Cape Town (320km), Oudtshoorn (100km), George (160km) and Port Elizabeth (420km).

To get to the trail head, follow Church Street and turn left into North Street, continuing out of town onto a dirt road. Pass through the gate on your left (about 3km) with a hiking icon (GPS 33°28′11.55″S, 21°15′56.17″E), closing the gate behind you. The road becomes rough and you may need a high-clearance vehicle, depending on the river crossing. Continue along this dirt track for 1km to the trail head. Park your car next to a small timber hut with a corrugated roof. No permit is required, but there is a book to sign. Do so – it's for your safety!

ACCOMMODATION Extensive farming in the area focuses on the production of apricots, peaches, plums, nectarines, figs, pomegranates, olives and grapes. There are also two cheese factories and a winery. For numerous accommodation options, check out www.ladismith.org.za

FAST FACTS

Grading Difficult to extreme
Duration 4–7hrs
Configuration Circular route (24km)
Start point Ladismith High School
GPS co-ordinates 33°29'21.18"S, 21°16'6.41"E
Terrain Mountainous and steep singletrack
Map Available from Information Office
Access requirements Free entry
Trail markings Wooden signs; stone cairns on hiking trail
Facilities All amenities in village
Cell reception Minimal coverage along remote sections of trail
Beware Black ice; extreme temperatures; flooding streams and rivers
Time of year Avoid both summer and winter extremes
Local info www.ladismith.org.za /Tel (+27 28) 551 1378
More info www.quantumadventures.co.za / Tel (+27 21) 789 0188

THE TRAIL A range of scenic hiking routes is accessible from the edge of town, with maps available from the local Tourism Information Office. The Stanley's Run route negotiates a 1.5km trail before crossing the stream onto a steep, mountain singletrack.

For the next hour or two, runners will climb towards the highest point of the run (1 480m) near the historic Stanley's Light. The trail then meanders along the base of rugged cliffs and outcrops, before juddering across a 1km scree field. Boulder-hopping is the name of the game until you start winding down towards the valley floor.

The altitude gain from the start to Stanley's Light is nearly 800m, so expect to 'pay your school fees' on the way up. After 18km, the singletrack drops down to meander through the Renosterveld koppies on the edge of the town. You will contour around the numerous valleys, but for most of the way you will remain on the ridge line until you hit the outskirts.

The trail is open to the public from first light, and you should plan to be out there for about five hours or more. Do not attempt the run during extreme weather, as summer temperatures may rise to a sizzling 48°C! There is generally water around 8km from the start.

EXPERT'S VIEW

Ugene Nel is an adventure racer, trail runner, mountain biker and event organiser, sponsored by First Ascent (www.firstascent.co.za), Spur (www.spur.co.za) and Vibram. He has competed in multi-day expedition races around the world, and has completed the gruelling, 2 400km 'Freedom Challenge MTB Race across South Africa' three times.

My shoe
Brand ~ Salomon
Model ~ Raid
Rating ~ Fantastic underfoot protection; heavier than new range, but still my favourite shoe ever

THE EVENT The 24km run is not recommended if you are a novice off-road runner; rather start off with the 13km trail that follows a similar route. Youngsters, families and ex-couch potatoes can partake in the easy 3km trail run from the Ladismith High School.

EVENT FACTS

Event name Stanley's Mountain Run
Series name Quantum Country Classics
Venue Ladismith High School (sport fields)
Distances 13km, 24km
Time of year End of April
Enter as Solo
Cut-offs Yes – runners will be briefed at the race
Event organiser Quantum Adventures
Average duration 2–3hrs (13km), 4–7hrs (24km)
Entry info www.quantumadventures.co.za

GRADIENT PROFILE

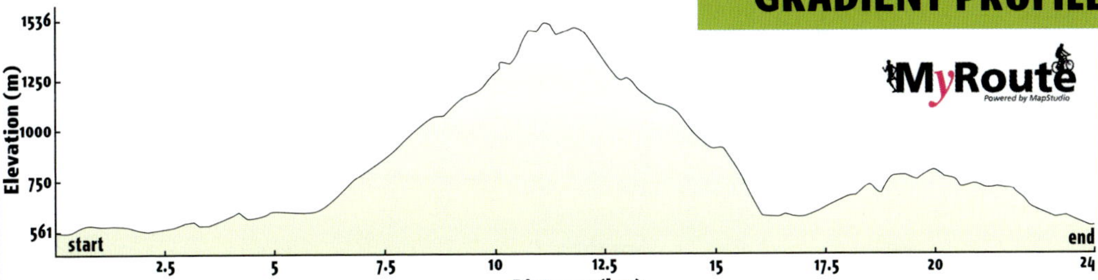

To view maps and gradient profiles go to **www.myroute.co.za**

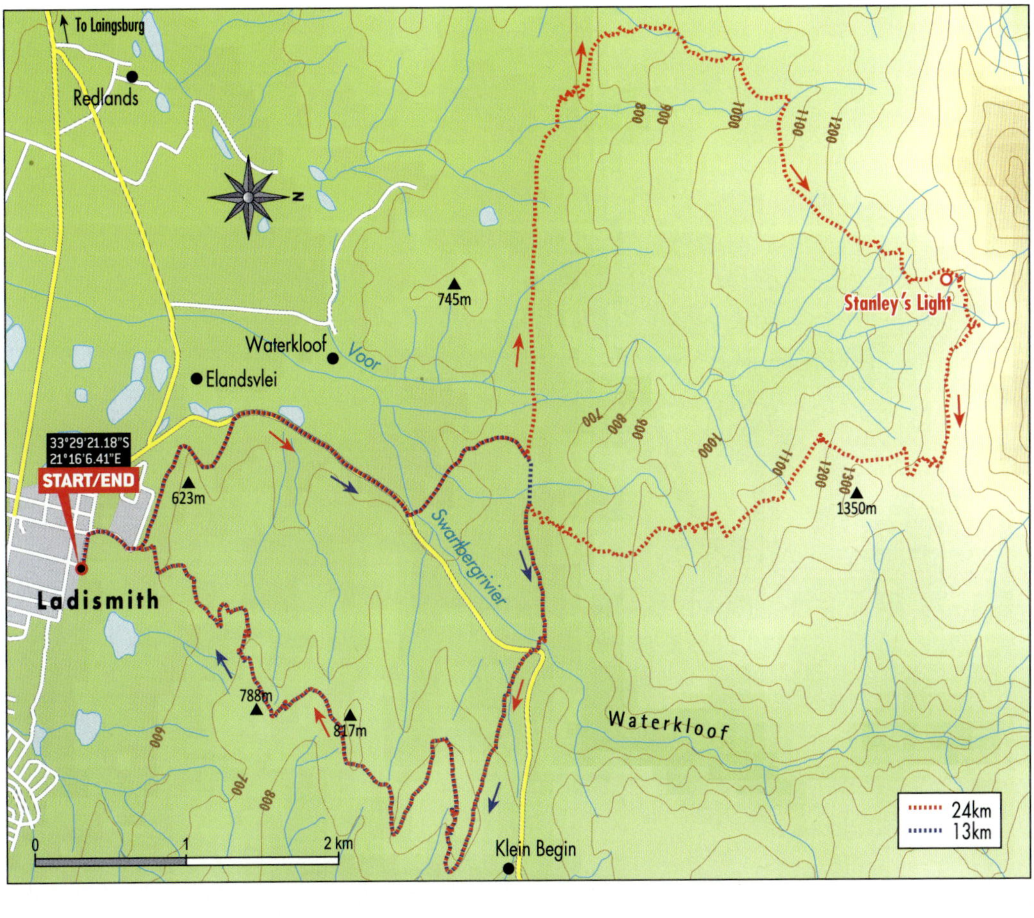

Trail Only

Suikerbosrand Nature Reserve

10km / 12km

Province Gauteng
Region Gauteng South
Closest town Heidelberg
Trail destination Suikerbosrand Nature Reserve
Contributed by Lisa de Speville

© PETER KIRK

EXPERT'S VIEW

Lisa de Speville is the owner and editor of www.AR.co.za, South Africa's adventure racing website. She is also the creator and organiser of FEAT (www.featsa.co.za), an annual evening of fast-paced and inspiring talks by adventurers. Lisa is an adventure racer, orienteer and trail runner. She has been a passionate participant in these sports for well over a decade and in this time she has completed many ultra-distance, multi-day and staged races. She lives a zippy 35 minutes from Suikerbosrand, her favourite trail spot.

THE DESTINATION A shining diamond in Johannesburg's outdoor crown is Suikerbosrand. Located off the R550, this gem of a reserve – with its kloofs, koppies, ridges and open plains – takes its name from the sugar bush (suikerbos) protea, a shrub that grows abundantly in this area.

Suikerbosrand is the site of many late Iron-Age settlements, and ruins of kraals decorate the hills. The stone walls are easy to spot from the trail, especially around the 6.5km point of the Bokmakierie Trail. Runners are also sure to see game, usually zebra, a variety of antelope and black-backed jackal (if you're very lucky).

THE TERRAIN Although there are some smooth and open sections, the trails at Suikerbosrand are challenging. Ascents and descents are interspersed with good old Highveld rocks and, for the less technically adept runner, there may be quite a bit of walking.

DIRECTIONS Take the N3 South from Johannesburg past Vosloorus township and turn right onto the R550. Brown 'Suikerbosrand' directional tourism signs mark the route. Continue for 6.4km, then turn left onto the reserve road (GPS **26°26'14.82"S, 28°13'10.98"E**). Alternatively, take the R59 from Alberton onto the R550; turn left, heading east along the R550 for 14.5km to the reserve road. Turn right and continue for 1.6km to the manned visitors' gate, which opens at 07:00 and closes by dark.

The only place you're likely to get lost is getting to the start of the trail. From the parking area, walk past the Visitors' Centre and look out for the signs indicating the Bokmakierie Trail. The trail from the pedestrian gate (use any of the footpaths) takes you on to the road. Keep walking uphill and look out for the cement route marker that shows the trail on the other side of the road. The first section of trail is short and it meanders back to the road. Continue walking uphill and after 140m you'll pick up the trail again. From here the trail is well defined with no diversions. Cement blocks with a yellow-green footprint on top are the route markers.

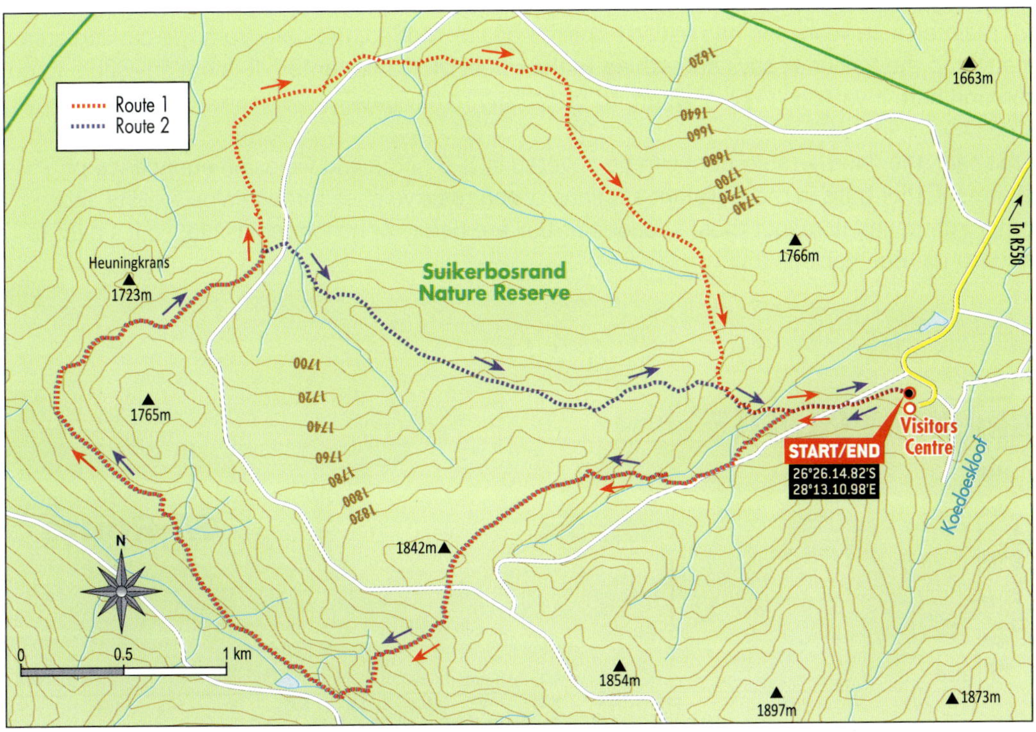

FAST FACTS

Grading Difficult
Duration 1.5 to 3.5hrs to run/walk the 10km and 12km trails
Configuration Circular route (10km or 12km)
Start point Parking area outside Visitors' Centre
GPS co-ordinates 26°26'14.82"S, 28°13'10.98"E
Terrain A challenging, but rewarding, rocky trail
Map A basic photocopied map is provided at the gate
Access requirements Entry fee per person and per car
Trail markings Cement blocks with yellow-green footprints on top
Facilities Toilets and water at the parking area
Cell reception Throughout
Beware Heat in summer; be considerate to hikers and birders
Time of year All year
More info There isn't; the reserve doesn't have a website and any content online is generally old and generic

THE TRAIL There are two main circular trails. The 4km Cheetah Trail loops around the koppies to the northwest of the parking area. The one you really want to do is the Bokmakierie Trail (yellow-green markers), which has two variations. The less-used, longer route diverges from the standard 10km loop at around the 7km mark, before a tar-road crossing. Here the yellow-green footprint marker changes to only yellow for the longer route and only green for the shorter route.

Websites will tell you that the longer route is 17km in total. It isn't. By GPS the longer version of the trail measures 11.8km. In reality there is only a 1.8km difference and the extension of the longer route is certainly easier terrain with less ascending over the last 3km or so.

After the river crossing on the longer route, keep to the right to pick up the trail again. Be considerate to walkers and birders on the trails. The trails are singletrack throughout. There are three large cairns along the route but they're more fun than navigational beacons.

There is, in fact, an extensive network of hiking trails in the reserve that leads to, from and around the hiking huts, but these trails are rarely used and hardly known so they're generally overgrown and difficult to follow. The overnight huts are no longer in use (they were closed for maintenance years ago and haven't opened again). Indeed, the gate from the parking area leading to the trail head says something to the effect of 'Do not enter'. It is not advisable to go through here if you don't know where to go or how to navigate.

That said, the 24km+ route here can be covered in 3–6 hours and yields an abundance of charms. Other trails in more distant sections of the reserve pass through aloe forests and other interesting flora, but most sections of trail are barely or no longer visible, so it's best to stick to the Bokmakierie Trail.

GRADIENT PROFILE

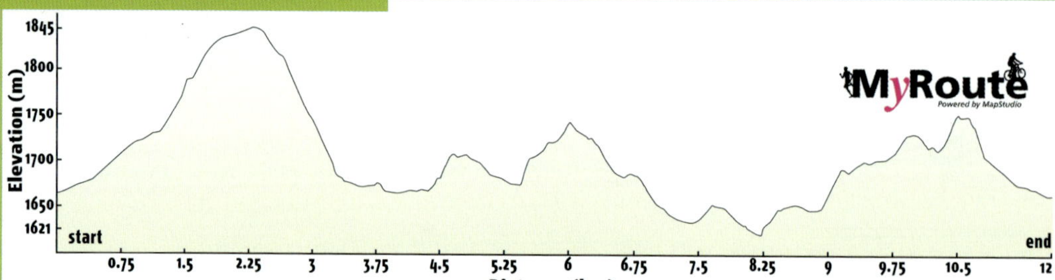

To view maps and gradient profiles go to **www.myroute.co.za**

© ANDREW BOOTH

Table Mountain – Talbot Trail Run Series

7km and 14km

Event Only

Province KwaZulu-Natal
Region KZN Midlands
Closest town Pietermaritzburg
Trail destination Pietermaritzburg's Table Mountain
Series Talbot Trail Run Series
Contributed by Andrew Booth

THE DESTINATION Pietermaritzburg's Table Mountain is a landmark of the western edge of the Valley of 1000 Hills, and its majestic outline is visible from as far away as the N3. The mountain is a mythical place according to the local community who believes a large python resides atop the peak.

Urban legend also has it that cannibals used the mountain as a holding pen for captives before devouring them. Whether this holds true or not, the mountain is very much seen as a holy place by the Zulu people. It took much negotiation with the local Nkhosi (Chief) to gain access to the mountain, and it is important for runners to treat the people and area with utmost respect.

THE TERRAIN Don't be fooled by what looks like a 'table top' from a distance. Just like its big brother in Cape Town, Pietermaritzburg's Table Mountain is far from flat. Getting to the summit requires a steep 1km ascent, firstly via a few lively local homesteads and then along a well-worn and rocky path. Once on top, the terrain is undulating and footing can be tricky along narrow cattle paths and through the open veld. A steep camber also makes running challenging in parts.

DIRECTIONS Make your way to Table Mountain Road from the N3 and continue for around 20km until it becomes a dirt road. Very soon after this, turn right onto the D1001 and keep going towards the mountain for 3km. The event start is at the Mcoseleli Secondary School on your right-hand side.

ACCOMMODATION No accommodation is available at Table Mountain, but there are a bunch of establishments at Nagle Dam, Cumberland and in Pietermaritzburg.

FAST FACTS

Grading Intermediate to difficult
Duration 45mins to 3hrs (14km)
Configuration Circular
Start point Mcoseleli School, Table Mountain
GPS co-ordinates 29°35'49.17"S, 30°30'16.47"E
Terrain Off-track running and cattle footpaths
Map None
Access requirements Only during event
Trail markings Tags and chalk arrows
Facilities Ablutions at Mcoseleli School
Cell reception Relatively good; occasional loss of signal
Beware Cliffs, mist and cattle; steep ascent onto ridge
Time of year Winter months when the grass is short
More info www.kzntrailrunning.co.za

THE TRAIL Don't go out too hard or you might never catch your breath!' This must be by far the best advice an experienced runner can give novices taking on this course for the first time. The first few hundred metres are slightly downhill before the steep climb to the top starts.

The final 100m of this ascent is rocky and requires concentration to avoid slipping. Once up, both the short and long courses traverse the edge of the mountain over-looking the Dusi for a while. The footing on top is generally good along narrow cattle paths, but these tend to peter out on the long course and runners have to go off-track across the open veld.

Grassy tufts make the footing precarious, and runners should use the high-visibility white tags to guide themselves along the route. The short course cuts back through the middle of the mountain on well-established paths, while the long course circumnavigates the edge of the entire mountain.

Anyone new to trail running may find aspects of the long course challenging. This is a unique trail and one to put on that bucket list despite it being quite short.

THE EVENT This is one of KZN's most popular short trail runs for many reasons. Firstly it offers superb views of both the Dusi and uMngeni rivers, and on a clear day one can see the Berg to the west and the Indian Ocean to the east. Secondly, the community vibe at Mcoseleli School (a beneficiary of the event) is unique and this alone means it deserves your support.

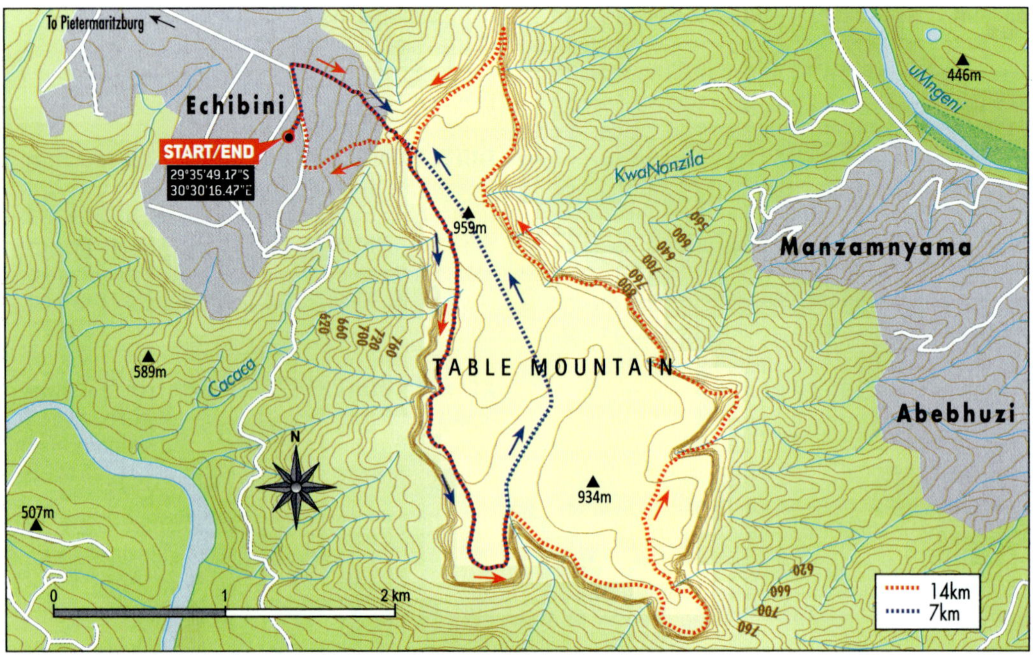

EVENT FACTS

Event name Talbot Trail Run Series – Table Mountain
Venue Starts at Mcoseleli School, Table Mountain
Distances 7km, 14km
Time of year Summer series in November, winter series in June
Enter as Solo
Cut-offs None
Event organiser Andrew Booth (KZNTrailRunning)
Entry info www.kzntrailrunning.co.za

EXPERT'S VIEW

Andrew Booth is primarily a trail runner, but a road running family history means he cannot resist great South African tarmac ultras such as the Comrades and Two Oceans. He started organising trail runs in KZN in 2009 and launched www.kzntrailrunning.co.za, which now coordinates a dozen events in and around the uMngeni and Dusi valleys. His long-term objective is to organise a 100-mile trail race in KZN.

GRADIENT PROFILE

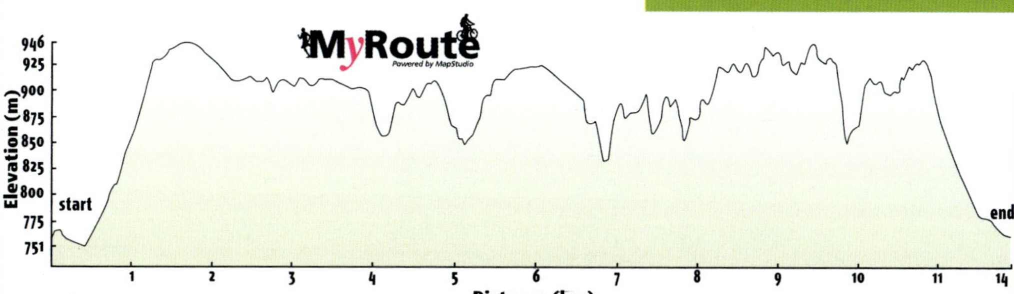

To view maps and gradient profiles go to **www.myroute.co.za**

Trail & Event

Table Mountain Challenge
37km

Province Western Cape
Region Cape Peninsula
Closest town Cape Town
Trail destination Table Mountain
Series Crazy Store
Contributed by Leo Rust

THE DESTINATION The Table Mountain National Park encompasses the incredibly scenic Peninsula mountain chain, stretching all the way from Signal Hill in the north to Cape Point in the south, over a distance of around 60km. Two world-renowned landmarks – the majestic Table Mountain and legendary Cape of Good Hope – symbolise this protected area, famous around the world for its extraordinarily rich, diverse and unique flora and singular land formation.

THE TERRAIN The area forms part of the Cape Floristic Region and thus supports a high diversity of flora, a lot of it rare and endemic. Protea, erica, restios, aster species and geophytes are found in abundance. The routes are mostly along well-trodden hiking trails, often with the occasional steep scramble along the way.

DIRECTIONS From the City Bowl, follow the tourism signage to Table Mountain along Kloof Street. A good place to leave your vehicle is the parking area immediately to your left where you turn off towards the Aerial Cableway along Table Mountain Road (GPS 33°56'32.41"S, 18°23'43.50"E).

EXPERT'S VIEW

Leo Rust is one of South Africa's top trail runners and has triumphed in endurance and road races around the country. He is marketing manager for Adventure Inc., a leading local outdoor retailer and distributor.

My run

The TMC is a classic in every sense of the word and certainly rates as one of the big races on the local trail calendar. It is not overly difficult technically and can offer a good stepping stone for those aspiring to ultra-distance trail events.'

Insider tips

The start of the race is normally fast and furious – don't be drawn into this. You should expect to spend around half of your running time on Leg 3, so pace yourself appropriately. Keep something in the tank for running on top of Table Mountain.'

Gear and apparel

'If conscious of weight, arrange to have a bag dropped at CP2 at the Constantia Nek water point. (You must arrange this yourself). Leg 3 can be extremely hot, so keep cool and hydrate adequately early on. Bad weather can also be vicious on top of the mountain – take the right gear to keep yourself protected.'

Technical trail and terrain tips

'A relatively non-technical route goes ballistic once you reach the base of Hout Bay Corner and Llandudno Ravine. This steep, crucial section takes you onto the Table Mountain massif, but to get there you have to control your vertigo as you scramble up a metal ladder along a cliff, and then negotiate a cliff-top path into a craggy, ravine scramble. If you've only run on road, you may well freak out here.'

FAST FACTS

Grading Difficult
Duration 3.5–7hrs
Configuration Circular
Start point Kloof Nek parking spot
GPS co-ordinates 33°56′32.41″S, 18°23′43.50″E
Terrain Gravel roads, singletrack, serious scrambling
Map Full map available on website
Access requirements Limited to 400 entries
Trail markings Some markings; stone cairns – ability to navigate
Facilities Basic ablutions at start
Cell reception Coverage along much of route
Beware Hydration is critical; metal ladders
Time of year September for race; autumn and spring for the trail
Local info www.tablemountain.co.za
More info www.trailrunning.co.za

© JACQUES MARAIS

THE TRAIL Table Mountain National Park is a protected area with an exhilarating selection of trails to suit all levels of runners. There are many routes to choose from along the full extent of the rugged chain, all boasting exceptional views of Cape Town and the azure Atlantic Ocean.

THE ROUTE The Crazy Store Table Mountain Challenge is a 37km mountain trail, run clockwise around Table Mountain and Devil's Peak, mostly along hiking paths and a few kilometres of jeep track. Expect some scrambling as you traverse indigenous forest, ford streams and ascend the craggy slopes of this mother of all mountains.

The first leg starts at Kloof Nek, passes below Tafelberg Road via Deer Park and onto the contour path below the Blockhouse on Devil's Peak (Leg 1 – 9km). From here, runners navigate a scenic 10km along the contour path above Kirstenbosch, to complete the second leg at Constantia Nek.

The final stage constitutes a gruelling 17km run via Orange Kloof (off limits outside race day) to Suikerbossie and up Llandudno Corner. Thump along the top of Twelve Apostles and down Kasteelspoort, and finish along the Pipe Track at Kloof Nek.

THE EVENT The idea of having three legs in the event encourages relay teams to take on only part of the challenge, thus making TMC a more inclusive race. There will be a sweep runner and a cut-off time in place at Constantia Nek, and it is recommended to train along the route well before race day. NOTE: You are not allowed in Orange Kloof except on race day, but may access Myburg's Path and the Llandudno Corner to Grootkop section from Suikerbossie.

EVENT FACTS

Event name Crazy Store Table Mountain Challenge
Series name Crazy Store Series
Venue Kloof Nek parking lot
Distance from city centre 5km
Time of year Mid-September
Enter as Solo or teams of three
Cut-offs Yes – runners will be briefed at the race
Distances 37km
Average duration 3.5–7hrs
Entry info www.trailrunning.co.za

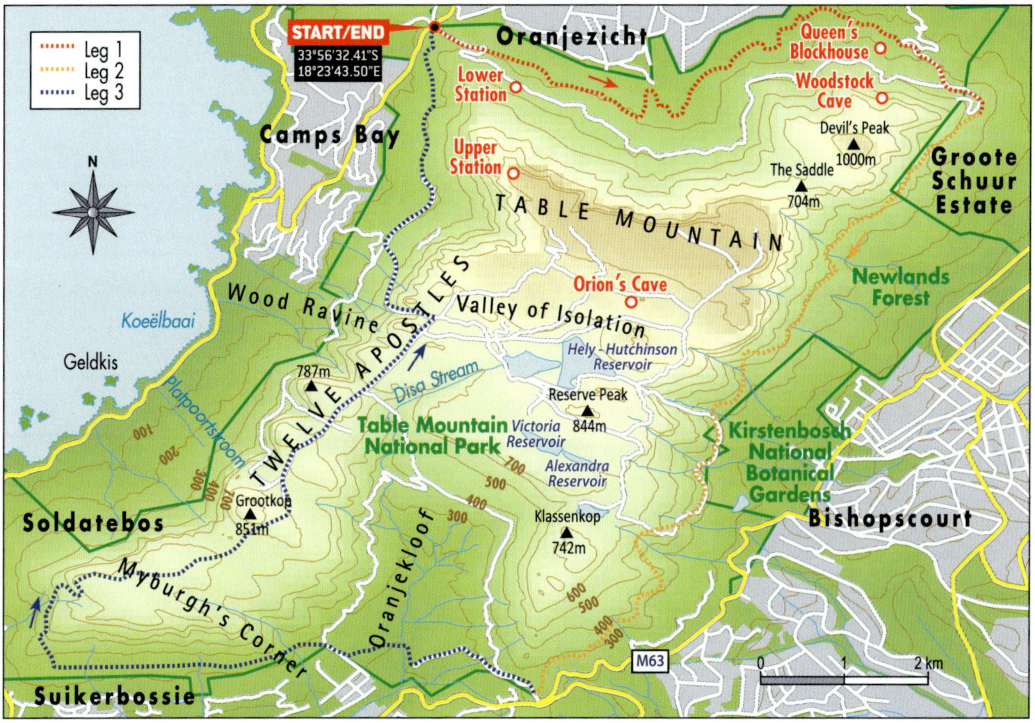

GRADIENT PROFILE

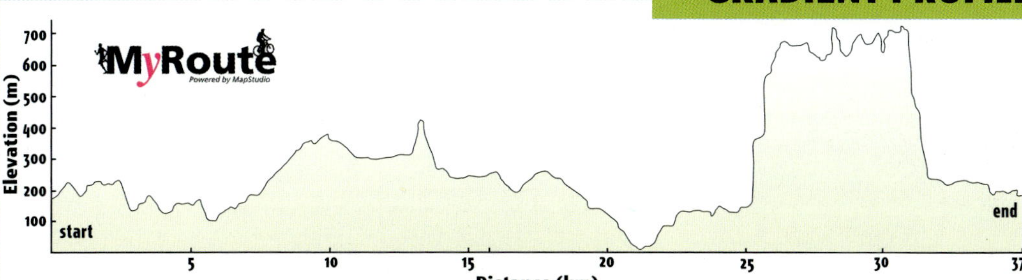

To view maps and gradient profiles go to **www.myroute.co.za**

Event Only

Three Cranes Challenge

30km, 40km and 32km (three-day stage race of 102km)

Province KwaZulu-Natal
Region KZN Midlands
Closest town Howick
Trail destination Bushwillow Park
Series Bonitas Wild Series
Contributed by Heidi Mocke and Nic de Beer

THE DESTINATION The Karkloof Conservancy covers an area of 40 000ha and features some of the most fantastic biodiversity you'll find in South Africa. Wetlands, mist-belt grasslands and huge tracts of mist-belt forest are a few of the protected biomes you could expect to encounter in the Karkloof Nature Reserve (an area of 3 275ha) section of the conservancy.

The beautiful Karkloof valley forms part of the breeding grounds of South Africa's endangered cranes. Sadly, all three of South Africa's crane species are in decline due to man's relentless exploitation of their delicate habitat. By running the Bonitas Sunday Tribune Three Cranes Challenge you will assist in saving these beautiful birds.

THE TERRAIN The run incorporates roads in and around the Gilboa and Karkloof Nature Reserve area, with easy off-road tracks through plantations and grasslands. The trail traverses misty forests and offers magnificent views as you run along the Gilboa escarpment. Expect some hectic climbing on narrow and uneven trails or along grassy paths, slippery rocks and overhead branches in the forests, but also some open forestry roads meandering through plantations.

DIRECTIONS From Howick Main Road, turn onto Karkloof Road (P141, GPS 29°28′57.6″S, 30°14′02.1″E) and travel for approximately 20km until this becomes gravel. The turn-off to Bushwillow Park (GPS 29°19′02.6″S, 30°17′42.5″E) is about 1km further on your left.

ACCOMMODATION The race package includes tented accommodation in the race village. The race village consists of hot showers, a massage area, a 24-hour snack/coffee station and a chill zone. If you wish to stay with your family or friends, you may opt for local accommodation; several possibilities are listed here: www.3craneschallenge.co.za/accommodation.php

FAST FACTS

Grading Intermediate to difficult
Duration 3 days, 3–7hrs per day
Configuration Circular; cloverleaf setup
Start point Bushwillow Park
GPS co-ordinates 29°19'02.6"S, 30°17'42.5"E
Terrain Singletrack, rugged jeep track and forestry roads
Map Available at www.3craneschallenge.co.za
Access requirements By invitation only; email heidim@wildlands.co.za for info
Trail markings Directional arrows, candy tape, reflective tape
Facilities Refreshment tables every 10km
Cell reception None in some of the valleys
Beware Extreme heat and thunderstorms in the afternoon
Time of year Last weekend in February
Local info www.bushwillowcaravanpark.co.za or www.karkloofconservation.org.za
More info www.3craneschallenge.co.za / Tel (+27 33) 343 6380

THE TRAIL The first day's 30km starts off on about 4km of open road before hitting singletrack and uneven road. The first big climb takes you through some misty forests to the top of Mbona Nature Reserve and some amazing views. Once at the top, you can stretch your legs down through the Bushbuck Trail and Mbona Nature Reserve before hitting the main road and back onto some gravel roads.

Next up is Twin Falls valley – a nice downhill followed by a 'nice' uphill. The hardest part of the day is this climb up the side of the mountain on a grassy path, but as always the great views of both Karkloof Valley and Grey Mare's Tail Falls make it worth your while. The descent is through magical forests; watch out for slippery rocks and overhead branches.

The 40km route on Day 2 takes you straight into a massive climb and you will keep climbing until you summit at Gilboa. Once on top, it is a 'walk in the Gilboa Park', with forestry roads meandering in and out of pine plantations. Continue through the crane-breeding grounds to revel in easy running before heading back past more great views to finish off on a nasty climb up Giggle Hills.

The third day starts not too early and not too late, but just in time to see the sunrise from the top. You set off on your last stage of 32km along gravel roads, broad and wide, flat and fast. That is until you start your climbing, first meandering through some scenic grasslands and then onto a steep, open road right to the top. The good news is that a breakfast water table will invite you to sit down, have a bite and enjoy the rising sun. Once on top, an easy run through plantations and misty forests awaits on the final stretch home.

THE EVENT The Three Cranes Challenge is a multi-stage trail event covering just over 100km in three days, with a total ascent of over 3 000m. Runners are faced with three challenging days of running through some of the most beautiful mountains, forests and valleys in the country. Runners are based and accommodated in their own tent at the lovely Bushwillow Park, where all three days start and finish. Entries are per invitation only – email Heidi on heidim@wildlands.co.za for info.

EVENT FACTS

Event name Bonitas Sunday Tribune Three Cranes Challenge
Venue Bushwillow Park, Karkloof Valley
Distance from Howick 22km
Time of year End of February
Enter as Solo
Cut-offs No, but there are checkpoints along the way
Distances 30km, 40km and 32km (102km in total)
Average duration 3 days, 3–7hrs per day
Entry info www.3craneschallenge.co.za

GRADIENT PROFILES

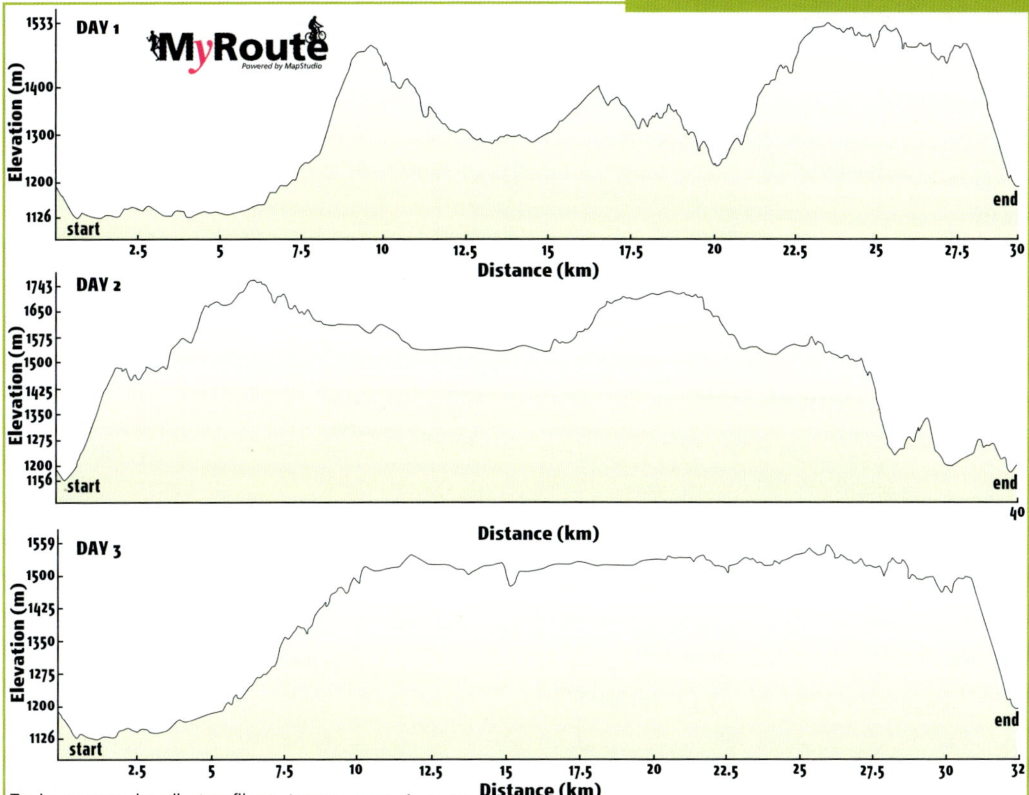

To view maps and gradient profiles go to **www.myroute.co.za**

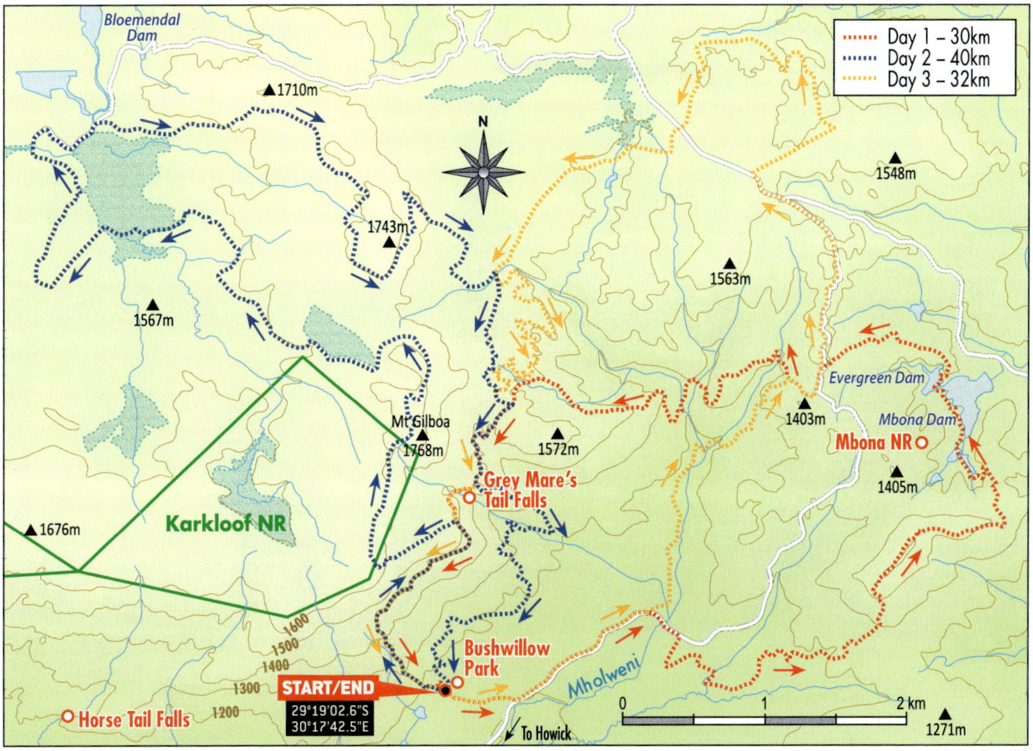

EXPERT'S VIEW

Nic De Beer is a relative newcomer to trail running. He comes from a road-running background, with a Comrades personal best of 6:12 in 2010, and has proven that he is a force to be reckoned with on the trails. Victories include the 2010 and 2012 Three Cranes Challenge, as well as the 2011 Puffer.

My run

'After grinding your way up through misty forests on the first day, you are rewarded with amazing views of Mbona Nature Reserve. Valleys, dams and mountains appear as the sun breaks through the mist. You realise where you are, why you came and how far you still have to go. And you love it! Enjoy a few deep breaths of the clean, crisp mountain air before you head down a very tricky, slippery decent, through magical forests. If you don't fall here, you didn't run hard enough!

'On Day 2, the 200 runners lining up at the start look like Zulu warriors going to war. Most of them are equipped with spears (trekking poles or walking sticks) to tackle the tough first 8km of the stage that goes straight up a twisty, slippery, steep mountain. Before you realise it, you have covered 30km and you get to one of the most spectacular sights you will ever see: a magnificent waterfall carved from the mountain face, pristine water thundering to the valley below. Your legs voice their discontent on a quick descent before you're faced with the toughest finish imaginable. Appropriately named Giggle Hills, you will either develop a sense of humour or completely lose the one you had!

'Day 3 starts with confusion – confusion as to why on earth your alarm is going off and your watch says 02:45! Two hundred runners with headlamps strapped to their foreheads line up for survival day. The creaky legs warm up after a few kilometres as you head up the first, and thankfully only, big climb of the day. The smiles return to every single face of the runners crossing the finish line. Each has experienced complete elation at having been a part of such an amazing event, doing something special for an incredible cause, meeting the most fantastic people and creating unforgettable memories while "Running for the Birds".'

My shoe

Brand ~ Hi-Tec

Model ~ Infinity

Rating ~ Lightweight trail shoe that offers excellent advantage on the fast gravel roads and jeep tracks, as well as on the technical parts where fast and light feet are important

Insider tips

'After Day 2, a lot of runners were engaged in a debate that the Three Cranes Challenge, as a whole, is as tough, if not tougher, than Comrades. I think that you should at least be strong and fit enough to be able to comfortably run an ultra marathon before you tackle Three Cranes.'

Gear and apparel

'Trail shoes with proper traction are imperative, as some of the forest sections are extremely slippery. A hydration pack or belt with bottles is compulsory and it is extremely important to drink adequately to prevent hitting the wall. Trekking poles or a walking stick are very useful, especially on the big climb on Day 2, as this alleviates pressure on your lower back and quads. And take a headlamp with good light lasting at least an hour.'

Training and pacing

'Simulate the race you train for: run similar terrain and do a few consecutive long runs in training to get used to running with tired legs. The event is three days long and you should pace yourself not only during each stage, but also over the entire event. Make sure you stay properly hydrated during and after each stage. Eat properly, stretch those sore and tired legs and try to get as much sleep as possible.'

© KELVIN TRAUTMAN

Umdoni Park Challenge

14km and 22km

Trail & Event

Province KwaZulu-Natal
Region Mid-South Coast
Closest town Scottburgh
Trail destination The Umdoni Park
Contributed by James Hallett

© FILIPPO FARALLA

THE DESTINATION In 1918, Sir Frank Reynolds, a prominent English sugar baron, established the Umdoni Park in the small coastal village of Pennington. His vision was to preserve one of a few remaining stands of lush indigenous coastal forest left untouched by the thriving sugar industry of the 19th century.

The result is a 220ha conservancy which tumbles its way onto the warm Indian Ocean and the rocky, unspoilt coastline of the Pennington-Sezela beachfront. Tall stands of umdoni trees and a wealth of other indigenous vegetation give way to patches of open grassland and the infamous Nkhumbane River gorge. This steep-sided river winds its way along the entire southern border until it reaches the sea.

THE TERRAIN Generally, the KwaZulu-Natal coastline consists of soft, undulating terrain, a landscape suited to sugar-cane farming. Umdoni Park, however, boasts a combination of flatter, open running coupled with steep and technical sections as you navigate your way towards the Nkhumbane River. It is quite sandy in places due to its proximity to the beach, but rocky and harder-packed trails – as well as the occasional dirt road – add to your running options. Finally, you could pick up on the numerous fishermen's trails along the rocky 3.5km shoreline.

DIRECTIONS Travel south along the N2 towards Port Shepstone onto Exit 104 for Park Rynie/Pennington, then turn left at the off-ramp onto the R612 and follow the signs to Pennington. From Pennington Drive, turn right into Minerva Road (4th right) to Umdoni Park (GPS **30°23'39.42"S, 30°41'23.40"E**).

To get to the trail head, follow Minerva Road until you reach the entrance to Umdoni Park. Sign the register as a visitor and proceed to Botha House (a guesthouse) where there is secure parking. The trail begins directly from the gate.

ACCOMMODATION For accommodation within the Umdoni Park, contact Lynne or Susanne on Tel (+27 39) 975 1227.

FAST FACTS

Grading Difficult
Duration 2.5–4hrs
Configuration Circular route
Start point Botha House B&B
GPS co-ordinates 30°23′39.42″S, 30°41′23.40″E
Terrain Jeep track, singletrack, rocky trails, beach running
Map A map is available from Botha House or from the Golf Course
Access requirements Free entry
Trail markings Wooden signs indicating trail splits
Facilities All amenities in village
Cell reception Fair coverage along most of the route; weak in river gorge
Beware Snakes, dense vegetation, flooding streams, high tides
Time of year Ideal months would be March to November
Local info Scottburgh Tourism Office, www.scottburgh.co.za / Tel (+27 39) 976 1364
More info www.bothahouse.co.za/upc / James, Tel (+27 82) 563 9174

THE TRAIL The trail network within the Umdoni Park is an historic one, dating back to the end of the 19th century. A combination of singletrack, jeep track and gravel roads awaits you as you explore the 15km of trail-running heaven found here.

Use the central service road (gravel) to link up the named trails. Molly's Road is an undulating stretch of well-maintained trail through indigenous vegetation. From Molly's Road, head onto more technical routes such as Meander Stream, Cottage Trail and Pan Handle.

The most exhilarating singletrack descends into the Nkhumbane River gorge and, once there, you must steel yourself for the challenge of the very technical and rocky Gorge Trail. Wind your way alongside the river up towards the dam wall, from where a few public trails outside of the park may be accessed.

For the adventurous, head down to the beachfront to explore the fishermen's trails that network along the treacherous Umdoni Point. Here you can boulder-hop to your heart's content, or chill while taking in the sights and sounds of this stunning coastline.

EVENT FACTS

Event name Umdoni Park Challenge
Venue Botha House B&B (within the Umdoni Park)
Distances 14km and 22km
Time of year End of July
Enter as Solo
Cut-offs Yes – runners will be briefed at the race
Event organisers James and Susanne Hallett
Average duration 1–2.5hrs (14km), 2.5–4hrs (22km)
Entry info www.bothahouse.co.za/upc

THE EVENT The Umdoni Park Challenge (UPC) is a short- and medium-course single-stage trail-running event catering for both amateur and more proficient trail runners. Consisting of the UPC 14km and UPC 22km routes, all runners will not only be spoilt by the diverse terrain this event offers, but also by the charisma of the event. Live music, a scrumptious breakfast and the serenity of the grounds will tempt you to return again and again.

EXPERT'S VIEW

James Hallett is an avid trail runner and race director of the Umdoni Park Challenge (UPC). He is also the editor of *Go Trail Magazine*, a popular digital trail-running magazine. To him, the Umdoni Park is the true source of his trail-running inspiration, a place to which he can escape to discover new connections with the earth and be reminded why we run trails.

GRADIENT PROFILE

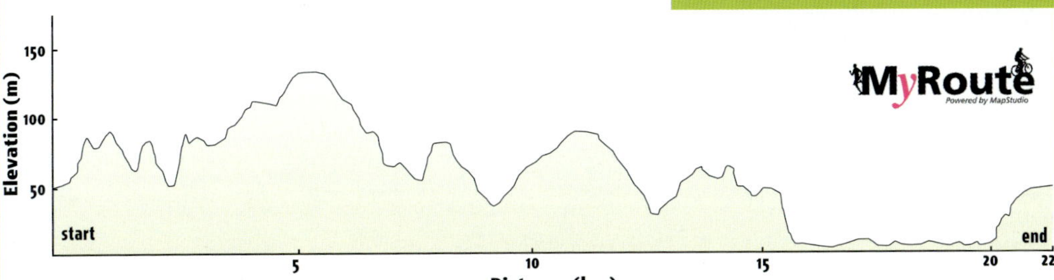

To view maps and gradient profiles go to **www.myroute.co.za**

Trail & Event

uMngeni River Run Ultra

22km and 70km

Province KwaZulu-Natal
Region uMngeni Valley / Valley of 1000 Hills
Closest town Durban and Pietermaritzburg
Trail destination iNanda Dam
Contributed by Andrew Booth

© JACQUES MARAIS

THE DESTINATION The uMngeni River spills into the Indian Ocean centrally within Durban at Blue Lagoon, a spot which marks the finish of the Dusi Canoe Marathon. Some 30km upriver you will find iNanda Dam, built in 1983 to supply water to the city, but also with a strong recreational focus. Since 2010, many formal trails were established around Inanda Dam by the Durban Green Corridor (DGC), an Ethekwini Municipal initiative. In addition, a huge network of less formal trails and paths exist throughout the uMngeni Valley, used by both livestock and the local people moving between grazing areas and homesteads.

THE TERRAIN It's not known as the Valley of 1000 Hills for nothing – steep climbs and descents of varying lengths and difficulty are plentiful. This said, the route is not relentless and there are long sections where contouring makes for faster, flat running. Watch out for the big climb and descent half way through the race; it is steep both up and down and your legs will feel it. Stream and river crossings make interesting obstacles, but the route is 85% runnable.

DIRECTIONS The run starts at iNanda Dam Adventure Resort (GPS **29°41'29.58"S, 30°53'20.28"E**) on the north bank of the dam just outside Durban. Access from Durban is easiest from the KwaMashu Highway (M25); turn right at the traffic circle (12km after passing under the N2), then take the first left and follow the signs for 4.5km.

To reach the finish, follow the N3 north from Durban, take the Ohrtmann Road off-ramp in Pietermaritzburg and turn right. Cross the highway and turn right into Manning Avenue, then turn left at the Shell garage. Travel up the hill for 2km and turn right onto the Table Mountain Road, continuing for about 2km before turning left onto the D408. Follow the D408 all the way into Cumberland (GPS **29°31'18.25"S, 30°30'15.77"E**).

ACCOMMODATION It is best to stay in Durban North, which leaves only a 20-minute drive to the race start in the morning. There are plenty of B&Bs in the area, while The Riverside Hotel overlooking Blue Lagoon is more up-market and close to registration.

FAST FACTS

Grading Difficult to extreme
Duration 7–14hrs
Configuration Point to point
Start point iNanda Dam
GPS co-ordinates 29°41′29.58″S, 30°53′20.28″E
Finish point Cumberland Nature Reserve
GPS co-ordinates 29°31′18.25″S, 30°30′15.77″E
Terrain Mountainous and steep singletrack
Map Available from organiser
Access requirements Fee payable at trail heads
Trail markings Tags and chalk arrows (during race)
Facilities Aid stations every 10km; ablutions at start and finish
Cell reception Generally good, with a few dead patches
Beware Flooding streams and rivers; dogs and cows
Time of year April to September; avoid the hot summer months
Local info www.kzntrailrunning.co.za / Tel (+27 82) 603 4098

THE TRAIL There is a range of trails to choose from at the start and end points of the uMngeni River Run, but the focus here is the route between these two points. A good trail undulates along the northern bank of the dam, making up the first 20km of the event. There are no major climbs in this section, but numerous steep ascents and descents will take their toll.

Beyond the dam, the route follows gravel roads and jeep tracks for 10km along the river before turning up a beautiful tributary known as the Mqeku. The next section (5km) meanders along this stream, crossing it four times before reaching a tar road which is where the serious climbs kick in. A full 5km of steep climbing along a gravel road brings Nagle Dam into sight leaving the final 20km, from Nagle Dam to Cumberland.

This stretch traverses the most pristine section of the valley, following fantastic singletrack with a few short, technical sections which may be difficult to run. After crossing the river twice, you will be faced with one final climb out to the top of the cliffs. The race finishes here in Cumberland on a field alongside an old farm school.

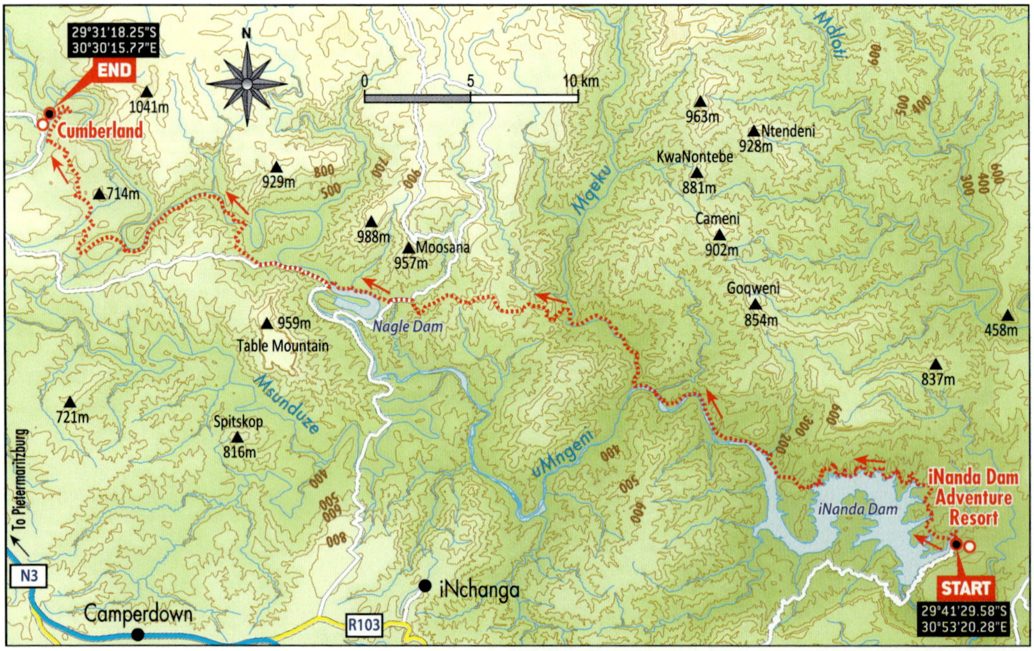

THE EVENT The main event is for experienced ultra runners, although the tracks and footing along the route are generally good and therefore do not require extensive off-road experience. The short and tricky sections towards the end (including two river crossings with safety crew) are challenging though. Good fitness and a positive mental approach are essential. The shorter 22km event follows the same route as the final stretch of the main event, so may be a better option for those with no ultra-running experience.

© JACQUES MARAIS

EVENT FACTS

Event name uMngeni River Run
Venue Start – iNanda Dam, Durban; finish – Cumberland Nature Reserve, Pietermaritzburg
Distances 22km, 70km
Time of year Mid-August
Enter as Solo
Cut-offs Yes – runners will be briefed at the race
Event organiser Andrew Booth (KZNTrailRunning)
Average duration 2–4hrs (22km), 7–14hrs (70km)
Entry info www.kzntrailrunning.co.za

EXPERT'S VIEW

Andrew Booth is primarily a trail runner with a slight road-running addiction, and can't resist great South African road ultras like the Comrades and Two Oceans. He started organising trail runs in KZN in 2009 and recently launched www.kzntrailrunning.co.za which offers more than 10 trail-running events in and around the uMngeni and Dusi valleys. His long-term objective in trail running is to organise a 100-Mile trail race in KZN.

GRADIENT PROFILE

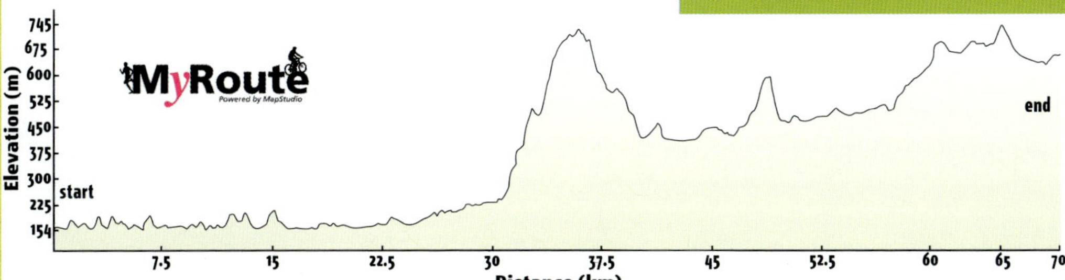

To view maps and gradient profiles go to **www.myroute.co.za**

Trail Only

Waterval Boven – eMgwenya Trails
30km

Province Mpumalanga
Region Highlands Escarpment
Closest town eMgwenya (Waterval Boven)
Trail destination Various circular loops
Series None
Contributed by Gustav Janse van Rensburg

© JACQUES MARAIS

THE DESTINATION Essentially, eMgwenya (Waterval Boven) is a rock-climbing town with a trout-fishing problem, among others. Stupendous crags cutting sheer lines along the escarpment have made more than 700 different climbing routes possible, but lately climbers have started mountain biking and trail running on 'rest days'. Glenn Harrison is (almost) single-handedly responsible for constructing a trail network second to none in the region

THE TERRAIN Singletrack-minded folk rave on a range of trails, with mind-blowing vistas from the Rim Trail to swooping s-bends through shady forests and past historical sites, or a big climb up to Imemeza's summit (a.k.a. The Place of Shouting).

By combining the various trails you can have the best of all worlds, with a smidgen of jeep track, some ankle-testing rock gardens and loads of groomed and bermed singletrack, all with minimal urban interference. With moderate temperatures, these trails are good year-round, although some winter days can become dusty when the wind picks up.

DIRECTIONS eMgwenya is neatly nestled in the gap where the N4 suddenly descends steeply into the Lowveld of Mpumalanga. eMgwenya is located roughly 100km away from both Middelburg and Mbombela.

Trails start wherever you pick up your permit: the offices of Roc 'n Rope Adventures (GPS 25°38'33.9"S, 30°19'48.7"E) in the main street of eMgwenya, or at the Tranquilitas car park (25°40'21.00"S, 30°21'43.00"E).

ACCOMMODATION The area has loads of B&Bs, self-catering farmhouses, a camp site at Tranquilitas with chalets/safari tents, and a range of affordable guesthouses or backpackers. Contact Roc 'n Rope and Mpumalanga Highlands Travel on (+27 13) 257 0363 or www.watervalboven.com or email climb@rocrope.com

FAST FACTS

Grading Easy to difficult
Duration 1–5hrs
Configuration Three circular routes (total of 30km)
Start point Downtown eMgwenya or Tranquilitas Adventure Farm
GPS co-ordinates 25°38'33.9"S, 30°19'48.7"E
Terrain Mountainous, exotic forest, ravines and steep singletrack
Map Available from Roc 'n Rope Adventures
Access requirements Permits required
Trail markings Metal signs; stone cairns on trail
Facilities All amenities in village
Cell reception Most sections enjoy good coverage
Beware Flooding streams; lightning in exposed areas
Time of year All year round
Local info website www.watervalboven.com / Tel (+27 13) 257 0363
More info website www.rocrope.com / Tel (+27 82) 753 3695

THE TRAILS Trails around eMgwenya are constantly changed or diverted to allow for erosion control, and new trails are therefore constantly being created. The three current loops are becoming exceptionally popular among trail runners. The town sleeps at 1430m above sea level and the highest point on the trails is roughly 1750m, with a valley in between, so expect to gain more than just miles.

The Mountain Trail, an 11km circular loop from the centre of town, climbs steeply along zigzags after a short section of dirt road. Here it traverses back towards town with vistas over Steenkampsberg towards Dullstroom. Halfway along the 7km of singletrack you will cross the direct route to the summit (for a sneaky short cut back to town). From here, the track gently dips towards the west via subtle cutbacks through ravines. Slow down to look at some controversial ancient stone circles on your right. The singletrack finishes at Camp Trevor Youth Camp, from where a jeep track leads back to town.

GRADIENT PROFILE

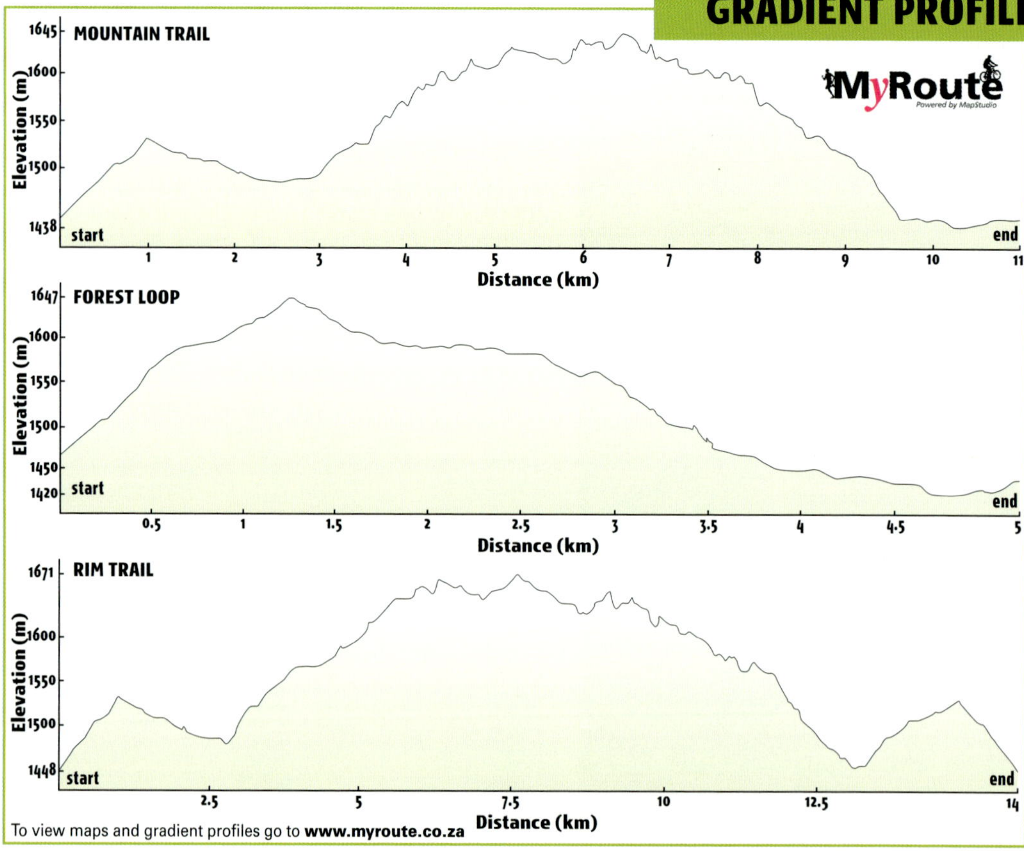

To view maps and gradient profiles go to **www.myroute.co.za**

EXPERT'S VIEW

Gustav Janse van Rensburg may be more of a climber and mountain biker, but is definitely not shy of the trails. He has been living and guiding in eMgwenya (Waterval Boven) since 1999, is a top rock-climbing instructor, and has spent quality time on cliff faces around the globe.

My shoe

Brand ~ Montrail

Model ~ Sabino

Rating ~ An all-round shoe that can handle rocks and typical 'off-piste' terrain

The Forest Loop constitutes 5km of sublime switchback singletrack: start along a section of jeep track across the way from Tranquilitas Adventure Farm. Beyond a gate, the blue arrows to the left will lead you into a wild wattle plantation for a run to remember.

Those doing the Rim Trail immediately need to get into downhill mode along a run roughly parallel to Slaaihoek Road. This route heads back towards eMgwenya on 6km of singletrack right up on the edge of the escarpment. Some fast, rocky sections will keep you on your toes as you thump to the bridge over Dwaalheuwelspruit (there's a great pool here for a quick dip). The trail climbs steeply from here for a hefty cardio workout to where the singletrack finally peters out. Here the choice is to cut back down the dirt road for some more, or you can plod the 2km of tar back into town.

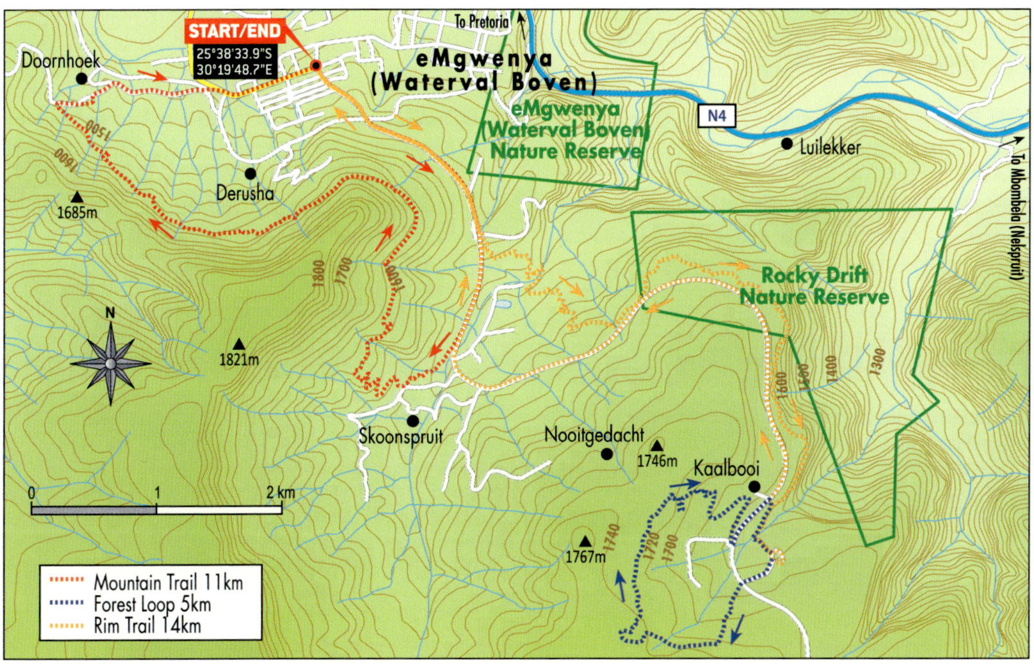

Bastille Day Trail Run (10km, 20km)

Province Western Cape
Region Cape Winelands
Closest town Franschhoek
Trail destination Franschhoek Mountain Trails (conservation land)
Contributed by Robyn Ferrar

THE DESTINATION About an hour from Cape Town, nestled in a valley between towering Cape Fold Mountains, you will find the historic and picturesque wine-farming village of Franschhoek. It is set in what is arguably one of the most beautiful valleys in the Western Cape.

THE TRAIL It is important to note that new trail events such as this tend to be quite dynamic, and routes can change yearly. The trail starts with a short gravel section heading towards the slopes and singletrack with switchbacks and panoramic views before passing through a plantation. There are technical sections with exposed drop-offs along very steep slopes before a roller-coaster descent back into the valley.

FAST FACTS

Grading Difficult to extreme
Duration 45min to 2hrs (10km); 1.5–4hrs (20km)
Configuration Circular route
Start point Berg River Dam
GPS co-ordinates 33°56'11.1"S, 19°04'25.5"E
Terrain Mountainous and technical singletrack
Map On organiser's website
Access requirements Race day only (this may change soon)
Trail markings None
Facilities Portaloos at start/finish
Cell reception Good
Beware Exposed, steep sections of trail and slippery river crossings
Time of year Mid-July for race; avoid extreme summer heat and bad weather or high wind
Local info www.franschhoek.org.za / Tel (+27 21) 876 2861
More info - www.trailrunning.co.za / Tel (+27 79) 558 3168

Baviaans River Huntly Glen Trails (5–25km)

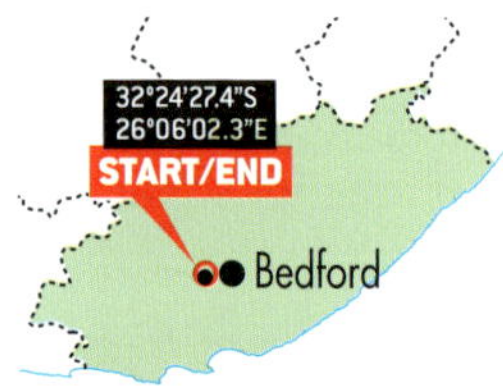

Province Eastern Cape
Region Amathole and Frontier Country
Closest town Bedford
Trail destination Baviaans River Conservancy Huntly Glen Farm
Contributed by Anne Pringle

THE DESTINATION Huntly Glen is a working farm, situated in the foothills of the Winterberg Mountains, approximately halfway between Bedford and Tarkastad. It offers trail running, hiking, bird-watching and mountain biking for the active crowd, or you could just come and relax and enjoy the uninterrupted views across the mountains and valleys.

THE TRAIL Bliss out on a network of farm roads and tracks that criss-cross 7 000ha of unspoilt Eastern Cape bush. You will get a map of the tracks and area and do not need a permit if you are a farm guest. There are five circular routes to choose from, with a total running distance of over 35km.

FAST FACTS

Grading Easy to difficult
Duration 1–4 hours
Configuration Circular
Start point Huntly Glen
GPS co-ordinates 32°24'27.4"S, 26°06'02.3"E
Terrain Rugged jeep tracks, game, sheep and cattle paths, rocky sections, stream crossings
Map Supplied by the owners
Access requirements Open to farm guests
Trail markings None
Facilities Runners are expected to be self-supported
Cell reception There is no cellphone reception in the mountains
Beware Extreme heat in summer or mist in winter; snakes
Time of year Year-round
Local info www.ectourism.co.za /Tel (+27 43) 701 9600
More info www.huntlyglen.co.za /Tel (+27 46) 685 0710

Bokpoort Trails (10–34km)

Province Free State
Region Thabo Mofutsanyana
Closest town Clarens
Trail destination Bokpoort Holiday Farm
Contributed by Christo Roos

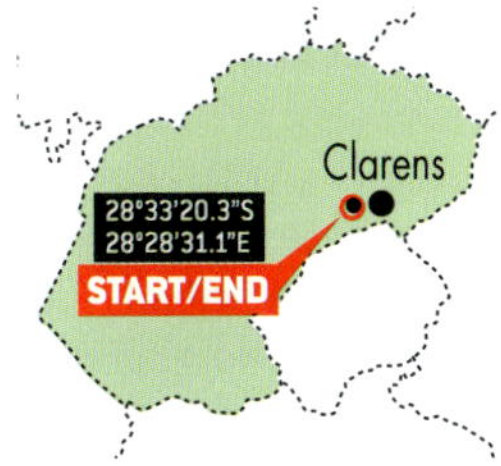

THE DESTINATION Bokpoort Holiday Farm is set amid sweeping skies punctuated by the soaring Maluti peaks, less than 8km from the picturesque village of Clarens. Surrounded by the Rooiberge, Bokpoort Farm has been part of the Roos family heritage for five generations.

THE TRAIL There are five trails ranging from 10km to 34km, all varying in difficulty and offering never-ending exploration amid grassland ridges teeming with game and bird life. Cool mountain streams offer refreshing dips along the way. The Bokpoort Mountain Challenge is a 20km race.

FAST FACTS

Grading Easy to difficult
Duration 1–6hrs
Configuration An out-and-back trail to which various loops can be added
Start point Bokpoort Farm Office
GPS co-ordinates 28°33'20.3"S, 28°28'31.1"E
Terrain Rocky singletrack and jeep tracks, steep ascents and descents, horse tracks and hiking footpaths
Map Supplied by operator
Access requirements Contact horses@bokpoort.co.za for access outside race days
Trail markings Black-and-white arrows
Facilities Water tables during races; self-sufficient otherwise
Cell reception 90% coverage
Beware Heat, rocky sections and snakes
Time of year End March for race; autumn or spring – trails open throughout the year except winter
Local info www.clarensmag.co.za
More info www.bokpoort.co.za /Tel (+27 83) 744 4245 or (+27 83) 628 5055

Bontebok National Park (1.8–40km)

Province Western Cape
Region Overberg
Closest town Swellendam
Trail destination Bontebok National Park
Contributed by Jacques Marais

THE DESTINATION The Bontebok National Park is a place of serene beauty and tranquility, with the majestic Langeberg ranges providing a suitably scenic backdrop from the higher trails.

THE TRAIL Various options – from the 1.8km Aloe Trail or 7km Bushbuck Trail to over 40km along gravel roads – may be explored. Surface quality and terrain may be rugged in places, with stretches of loose gravel and fields of loose rocks sure to give you a workout. The superb Bushbuck Trail (singletrack along the river's edge) is the undeniable *pièce de résistance* in the park.

FAST FACTS

Grading Easy to intermediate
Duration 30mins to 3hrs
Configuration Circular and return
Start point Rest camp
GPS co-ordinates 34°03'20.8"S, 20°28'23.9"E
Terrain Good gravel roads, hiking trails, loose stones
Map Available at www.sanparks.org
Access requirements Fee payable at park offices
Trail markings SanParks signs on hiking trails
Facilities Ablutions, snack shop, picnic sites
Cell reception 100% coverage
Beware Soaring summer temperatures
Time of year Lots of rain in winter
Local info www.swellendamtourism.co.za
More info www.sanparks.org /Tel (+27 28) 514 2735

Burman Bush (6km)

Province KwaZulu-Natal
Region Durban & Surrounds
Closest town Durban
Trail destination Burman Bush Nature Reserve
Contributed by Deon Braun

THE DESTINATION Burman Bush Nature Reserve preserves 55ha of indigenous forest and coastal bush along the final stretch of the uMngeni River.

THE TRAIL Burman Bush Nature Reserve features three undulating hiking trails of around 2km. However, as these tracks criss-cross continuously, you can easily get lost in this jungle maze. The reserve forms a roughly circular enclave and can be as tough or gentle as you choose. This little reserve may be just short of a kilometre in diameter, but the exploration and training opportunities are nonetheless impressive.

FAST FACTS

Grading Intermediate
Duration 1–2hrs
Configuration Various trail options
Start point Burman Bush car park and Visitor Centre
GPS co-ordinates 29°49'03.3"S, 31°01'02.0"E
Terrain Singletrack, stairs and roots
Map Display board and map from Visitor Centre
Access requirements Entrance free
Trail markings Coloured concrete blocks
Facilities Toilets, braai facilities and picnic area
Cell reception 100% of route
Beware Snakes, overhanging branches and treacherous roots
Time of year Early mornings in summer, any time in winter
Local info www.durban.gov.za / Mr Dlamini on Tel (+27 31) 312 4466
More info www.durbangreencorridor.co.za / Tel (+27 31) 322 6026

Caveman Run (20km)

Province Western Cape
Region Garden Route
Closest town Jongensfontein
Trail destination Blombos Coastal Area near Stilbaai
Contributed by Jan Heenop

THE DESTINATION Situated on the Goukou River estuary, Stilbaai is one of the most popular resorts in the Hessequa, having the advantage of both river and ocean. Jongensfontein is only 10km from Stilbaai.

THE TRAIL The trail runs from Odendaalspunt to Jongensfontein. This terrain is 30% open to the public as most of it forms part of an informal trail for fishermen along the coastline between Vermaaklikheid, Jongensfontein and Stilbaai. The first 10km of the Caveman Run will take you over rocky terrain. Athletes will start behind the first sand dunes of Odendaalspunt in the Cape Nature Reserve. From there they will run down to the coast and follow the waterline for the next 10km up to Pletzen Bay, going through the beautiful Blombos Arch. Most of the day is singletrack running, boulder-hopping over sandstone rocks, scrambling and beach running.

FAST FACTS

Grading Intermediate to difficult
Duration 3–6hrs
Configuration Point to point
Start point Jongensfontein Caravan Park
GPS co-ordinates 34°25'33.3"S, 21°20'18.7"E (Jongensfontein); 34°24'35.3"S, 21°12'27.5"E (Odendaalspunt)
Terrain Coasteering and singletrack running, including boulder-hopping
Map Available from the 24–7 Adventure website
Access requirements Entrance fee payable for the race
Trail markings 24–7 Adventure arrows
Facilities All amenities in village, none en route
Cell reception Minimal coverage along remote sections of trail
Beware of the Caveman ...
Time of year Second weekend in August for race; avoid summer and winter extremes
Local info www.stilbaaitourism.co.za
More info www.24-7adventure.com / Tel (+27 82) 455 2875

Deelfontein Trails (60km)

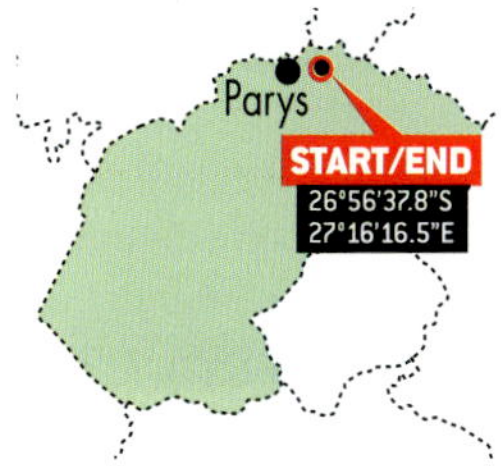

Province Free State
Region Northern Free State
Closest town Parys
Trail destination Vredefort Dome
Contributed by Gerhard Benade

THE DESTINATION Deelfontein lies in the heart of the Vredefort Dome on the southern side of the Vaal River, cradled between two of the concentric ridges typical of the Dome area. It is here, on 170ha of bergland covered with near-pristine bushveld, that you will find more than 50km of mountain-bike trails as well as a network of hiking trails to explore to your heart's content.

THE TRAILS Deelfontein is set within a network of more than 60km of hiking trails criss-crossing the Dome Conservancy. For trail runners this is an unexplored paradise as you will find that at least 15 trails can be accessed from Deelfontein, with distances varying from 1km to 16km.

FAST FACTS

Grading Easy to difficult
Duration 30mins to 10hrs
Configuration A network of trails
Start point Deelfontein Farm
GPS co-ordinates 26°56′37.8″S, 27°16′16.5″E
Terrain Jeep track, singletrack, farm and gravel roads
Map Supplied by host (www.deelfontein.co.za)
Access requirements Free for farm guests; fee payable for day visitors
Trail markings Signposts, paint markings and tree markings
Facilities Runners are expected to be self-sustaining; there are change rooms, showers and braai facilities on site
Cell reception Highly localised
Beware Steep sections, loose gravel and lightning on ridges
Time of year Open all year; beautiful winter days for running
Local info www.parys.co.za and www.domemeteoritepark.co.za
More info www.deelfontein.co.za /Tel (+27 83) 280 9784

Dwarsrivier Conservancy (8–24km)

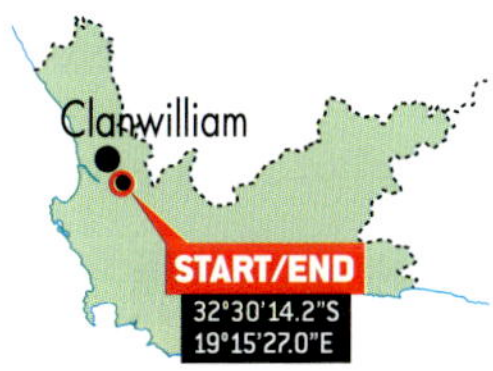

Province Western Cape
Region West Coast
Closest town Clanwilliam
Trail destination Cederberg Wilderness Area
Contributed by Jacques Marais

THE DESTINATION Sanddrif, tucked away on the lush banks of the Dwars River at the foot of the Wolfberg, is the ideal base for nature lovers and the adventurous runner, with mile upon mile of unexplored hiking trails and gravel roads.

THE TRAIL Start out at the Sanddrif Camp Site and head off towards Cederberg Private Cellars along either the MTB Route or the gravel road. Both the Maltese Cross and Lot's Wife trails are well signposted and eminently runnable. If you want 'gentle', opt for Lot's Wife, or take on gravity along the steep climb to the imposing Maltese Cross.

FAST FACTS

Grading Intermediate
Duration 1–4hrs
Configuration Return or circular
Start point Sanddrif Camp Site
GPS co-ordinates 32°30′14.2″S, 19°15′27.0″E (Dwarsrivier Sanddrif)
Terrain Hiking trail singletrack, loose stones, scrambling
Map At Dwarsrivier office
Access requirements Permits at Dwarsrivier office
Trail markings SanParks signs on hiking trails
Facilities Shop, wine sales, wood, ablutions, camp site, self-catering cottages
Cell reception Poor coverage
Beware Snakes, dehydration in summer, snow in winter
Time of year Avoid summer and winter extremes
Local info www.cederberg.co.za
More info www.cederbergwine.com /Tel (+27 27) 482 2825

Fish Eagle Trail (10km)

Province KwaZulu-Natal
Region Durban & Surrounds
Closest town Durban
Trail destination Durban Green Corridor
Contributed by Green Corridor Initiative

THE DESTINATION Adjacent to the uMngeni River estuary you will find the 'Green Hub' at the centre of the Durban Green Corridor Initiative. This programme seeks to integrate nature rehabilitation, conservation and environmental awareness with youth development and local economic growth through eco-tourism and adventure sport within the uMngeni River Valley.

THE TRAIL This 10km circular trail starts from the Green Hub Information Centre. It is an extension of the 4km Riverside Trail, leading runners further upstream to navigate through the reed beds, coastal forest and the last of the remaining coastal grasslands.

FAST FACTS

Grading Easy to intermediate
Duration 1–2hrs
Configuration Circular
Start point Green Hub
GPS co-ordinates 29°48'43.9"S, 31°02'10.9"E
Terrain Singletrack, rocky sections, mostly grass
Map Available on site
Access requirements Entrance free
Trail markings None
Facilities Parking
Cell reception 100% of route
Beware Urban legends of crocodiles abound
Time of year Open seven days a week, year-round
Local info www.durban.gov.za
More info www.durbangreencorridor.co.za / Tel (+27 31) 322 6026

Fynbos Trail Run (13km, 24km)

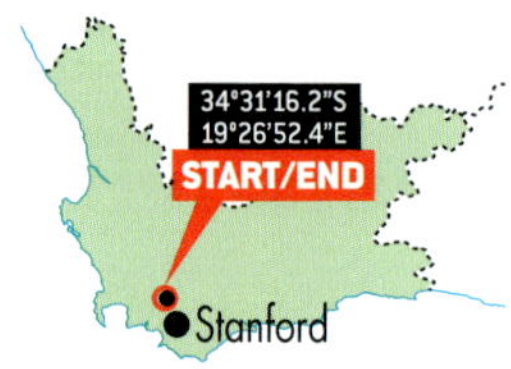

Province Western Cape
Region Overberg
Closest town Stanford
Trail destination Walker Bay Fynbos Conservancy
Contributed by Sean Privett

THE DESTINATION The village of Stanford is set in picturesque rolling hills covered in a mind-blowing variety of fynbos, with hidden patches of indigenous forests, spectacular views over the dunes and Walker Bay, and a sense of wilderness.

THE TRAIL You can start the Fynbos Trail from various locations along its route, including Flower Valley, Fynbos Retreat, Witkrans, Bodhi Khaya and 'Growing the Future'. The standard version starts and ends at Growing the Future. The trail starts with a gentle 1.5km of relatively flat terrain through an ancient milkwood forest before hitting the first climb to Pinnacle Peak. Thereafter there is a drop to the Witvoetskloof Valley, another steep ascent to Grootberg Peak, then down through Flower Valley. There is another steady climb to Swartkransberg and finally you head back to Growing the Future.

There is a range of shorter circular hiking routes available within the conservancy.

FAST FACTS

Grading Intermediate to difficult
Duration 1–3hrs (13km), 4–7hrs (24km)
Configuration Circular
Start point Growing the Future or Flower Valley
GPS co-ordinates 34°31'16.2"S, 19°26'52.4"E (Growing the Future); 34°32'53.5"S, 19°28'17.1"E (Flower Valley)
Terrain Mountainous singletrack and jeep track
Map Available from www.walkerbaytrails.co.za
Access requirements Trail must be pre-booked via info@walkerbaytrails.co.za; a trail fee is payable per person
Trail markings Metal signs on Fynbos Hiking Trail
Facilities Parking and ablutions at Growing the Future; water and overnight hiking accommodation en route
Cell reception Coverage over roughly half of route, mainly higher sections
Beware Heat and snakes
Time of year March for the race; autumn and spring for the trail
Local info www.stanfordinfo.co.za and www.gansbaaiinfo.com
More info www.walkerbaytrails.co.za / Tel (+27 82) 411 1008

George Trail Run (8km, 16km)

Province Western Cape
Region Garden Route
Closest town George
Trail destination George Botanical Gardens
Series GTR Trail Series
Contributed by Jacques Mouton

THE DESTINATION George is the heart of the Garden Route and with good reason. It is close to the sea, only 15km from Victoria Bay and Herold's Bay, and besides running along the area's numerous trails, you can also go mountain biking, kayaking, canoeing, fishing, big-game fishing, hiking, water-skiing or paragliding.

THE TRAIL The trail sets off in a northerly direction from the George Botanical Gardens towards the mountain, following jeep track, singletrack and gravel road. There are panoramic views and a run through Tonnelbos, a beautiful indigenous forest. This is a tough run and not recommended for novices.

FAST FACTS

Grading Intermediate
Duration 40–90mins (8km), 1.5–4hrs (16km)
Configuration Circular
Start point George Botanical Gardens
GPS co-ordinates 33°56'40.8"S, 22°27'46.5"E
Terrain Mountainous singletrack and jeep track
Map Google Earth track log
Access requirements Free
Trail markings TekkieTown arrows on race day
Facilities Parking, amenities in George Botanical Gardens
Cell reception 100% coverage
Beware Weather can change quickly; the trail is slippery when wet; mist and low clouds can impair visibility
Time of year December for the race; year-round for the trail
Local info www.visitgeorge.co.za and www.georgetourism.org.za
More info www.gardenroutetrailrunning.co.za / Tel (+27 82) 787 5300

Gericke's Point Beach Run (16km)

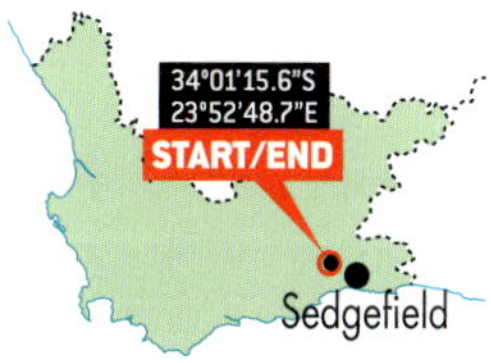

Province Western Cape
Region Garden Route
Closest town Sedgefield
Trail destination Swartvlei and Groenvlei (Goukamma)
Contributed by Riaan and Thea-Mari van der Sandt

THE DESTINATION Sedgefield is not only a coastal town; it is also surrounded by lakes. On the western side lies Swartvlei and in the east lies Groenvlei, which makes it a fisherman's dream destination. It is therefore through fishing that many get to know the area more intimately and discover that it can also be a trail runner's dream destination!

THE TRAIL This is all about a beach run from Gericke's Point to Groenvlei Beach and back. You start running from the car park at Swartvlei Beach. In the west you will see the most beautiful rock formation that juts into the ocean; this is, of course, Gericke's Point. So head east and leave the best for last.

There are plenty of other trails to choose from in the Goukamma Nature Reserve itself.

FAST FACTS

Grading Intermediate to difficult, depending on the tide
Duration 90mins to 3hrs
Configuration Out and back
Start point Swartvlei Beach Car Park
GPS co-ordinates 34°01'15.6"S, 23°52'48.7"E
Terrain Beach sand and boulders
Map No map available
Access requirements No permits necessary
Trail markings None
Facilities Ablution facilities at the car park
Cell reception Full coverage
Beware High tide
Time of year Summer
Local info www.discover-sedgefield-south-africa.com and www.capenature.co.za
More info www.sedgefieldonsea.co.za / Tel (+27 44) 343 2568

Giants Cup Trail Run (20.5km and 19km or 27km)

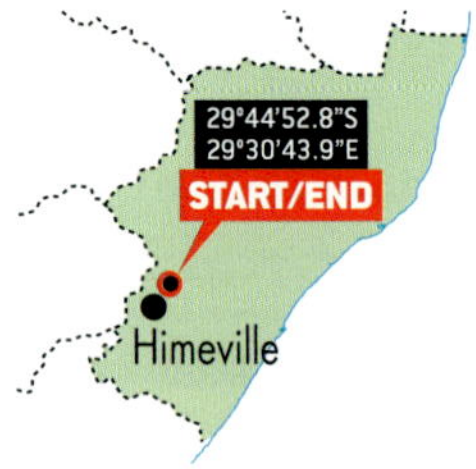

Province KwaZulu-Natal
Region uKhahlamba-Drakensberg
Closest town Himeville
Trail destination The Southern Drakensberg
Contributed by Sarah Drew

THE DESTINATION The southern Drakensberg is an alpine landscape of dramatic beauty just off the beaten tourist track. There are several nature reserves and numerous crystal-clear lakes and rivers, with the Sani Pass (the highest pass between South Africa and Lesotho) one of the obvious highlight.

THE TRAIL The Giants Cup Trail is a renowned five-day hiking trail that is accessible by road at a few key points, so runners will be able to complete the full distance over two days (20.5km and either 19km or 27km). The standard tour package includes two nights' accommodation, all meals, pick-up and drop-offs, and luggage transfers. Customised variations on this tour can be made.

FAST FACTS

Grading Intermediate to difficult
Duration Two days
Configuration Point to point
Start point Himeville
GPS co-ordinates 29°44′52.8″S, E29°30′43.9″E
Terrain Hiking trail, steep climbs, contour paths, long grass, loose gravel
Map Provided by organiser
Access requirements The trail can be booked all year round; avoid school/public holidays
Trail markings Ground markers
Facilities None en route; full amenities at overnight stops
Cell reception Intermittent
Beware Loose ground and erosion berms
Time of year Winter months (April to August) when the weather is stable
Local info www.drakensberg-tourism.com and www.kznwildlife.com
More info www.activegetaway.co.za /Tel (+27 84) 240 7277

Grabouw Grapple (6–35km)

Province Western Cape
Region Overberg
Closest town Grabouw
Trail destination MTO Forestry
Contributed by Raoul de Jongh

THE DESTINATION Grabouw is an area renowned for its unforgiving landscapes, set in-between Sir Lowry's Pass, Nuweberg Pass and Houw Hoek Pass.

THE TRAIL Be adventurous and get lost on the trails setting off from the Grabouw Country Club and heading towards the Eikenhof and Nuweberg dams and beyond. Sweeping panoramic views and magnificent singletracks will be your reward.

FAST FACTS

Grading Intermediate to difficult
Duration 1–5 hours
Configuration Various options
Start point Grabouw Country Club
GPS co-ordinates 34°08′26.1″S, 19°01′27.0″E
Terrain Rocks, sand and gravel
Map Available from MTO office
Access requirements Fee payable at MTO office
Trail markings Wooden signs
Facilities All amenities in Grabouw
Cell reception Minimal coverage along remote sections
Beware Extreme temperatures, flooding rivers
Time of year Spring and autumn
Local info www.elginvalley.co.za
More info www.urban-ninja.co.za /Tel (+27 21) 859 1612

Hi-Tec Mystic Sable (50km)

Province Gauteng
Region Gauteng North
Closest town Pretoria
Trail destination Groenkloof Nature Reserve
Series Hi-Tec Trail Series
Contributed by Francois Jooste

THE DESTINATION Groenkloof Nature Reserve is located near the famous Fountains Valley. Paul Kruger proclaimed this valley as a game sanctuary on 25 February 1895 – the first in Africa.

THE TRAIL There are several hiking routes of differing distance and degree of difficulty to choose from. The 10.5km Yellow Trail cuts across a rocky hill and is recommended for those who are walking fit and experienced at hiking. The shorter trails – such as the 4km White Trail and the 3.5km Red Trail – are recommended for younger and older groups. Maps are available for self-guided hikes, but guided hikes can be provided if booked two weeks in advance.

The Hi-Tec Mystic Sable Stage Run is one of a series of events presented by Vertial Horison in the Pretoria region.

FAST FACTS

Grading Intermediate
Duration 4–7hrs
Configuration Circular route, divided into three stages (50km)
Start point Moyo Fountains
GPS co-ordinates 25°46'54.05"S, 28°11'43.03"E
Terrain Variety of singletrack, through both forest and mountains
Map From Information Office at Groenkloof
Access requirements Free entrance
Trail markings Wooden signposts along trails
Facilities All amenities in reserve, including great hot showers
Cell reception Yes
Beware The odd hungry wildebeest ...
Time of year Early November for race, otherwise year-round
Local info groenkloofnaturereserve@tshwane.gov.za / Tel (+27 12) 440 8316
More info www.verticalhorison.co.za / Tel (+27 83) 653 4367

Howick Mountain Trails (10–70km)

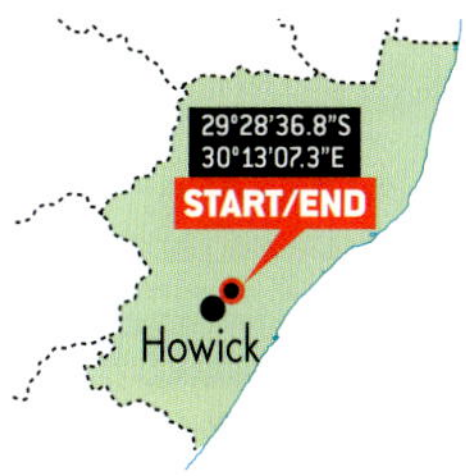

Province KwaZulu-Natal
Region Midlands
Closest town Howick
Trail destination Howick Trail Network
Contributed by Paul Rencken

THE DESTINATION Howick is in the heart of the uMngeni Municipal region in the Midlands, within easy reach of both Pietermaritzburg and the uKhahlamba Drakensberg. The 100m-high Howick Falls is almost in the centre of the picturesque town and is known to the Zulu people as KwaNogqaza, or 'Place of the Tall One'.

THE TRAIL Tick off great singletrack, a 'not-so-bad' climb, quiet trails and awesome views – that's what you will do on the Howick trail network. The good news is that there is over 70km of singletrack in the Howick area, with named trails making it quite simple to navigate, even for novices.

FAST FACTS

Grading Intermediate
Duration 60–90mins
Configuration Circular and other options
Start point Howick Private Hospital, Main Road
GPS co-ordinates 29°28'36.8"S, 30°13'07.3"E
Terrain Singletrack, forest tracks and contour roads
Map Available from iRide Africa: www.iride.com/trail-maps
Access requirements Access indemnity forms available at the hospital, or from some local bike shops
Facilities None (public parking areas)
Trail markings Trails are named and simple to navigate; no directional arrows
Cell reception 100% coverage
Beware Traffic on tar road crossings, snakes in summer, mountain bikers
Time of year Open year-round
Local info www.midlandsmeander.co.za or www.howicktourism.co.za
More info www.howickmountainbiking.co.za or info@howickmountainbiking.co.za

Iron Crown Trail Run (21.1km, 10km, 5km)

Province Limpopo
Region Magoebaskloof
Closest town Haenertsburg
Trail destination Haenertsburg Village
Contributed by Peter Kirk

THE DESTINATION Haenertsburg is situated at the foot of the Iron Crown (or 'The Mountain' as the locals call it), the highest peak in Limpopo Province.

THE TRAIL The out-and-back route starts on the edge of town, where you immediately head onto gravel to follow the road past a few farms before the first climb of the day at the 2km mark. At an abandoned school (3km), the gradient eases off as you tunnel into indigenous forest, exiting into plantations.

To run this trail outside the race, you must obtain a permit; the route is marked on race day only. Your GPS will inform you that the 21.1km route climbs 687m from 1 439m in the village to the top of the Iron Crown, the highest point at 2 126m. The 10km is less testing and climbs to 1600m.

FAST FACTS

Grading Difficult to extreme
Duration 2–5hrs (21.1km)
Configuration Out and back
Start point Start of gravel road leading out of Haenertsburg (at end of Church Street)
GPS co-ordinates 23°56'49.50"S, 29°56'13.70"E
Terrain Gravel road, wagon trail and singletrack
Map Basic map available from the race organisers
Access requirements Contact race organisers if you intend to run outside of the race date. Permits are available from Rotary or the 'Foodzone' Supermarket. Ask for Ann.
Trail markings Route marked on race day only
Facilities Water tables on race day
Cell reception Irregular
Beware Long grass, sketchy and slippery singletrack; look out for snakes
Time of year July for race; all year; summer-rainfall region
Local info Shelley Milstein, Tel (+27 84) 262 8488
More info www.runnersworld.co.za or www.entrytime.com

Kenneth Stainbank Nature Reserve (6km)

Province KwaZulu-Natal
Region Durban and Surrounds
Closest town Yellowwood Park
Trail destination Kenneth Stainbank Nature Reserve
Contributed by Deon Braun

THE DESTINATION It really is quite surreal seeing zebra grazing within an unspoilt African wilderness setting with Durban's skyscrapers and harbour infrastructure as a backdrop to the northeast. Keep on running though, as once you're enveloped by the magnificent old-growth forests or the rolling savannah of the sprawling 253ha Kenneth Stainbank Nature Reserve, nature will erase any thought of the city.

THE TRAIL There are four main trails including a 500m trail for the physically disabled and sight-impaired. The 6km Mkumbi Trail takes the average trail runner 45–50 minutes to complete; super-size (well, not quite) your run by combining it with the 3km Yellow Trail (25min) and the 500m Brown Trail.

FAST FACTS

Grading Easy to intermediate
Duration 15–90mins
Configuration Circular
Start point Kenneth Stainbank Nature Reserve car park
GPS co-ordinates 29°54'41.9"S, 30°56'39.2"E
Terrain Hard-pack and grassland jeep track to technical forest singletrack
Map Display board with map at entrance
Access requirements Entrance fee; open year-round
Trail markings Coloured concrete blocks
Facilities Ablutions and picnic area
Cell reception 100% coverage
Beware Pepper ticks; better to not run alone
Time of year Early mornings in summer, any time in winter
Local info www.yellowwoodpark.com
More info www.kznwildlife.com /Tel (+27 33) 845 1000

Kings Kloof (7km, 14km, 17km, 20km or 23km)

Province Gauteng
Region Krugersdorp / Muldersdrift
Closest town Krugersdorp
Trail destination Kings Kloof Trail Centre
Contributed by Nicky Swanevelder

THE DESTINATION Kings Kloof Trail Centre is situated near Krugersdorp and Muldersdrift on the stunning Laurentia Farm. The trails here stand out in comparison to other running destinations in the northern Gauteng region, with beautiful valleys, mountain ascents, river crossings, natural pools, dense thickets and spectacular views to boot.

THE TRAIL Kings Kloof offers off-road junkies a range of trail configurations, including everything from easy jeep track to ankle-snapping singletrack. The trails are perfect for runners keen on challenging training sessions, with five primary routes to choose from.

FAST FACTS

Grading Various (easy to difficult)
Duration 90mins to 4hrs (depending on route)
Configuration Circular routes
Start point Kings Kloof, behind Laurentia Farm Stall
GPS co-ordinates 26°02'28.39"S, 27°47'10.64"E
Terrain Quartzite ridges, rolling grassland, steep hills
Map Download at www.runtrail.co.za
Access requirements Entrance fee payable
Trail markings Well marked with coloured arrows
Facilities No facilities
Cell reception Good reception along the trail
Beware Snakes, ticks, dehydration, natural obstacles, mountain bikers; always carry a cellphone
Time of year Summer and winter
Local info www.kingskloofmtb.co.za
More info www.runtrail.co.za / Tel (+27 72) 699 2437

Klipriviersberg Nature Reserve (6km)

Province Gauteng
Region Gauteng Central
Closest town Kibler Park / Mondeor
Trail destination Klipriviersberg Nature Reserve
Contributed by Lisa de Speville

THE DESTINATION Scenic Klipriviersberg was declared a nature reserve in 1984 to protect an area of archaeological, historical, cultural and geological interest. Eagle-eyed runners may spot any number of antelope including red hartebeest, black wildebeest, springbok, duiker and mountain reedbuck, or indulge in the occasional bout of fast-paced twitching should this be to their liking.

THE TRAIL This 680ha reserve has eight colour-coded routes, which are marked in the terrain by painted cement blocks; they are not separate loops but rather extend off each other. Coloured route markers serve more for orientation than to dictate where you should run.

FAST FACTS

Grading Easy to intermediate
Duration Easy 6km return run; or own distance up to 2hrs
Configuration Various options
Start point Precinct entrance or Frandaph Drive in Mondeor
GPS co-ordinates 26°18'13.44"S, 28°00'39.18"E (Precinct entrance); 26°16'58.26"S, 28°00'34.44"E (Frandaph Drive)
Terrain Wide, easy-running paths to steep, rocky trails
Map Colour map of the reserve and trails is available online from www.knra.co.za
Access requirements Free entrance
Trail markings Colour-coded cement route markers
Facilities Toilets at the Precinct gate only
Cell reception Good throughout
Time of year Year-round
Local info www.gauteng.net / Tel (+27 11) 085 2500
More info www.knra.co.za / Tel (+27 82) 458 2816

Kogelberg (26km)

Province Western Cape
Region Overberg and Southern Cape
Closest town Kleinmond
Trail destination Kogelberg Nature Reserve
Contributed by Jacques Marais

THE DESTINATION There used to be a super 39km one-way run all the way down the valley from Grabouw, but land access became an issue. Runners still have access to the rugged jeep track meandering up to Stokoei Bridge, or can go technical along the network of hiking trails following the lower valley or climbing up towards the Old Forest and Leopards Kloof.

THE TRAIL Start from the reception at Oudebosch Cabins and follow the trail that links up with the jeep track, tracking the reeded banks of the Palmiet River flowing down the valley. There is a fair bit of up-and-down as you tramp to where you cross the Louws River (6km), all the while keeping the Palmiet to your right. Your turn-around point is at the Stokoei Bridge, where there is a lovely swimming pool. The other hiking routes all start from Kogelberg reception.

FAST FACTS

Grading Intermediate
Duration 2–3 hours
Configuration Return
Start point Reserve office at Oudebosch Cabins
GPS co-ordinates 34°19'20.81"S, 18°57'58.56"E
Terrain Jeep track and gravel road; singletrack hiking trail
Map Download from www.capenature.co.za
Access requirements Trail must be pre-booked through CapeNature
Trail markings Trail is signposted with CapeNature signage
Facilities Ablutions, self-catering accommodation, camping
Cell reception Intermittent
Beware The richest biodiversity in the world – tread carefully
Time of year Year-round
Local info www.patourism.co.za /Tel (+27 23) 541 1366
More info www.capenature.co.za /Tel (+27 21) 483 0000

Kurland Summer Trail Run (16km)

Province Western Cape
Region Garden Route
Closest town Plettenberg Bay
Trail destination Kurland Hotel and Estate
Series Pennypinchers AR Team trail runs
Contributed by James Stewart

THE DESTINATION The Kurland Hotel lies east of the prime holiday destination of Plettenberg Bay and just inland of Nature's Valley. The estate lies in the foothills of the Tsitiskamma Mountains, with vistas of the whole of Bahia Formosa and The Crags. Beyond the manicured grounds of the hotel are hectares of mountains and valleys covered in indigenous forests, fynbos and some commercial forestry plantations.

THE TRAIL The first 4km of the run follows jeep tracks through pine and gum plantations and climbs to a saddle with a view of the polo fields below. The next 1km is a specially created path through indigenous forest and through some head-high clumps of ferns. The trail crosses a stream five times; the cool mountain water is delicious. Unfortunately, this trail is only open to hotel guests apart from race day.

FAST FACTS

Grading Intermediate
Duration 1–2.5hrs
Configuration Circular
Start point Kurland Hotel
GPS co-ordinates 33°56'26.0"S, 23°29'17.0"E
Terrain Mountainous, forest, singletrack and jeep track
Map None
Access requirements Permission required from Kurland Hotel
Trail markings None
Facilities All amenities at the Kurland Hotel
Cell reception 70% coverage
Beware Puff adders and bush pigs
Time of year December for the race; year-round for the trail
Local info www.plettenbergbay.co.za and www.cruisethecrags.co.za
More info www.trailrunning.co.za /Tel (+27 79) 558 3168

Marloth Nature Reserve Trail
(11km to over 40km)

Province Western Cape
Region Overberg and Southern Cape
Closest town Swellendam
Trail destination Marloth Nature Reserve
Contributed by Jacques Marais

THE DESTINATION Various route options beckon, all wending through the 14 000ha Marloth Nature Reserve at the foot of the Langeberg, traversing pine plantations, indigenous forest and fields of mountain fynbos. Choose between routes heading into the Hermitage Valley, up to Die Plaat or along the Two Feathers Horse Trails.

THE TRAIL Most of the running is along gravel roads, jeep tracks and stunning hiking trails, with surfaces varying from eroded rock and sand to muddy sections after heavy rains. The routes in Marloth Plantation link via various steep footpaths and some overgrown dual-track onto Die Plaat and into the towering peaks beyond. The route is marked in key places.

FAST FACTS

Grading Easy to intermediate
Duration 3–5 hours (17km or 39km)
Configuration Circular
Start point Marloth Offices
GPS co-ordinates 33°58'4.08"S, 20°24'1.08"E
Terrain Gravel road, jeep track, hiking paths
Map Available from Marloth reception
Access requirements Entry fee payable
Trail markings Route is marked, generally with wooden signage
Facilities Ablution facilities and secure parking at entrance
Cell reception Good
Beware Snakes, scorpions, floods
Time of year Year-round
Local info marlothnr@telkomsa.net / Tel (+27 28) 514 1410
More info www.capenature.co.za / Tel (+27 21) 483 0000

Mateke Trails (9km, 13km)

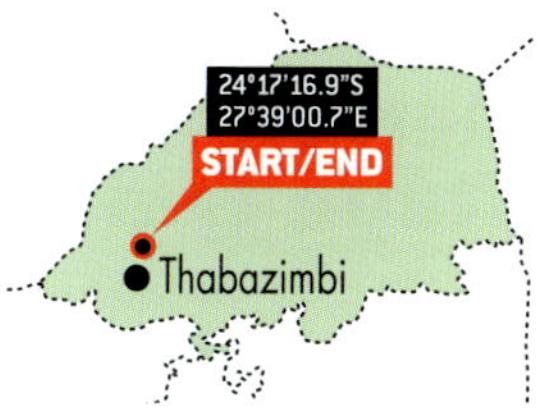

Province Limpopo
Region Waterberg
Closest town Thabazimbi
Trail destination Mateke Game Farm
Contributed by Mateke Trails

THE DESTINATION The Waterberg Biosphere Reserve stretches from Marakele National Park in the southwest to the Wonderkop Nature Reserve in the northeast. The landscape is one of rolling hills and endless vistas, with a distinct bushveld feel. Mateke Game Farm is a secluded 2 000ha game farm set within this world-renowned biosphere reserve.

THE TRAIL Breathtaking scenery, plentiful game and diverse vegetation will have you relaxed in no time. The perennial Mamba River flows through the entire length of the farm, with several tranquil rock pools perfect for a refreshing dip. If you love game viewing while running, the best time would be at sunrise or sunset. The Kransveld bushveld is very dense in summer, so runners can expect better game viewing during the winter months.

FAST FACTS

Grading Intermediate
Duration 1.5–3hrs
Configuration Circular
Start point Mateke Tree Camp
GPS co-ordinates 24°17'16.9"S, 27°39'00.7"EE
Terrain Singletrack hiking trails, sandy, rocky, flats and hills
Map Supplied by operator
Access requirements Free for farm guests; day visitors by prior arrangement
Trail markings Black and white arrows
Facilities No drinking water on trails; runners must be self-sufficient
Cell reception Some areas have no coverage
Beware Heat, rocky sections and snakes
Time of year Winter is best as the bush will be less dense
Local info www.waterbergbiosphere.org
More info www.mateke.co.za / Tel (+27 14) 779 0719

Merrell Norm-Hudlin Trails (20km, 10km, 15km)

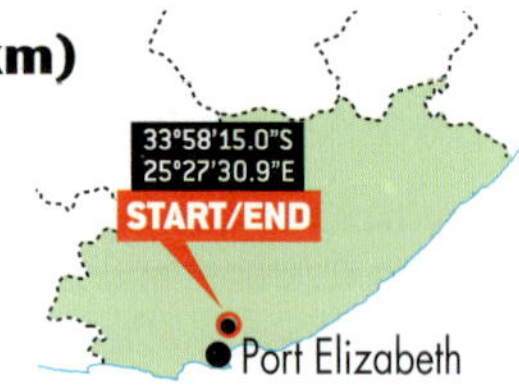

Province Eastern Cape
Region Nelson Mandela Metropole
Closest town Port Elizabeth
Trail destination Merrell Norm-Hudlin Trails
Series Merrell Events
Contributed by Andrea von Holdt

THE DESTINATION The Merrell Norm-Hudlin Trail Centre was established in 2010 on approximately 150ha of privately owned land close to Seaview on the outskirts of Port Elizabeth. All the trails are purpose-built, hand-cut and maintained by the owner of the property, Lex Holmes. The centre offers a safe and friendly destination to trail runners and mountain bikers, and caters for all levels of outdoor athletes.

THE TRAIL The route consists of a network of up to 20km of purpose-built trail, with shorter options of 10km and 15km. Beginners love the trails as everything is runnable. The trail centre has become a popular outdoor destination for families. While you push hard, the rest of the family can enjoy the trails at a slower pace, all the while knowing you're in a safe and secure environment.

FAST FACTS

Grading Easy to intermediate
Duration 1–2hrs
Configuration 20km circuit; shorter configurations available
Start and end point Norm-Hudlin Farm
GPS co-ordinates 33°58'15.0"S, 25°27'30.9"E
Terrain Flat, sandy in places, singletrack
Map Available at trail head
Access requirements Day fee per visit or buy a six-month membership
Trail markings Marker boards
Facilities Portable loos, safe parking, coffee and other refreshments
Cell reception Full reception
Beware Horses, mountain bikers
Time of year Year-round
Local info Lex Holmes, Tel (+27 83) 342 8306
More info www.merrell.co.za /Tel (27 83) 342 8306

Merrell Xtreme – Three-day Beach Stage Trail (146km)

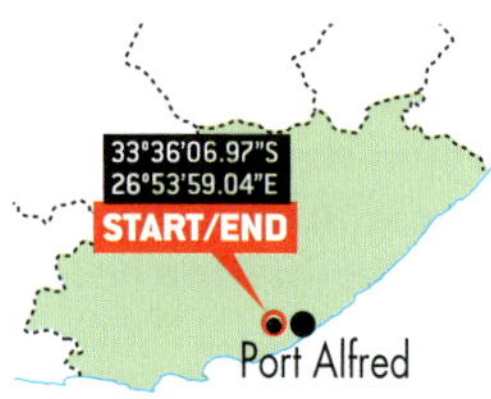

Province Eastern Cape
Region Sunshine Coast / Border
Closest town Port Alfred (trail head)
Trail destination Eastern Cape Coastal Trails
Series Backyard Adventures Events
Contributed by Craig Muller

THE DESTINATION The Sunshine Coast offers world-class nature reserves and unrivalled natural beauty, epitomising what is one of the country's most exhilarating adventure playgrounds.

THE TRAIL The trail is a single unmarked 146km route along the beach from Port Alfred to East London, and this monster is tackled over three days.

The trail makes its way along sandy beaches, over undulating dunes, river mouths and rocky outcrops. The Merrell Xtreme is not a race, and should be seen more as a challenge to every individual who takes on this gruelling event. It is an experience outdoor enthusiasts are sure to remember for life, and it will certainly test your fitness levels and stamina to the extreme.

FAST FACTS

Grading Difficult to extreme
Duration Three days
Configuration Point to point
Start point East Pier, Port Alfred
GPS co-ordinates 36°36'6.97"S, 26°53'59.04"E
Terrain Sandy beaches, dunes, rocky outcrops, river crossings
Map Use Google Earth
Access requirements Arrange through Backyard Adventures
Trail markings No trail markings; stick to the beach
Facilities All amenities at beach resorts along the trail
Cell reception Minimal coverage along some sections of trail
Beware High tides, fast-flowing rivers, strong winds, temperatures
Time of year End of April for race; temperate seasons
Local info www.sunshinecoasttourism.co.za
More info www.backyard-adventures.co.za /Tel (+27 82) 397 5454

Misty Valley Lodge Trails (5–20km)

Province Mpumalanga
Region Emakhazeni
Closest town eNtokozweni and eMgwenya
Trail destination Misty Valley Lodge & Family Resort
Contributed by Philip Vosloo

THE DESTINATION The Emakhazeni district encompasses the towns of Dullstroom, Belfast, eNtokozweni and eMgwenya. The Drakensberg Escarpment starts in this area of mountains, and many lakes adorn the valley regions. The evergreen Sappi forests, bushveld and luscious grasslands are home to the abundant game species that roam this part of Africa.

THE TRAIL Set in unity with the mountain-biking trails, there are 10 trails to choose from, depending on your level of fitness. Trails vary in distance from 5km to 20km and are in loops that all come back to the starting point. The trails were designed in this way so that runners could easily find their way back to the lodge and could then choose another trail to carry on with according to their fitness levels.

FAST FACTS

Grading Easy to difficult
Duration Various
Configuration Circular routes
Start point Misty Valley Lodge and Family Resort
GPS co-ordinates 25°45'14.85"S, 30°26'6.94"E
Terrain Rocky, forests, open grasslands and wetlands
Map Available on website
Access requirements Need to pre-book; Tel (+27 86) 136 4789
Trail markings The trails are all named and colour-coded with directional arrows
Facilities Tented accommodation with full toilet facilities
Cell reception Some networks better than others
Beware Veld fires (May–Aug); roaming game
Time of year Year-round, but winter can be very cold
Local info www.emakhazenitourism.com
More info www.mistyvalleylodge.co.za / Tel (+27 13) 256 6000

Mole Rat Night Trail Run (6km, 10km)

Province Western Cape
Region Garden Route
Closest town Sedgefield
Trail destination Pine Lake Marina
Series Southern Cross Adventures
Contributed by Hano Otto

THE DESTINATION Sedgefield is located midway between George and Knysna and is surrounded by lakes and no fewer than five splendid beaches. Multiple-day hikes and smaller one-day walks are all available in awe-inspiring natural beauty, with mountains, valleys, lakes, forests, streams and beaches.

THE TRAIL The Mole Rat Hiking Trail is open to everybody. You can get information and a map at the local tourism office in Sedgefield or at the SanParks office in Wilderness. This is a beautiful trail in and among indigenous forest and on the prehistoric dunes, all this next to the lakes. Most of the trail is in the SanParks area. While running you will see lots of different bird species and frequently hear the Fish Eagle's call.

FAST FACTS

Grading Easy
Duration 30–90mins
Configuration Circular
Start point Pine Lake Marina Resort
GPS co-ordinates 34°00'12.7"S, 22°44'38.2"E
Terrain Singletrack, jeep tracks and sandy sections
Map Maps available at the start and posted on the website; hiking trail map available at the local tourism office
Access requirements Entry fee payable at SanParks office in Wilderness or at Sedgefield Tourism office; race entries online
Trail markings The race is marked with marshals, lights and glowing tape
Facilities Toilets and restaurant at the Marina; none en route
Cell reception Minimal coverage along remote sections of trail
Beware Mosquitoes
Time of year March for race; winter is best as the bush will be less dense
Local info www.visitsedgefield.co.za
More info www.southerncrossadvenure.co.za / Tel (+27 82) 579 7595

Moreleta Kloof Nature Reserve
(1.5km to 6.5km)

Province Gauteng
Region Gauteng Central
Closest town Pretoria
Trail destination Moreleta Kloof Nature Reserve
Contributed by Nicky Swanevelder

THE DESTINATION The picturesque foothills of Moreleta Kloof enfold one of the underrated outdoor gems in the Pretoria area. The 100ha Moreleta Kloof Nature Reserve boasts a host of game species, including zebra, blesbok, duiker, impala and bushbuck, to name but a few. Marked trails cater for everyone from the newbie runner to the avid trail gunner, with distances varying from 1.5km to 6.5km.

THE TRAIL Moreleta Kloof Nature Reserve boasts a range of technical singletrack trails, all set within tranquil woodland interspersed with forested thickets. There are three primary routes (the Duiker, Suikerbos and Rademeyer trails) to choose from, with distances varying from an easy 1.5km to a tougher 6.5km loop combining all the various Moreleta routes.

FAST FACTS

Grading Intermediate
Duration 1–2hrs
Configuration Circular route with loops
Start and end point Moreleta Kloof Nature Reserve parking area
GPS co-ordinates 25°49'1.72"S, 28°17'27.61"E
Terrain Savannah woodlands and forest thickets
Map Download at www.runtrail.co.za
Trail markings Signage at all junctions
Access requirements Entry is free; open seven days a week 06:00–18:00
Facilities Restaurant, clean toilets and running water
Cell reception Good reception along trail
Beware Snakes, ticks and loose rocks
Time of year Avoid the summer thunderstorm season
Local info www.tshwanetourism.co.za/Tel (+27 12) 358 1430
More info www.moreletakloof.co.za

Nagle Dam Trail Run (10km, 25km)

Province KwaZulu-Natal
Region KZN Midlands
Closest town Pietermaritzburg / Cato Ridge
Trail destination Nagle Dam
Contributed by Andrew Booth

THE DESTINATION Nagle Dam nestles near the base of Pietermaritzburg's Table Mountain, a half-hour drive from the city. A game reserve (managed by Msinsi) surrounds the dam, with cracker views of the Valley of a Thousand Hills.

THE TRAIL The short and long courses (10km and 25km) start together at the shady picnic site near the dam wall, with runners following gravel roads or sections of tar for the first 3km to separate the field. The courses split at the weir, with short-course runners entering the tunnel through the weir to go 'under' the dam. The short course circumnavigates the bottom half of the dam, with a steady climb shortly after the halfway mark as the first real test. Although the footing may be tricky in places, the course is considered mild.

FAST FACTS

Grading Intermediate to difficult
Duration 2–4 hours
Configuration Circular
Start point Msinsi Picnic Site, Nagle Dam
GPS co-ordinates 29°35'0.38"S, 30°37'0.51"E
Terrain Undulating
Map None
Access requirements Free for Wild Card holders, otherwise there's an entry fee to Msinsi
Trail markings Tags and chalk arrows (during event)
Facilities Toilets, showers and braai facilities
Cell reception 80% reception along route
Beware Flooding rivers and streams; cows and dogs
Time of year Winter months
Local info www.msinsi.co.za /Tel (+27 31) 782 8085
More info www.kzntrailrunning.co.za /Tel (+27 82) 603 4098

Nguni Classic MTB and Trail Run

(5km, 14km, 30km)

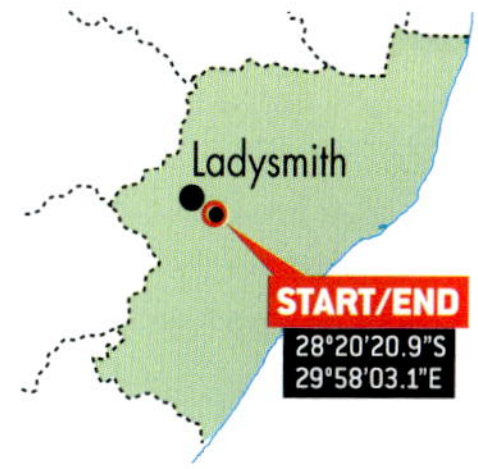

Province KwaZulu-Natal
Region Zululand and Battlefields
Closest town Ladysmith
Trail destination Blanerne Farm
Contributed by Angie Mitchell-Innes

THE DESTINATION Blanerne Farm lies 30km north of Ladysmith, between Ladysmith and Newcastle in the middle of the Northern Natal Battlefields area, and covers an area of 6 500ha. The countryside is beautiful, with lovely views of the horseshoe-shaped ring of hills at the Elandslaagte Battlefield and the Drakensberg in the distance.

THE TRAIL The challenging and technical 30km route is reserved for real adventurers only. Runners will face steep valleys with the odd river crossing, as well as a range of other exciting obstacles. The 14km intermediate run includes a beautiful section of singletrack and a challenging uphill to get out of the valley. This route is different from that of the 30km race (run on the previous day), so you could run both and thus lay claim to being the King or Queen of the Trail.

FAST FACTS

Grading Easy to difficult
Duration 30min to 5hrs
Configuration Circular
Start point Blanerne Farm
GPS co-ordinates 28°20'20.9"S, 29°58'03.1"E
Terrain Singletrack and farm roads; some steep climbs
Map Supplied on the day
Access requirements Online entries at www.nguniclassic.co.za or enter on the day
Trail markings Arrows, signs and candy tape
Facilities Water tables every 7km
Cell reception 100% coverage
Beware It can get quite windy
Time of year Long weekend in September
Local info www.zulu.org.za
More info www.nguniclassic.co.za /Tel (+27 82) 282 3395

Oak Valley Run (14km, 24km, 32km)

Province Western Cape
Region Overberg and Southern Cape
Closest town Grabouw
Trail destination Oak Valley Wine Estate
Contributed by Jacques Marais

THE DESTINATION The superb Oak Valley mountain-biking trails network forms the basis of your run at this working vineyard and soft-fruit farm. It is undoubtedly one of the most gorgeous trails you will find within less than an hour from Cape Town, and the wine is excellent to boot.

THE TRAIL Pick your trail and run: go gently along meandering singletrack following the course of a small stream; blast at speed through an oak forest brimming with ancient trees; or traverse the fence lines crisscrossing the higher-lying grassveld. The trail takes you through varying terrain and up a few steep-ish ascents, but any moderately fit runner will soon fall in love with the flow.

FAST FACTS

Grading Easy to intermediate
Duration 2–5 hours
Configuration Circular
Start point Oak Valley Estate
GPS co-ordinates 34°09'17,68"S, 19°02'46.85"E
Terrain Singletrack
Map None
Access requirements Trail permit available at gate; open seven days a week during daylight
Trail markings Well marked with green, red and black arrows
Facilities Spick-and-span toilets and showers
Cell reception 100% coverage
Beware Baboons and cattle – approach cattle herds on the pastures very slowly
Time of year Year-round
Local info www.overberg.co.za /Tel (+27 86) 123 4777
More info www.oakvalleywines.com /Tel (+27 82) 567 8639

Port Elizabeth Beach Run (3–19km)

Province Eastern Cape
Region Sunshine Coast
Closest town Port Elizabeth
Trail destination Hobie Beach
Contributed by Lize-Marie Marais

THE DESTINATION The Friendly City (often known as the Windy City, as well!) boasts kilometres of free-range running along unspoilt beaches and hiking trails. All you need is a sense of adventure!

THE TRAIL Set off from Hobie Beach, keeping the sea on your left. After about 1.5km, you'll hit beautiful boardwalks all the way past Pollock Beach; keep an eye out for pods of dolphins and the occasional whale. If you time the tide right, you can head onto the beach at the end of the boardwalk (3km) and make your way to the Cape Recife Lighthouse (7km) amid the flocks of energetic Oystercatchers. Back at Hobie Beach, you can add a further 5km return to your run by continuing to the harbour wall at the end of King's Beach.

FAST FACTS

Grading Easy to intermediate
Duration 25mins to 3hrs
Configuration Return
Start point Hobie Beach
GPS co-ordinates 33°58'51.1"S, 25°39'29.6"E
Terrain Beach, boardwalks, cement pathways
Map None – just follow the shoreline
Access requirements Free access
Trail markings None
Facilities Shops, toilets and parking at start
Cell reception 100% coverage
Beware High tide
Time of year Year-round
Local info www.nmbt.co.za
More info www.caperecife.co.za

Rietvlei Nature Reserve (6.2/12km)

Province Gauteng
Region Gauteng North
Closest town Pretoria
Trail destination Rietvlei Nature Reserve
Contributed by Nicky Swanevelder

THE DESTINATION Spectacular views, an antediluvian lava stream and the Rietvlei Dam combine to create an outdoor arena with massive appeal to trail runners keen to escape the surrounding urban jungle.

THE TRAIL Rietvlei Nature Reserve boasts two main routes, both around 5–6km, and each featuring completely different terrain; both are nonetheless ideal for beginners or those in search of easy and relaxing runs. The first route sets off from the fishing hut and loops mainly to the northeast side of the dam, following a fairly flat course through grassland plains and some thickets. The second trail starts at the parking area, traversing grassy plains and a few hills overlooking the dam along a few solid climbs onto the plateau singletrack. More experienced trail runners can combine the two via a short tarmac stretch for a satisfying 12km run.

FAST FACTS

Grading Easy
Duration 1–2 hours
Configuration Circular route with loops
Start point Start from fishing hut or from parking area down the road
GPS co-ordinates 25°51'54.51"S, 28°15'51.76"E
Terrain Grassland plains and undulating hills
Map Download at www.runtrail.co.za
Access requirements Entrance fee payable
Trail markings The trail is well marked
Facilities Ablutions
Cell reception Good; reception on all parts of the trail
Beware Snakes, ticks and mountain bikers; always carry a cell phone with you
Time of year Summer and winter
Local info www.rietvlei-reserve.co.za
More info www.runtrail.co.za /Tel (+27 72) 699 2437

Rooikat Trail (8/19km)

Province Western Cape
Region Cape Winelands
Closest town McGregor
Trail destination Vrolijkheid Nature Reserve
Series Quantum Country Classics
Contributed by Ugene Nel

THE DESTINATION The Vrolijkheid Nature Reserve, only 5km from McGregor, lies in the Breede River valley. It offers a rugged but striking habitat to numerous birds and animals, including the rare rooikat or caracal.

THE TRAIL The Rooikat Trail follows a popular hiking trail ascending into the foothills abutting the nature reserve, offering spectacular views of the Riviersonderend and Langeberg mountains. The terrain is firm, with loose shale and sand in places.

FAST FACTS

Grading Intermediate
Duration 90mins to 5hrs
Configuration Circular
Start point Vrolijkheid Nature Reserve
GPS co-ordinates 33°55'03.4"S, 19°52'34.8"E
Terrain Hiking trails, gravel roads, loose shale
Map Available from www.capenature.co.za
Access requirements Reserve entry fee payable
Trail markings Hiking trail markers
Facilities Parking and toilets
Cell reception Minimal along remote sections
Beware Extreme temperatures
Time of year September for race; avoid November to March
Local info www.tourismmcgregor.co.za
More info www.quantumadventures.co.za / Tel (+27 21) 789 0188

Salt River Trail (5km)

Province Western Cape
Region Garden Route
Closest town Nature's Valley
Trail destination Salt River Mouth
Series Otter African Trail Run Prologue
Contributed by Ian Little

THE DESTINATION Nature's Valley lies virtually in the heart of the Tsitsikamma forest, a lush and indigenous woodland characterised by ancient forest giants, dangling strips of 'old man's beard' moss and a gorgeous lagoon. The pristine shore is lined by wooded mountains slopes and mile upon mile of rugged sea cliffs.

THE TRAIL The 5km Salt River Mouth Hiking Trail traverses coastal bush, a river estuary and an extreme, rocky shoreline, combining steep forest singletrack and sand with pebble beaches and some scrambling along wave-splashed outcrops. The Salt River Prologue takes place the day before the Otter African Trail Run (see page 135).

FAST FACTS

Grading Intermediate
Duration 20–60mins
Configuration Circular
Start point Nature's Valley beach
GPS co-ordinates 33°59'06.1"S, 23°32'51.5"E
Terrain Steep singletrack, rocks, beach and forest
Map Available at De Vasselot Camp Site
Access requirements Permits at De Vasselot Camp Site
Trail markings Hiking trail markers
Facilities All amenities in village
Cell reception Intermittent
Beware Slippery rocks; rogue waves at high tide
Time of year October for event, year-round for trail
Local info www.plettenbergbay.co.za
More info www.theotter.co.za / Tel (+27 44) 382 2932

Save the Rhino Two-day Trail Run
(45km – 25km and 20km)

Province Western Cape
Region Garden Route
Closest town Great Brak River
Trail destination Botlierskop Private Big Four Game Reserve
Series Southern Cross Adventures
Contributed by Hano Otto

THE DESTINATION Botlierskop Private Game Reserve is nestled between the magnificent Outeniqua Mountains and the beaches of the Indian Ocean.

THE TRAIL Short sections of jeep track lead you to the hiking routes and onto singletracks in the game reserve. The singletrack sections are 80% runnable for a medium to fit trail runner. The routes are not too technical, but do go up and down a lot as you go from one valley to the next.

The views over the sea and mountains are amazing. The highest peak you will cross is 1 200m. The route will take you through beautiful fynbos and among herds of game. Outside race day you can only walk the hiking routes inside the resort with a guide. Day visitors have to book with Botlierskop.

FAST FACTS

Grading Intermediate to difficult
Duration 3–6hrs per days
Configuration Circular
Start point Botlierskop Private Game Reserve
GPS co-ordinates 34°01'56.8"S, 22°08'30.8"E
Terrain Singletracks, jeep tracks, river beds and rocky sections
Map Available at the start and posted on the website
Access requirements Can be run on race day only
Facilities Toilets and restaurant at the reserve; none en route
Trail markings The race is marked with arrows, marshals and bright orange ribbon
Cell reception Minimal coverage along remote sections of trail
Beware Extreme temperatures; flooding streams and rivers
Time of year August for the race
Local info www.visitmosselbay.co.za and www.botlierskop.co.za
More info www.southerncrossadvenure.co.za / Tel (+27 82) 579 7595

Seven Dams Conservancy (5km and 12km)

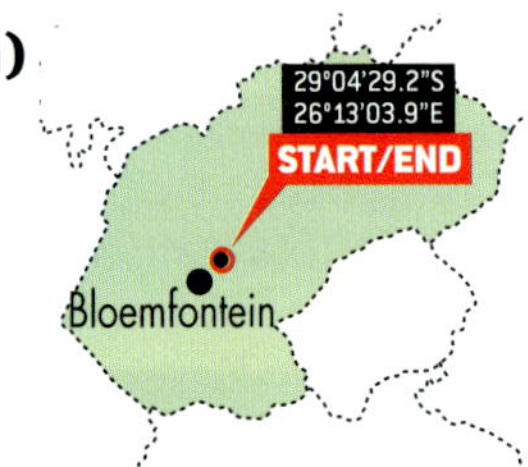

Province Free State
Region Mangaung Municipality
Closest town Bloemfontein
Trail destination Seven Dams Conservancy
Series Castle Light Trail Running League
Contributed by Peter Kirk

THE DESTINATION The Seven Dams Conservancy is great for trail running, mountain biking, walking the dog, or just chilling with the family on an afternoon picnic. Four distinctive habitats exist here, from woody shrubland, grassland and wetlands to the unique Bloemfontein Karroid shrubland. The wetlands around the dams are the highlight of the area and easy to find in the lower-lying areas of the conservancy.

THE TRAIL Runners can take various options, ranging in distance from 3km to 12km, off the two main loops along the extensive network of routes crisscrossing the conservancy. Expect the terrain to be gently undulating as you wind your way through varying habitats on a shallow soil layer covering underlying dolerite sheets exposed in places.

FAST FACTS

Grading Easy
Duration 0.5–1.5hrs
Configuration Two circular loops (5km and 12km)
Start point Entrance turnstile
GPS co-ordinates 29°04'29.2"S, 26°13'03.9"E
Terrain Dirt tracks, rocky singletrack, forest paths
Map Available on website
Access requirements None
Trail markings No trail markings or signage
Facilities N/A
Cell reception Good coverage
Beware Snakes and hot temperatures in summer; avoid running alone
Time of year Year-round
Local info www.bloemfonteintourism.co.za /Tel (+27 82) 413 3179
More info www.7dams.co.za /Tel (+27 51) 430 0712

Silvermine Nature Reserve (7–21km)

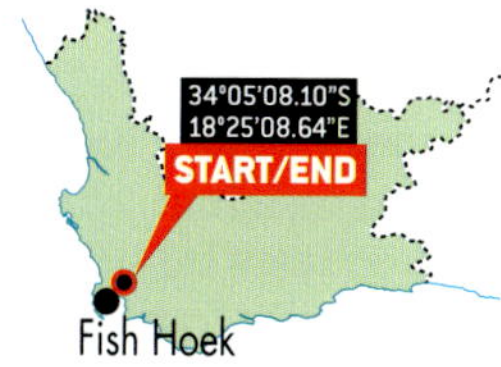

Province Western Cape
Region Cape Peninsula
Closest town Fish Hoek
Trail destination Silvermine Nature Reserve
Contributed by Jacques Marais

THE DESTINATION Silvermine Nature Reserve offers numerous trails for walking, running or hiking in some of the most spectacular coastal and mountain scenery around.

THE TRAIL Start out along the gorgeous 3.5km River Trail hiking route from the entrance gate, or follow the gravel road from the MTB parking area to the right of the tar road leading up to the dam. After 2km, this becomes concrete strips as it leads up to the turn-off right along Elephant's Eye Cave Trail or onwards to the highest point (775m) of the run. Take in the amazing views over False Bay and the Atlantic, then make gravity your friend as you s-bend down to the dam, either along the gravel road or some choice stretches of singletrack. There's quite a bit of rock and some sandy patches to negotiate.

FAST FACTS

Grading Easy to difficult
Duration 1–4 hours
Configuration Circular
Start point Parking area, Silvermine Nature Reserve
GPS co-ordinates 34°05'14.11"S, 18°25'12.66"E
Terrain Gravel road, concrete strips and singletrack
Map Available at the gate
Access requirements Entry fee payable
Trail markings Trails are marked with national parks signage
Facilities Secure parking, ablutions and picnic site
Cell reception Good
Beware Dogs, hikers and mountain bikers
Time of year Year-round
Local info www.tourismcapetown.co.za /Tel (+27 21) 487 4800
More info www.sanparks.org /Tel (+27 21) 701 8692

Sunshine Coast Trail Run (42km)

Province Eastern Cape
Region Sunshine Coast
Closest town Alexandria
Trail destination Springmount Farm and Alexandria Dunefield
Contributed by Jane Barnardo

THE DESTINATION The setting for this beautiful trail run is a dairy farm – the privately owned Springmount Farm, on the Sunshine Coast in the Eastern Cape. You will be running amongst some of the most pristine dune fields in Southern Africa, specifically the Alexandria Coastal Dune Field.

THE TRAIL The trail run covers varied terrain. It starts off with undulating jeep track through grassy farmland and cow pastures. At about the 7km mark the trail narrows into singletrack and then progresses to jeep track before the steep hill onto the dune section of the run. This is followed by a cleared path through dune vegetation towards the flag planted on the highest dune ahead. This is where you turn around and head back.

FAST FACTS

Grading Easy to intermediate
Duration 30mins to 3hrs
Configuration Out and back
Start point Springmount Farm
GPS co-ordinates 33°40'03.4"S, 26°02'21.0"E
Terrain Jeep track, singletrack, dunes and beach
Map Route map available on Facebook page – search for Sunshine Coast Trail Run
Access requirements Route restricted to race day only
Trail markings Directional arrows and danger tape blocking no-go paths
Facilities Refreshment tables en route and at finish line
Cell reception Very limited
Beware If the southeasterly wind picks up this is good practice for desert running!
Time of year Early September
Local info www.visiteasterncape.co.za and www.sanparks.org
More info www.trailadventures.co.za /Tel (+27 82) 642 3958

Tokai Mast Challenge (10.5km)

Province Western Cape
Region Cape Peninsula
Closest town Cape Town
Trail destination Tokai Forest (Table Mountain National Park)
Contributed by Robyn Ferrar

THE DESTINATION Cape Town's premier MTB trail hotspot in Tokai Forest plays host to this trail run event with a bit of a mountain biking twist to it. Although the event is a run/ride along service roads, there are stunning singletracks here for solo running.

THE TRAIL Starting from the Arboretum gate near the Tokai picnic area, the route follows the main jeep tracks that wind up the mountain towards the mast at the top of Constantiaberg Peak. By mostly keeping right, the network of jeep tracks will eventually (about halfway up) lead you to the tar road that takes you directly to the infamous mast 10.5km later. The mixture of jeep track and tar makes the terrain very easy underfoot; however, the 900m elevation over 10.5km makes this a feat of lung-busting strength and stamina not to be sniffed at.

FAST FACTS

Grading Intermediate to difficult
Duration 50–90mins
Configuration Linear route
Start point Tokai Forest car park
GPS co-ordinates 34°03'36.33"S, 18°25'30.54"E
Terrain Jeep track and tar road (often steep)
Map Available from Tokai picnic entrance or www.sanparks.org.za
Access requirements Free access for runners
Trail markings Minimal
Facilities At start/finish: Toilets, vendors, Lister's Tea Garden, cash prizes; en route: water table halfway, timekeeper at the finish
Cell reception Good
Beware Speeding mountain bikers
Time of year Mid-July for race, otherwise all year round; avoid running in bad weather
Local info www.sanparks.org / Tel (+27 21) 712 2337
More info www.trailrunning.co.za / Tel (+27 79) 558 3168

Tsitsikamma Storms River (5–22km)

Province Eastern Cape
Region Tsitsikamma and Baviaanskloof
Closest town Storms River
Trail destination Tsitsikamma State Forest and Garden Route National Park
Contributed by Jacques Marais

THE DESTINATION Tsitsikamma is a place of craggy peaks, secret beaches and temperate rain forest, where giant yellowwoods tower high above deep gorges and tranquil black-water pools.

THE TRAIL Three hiking trails in Plaatbos offer running options of 5km, 7.8km and 8km amid the indigenous forest surrounding Storms River Village. For those looking for a longer option, the 22km Storms River Pass winds on a quality gravel road through spectacular indigenous forest. Once across Storms River, a hard climb up the coastal bluff awaits before some flat running through pine plantations, spiked by views over Tsitsikamma and the Storms River Mouth.

FAST FACTS

Grading Easy to difficult
Duration 30mins to 6hrs
Configuration Circular and return options
Start point Storms River Village
GPS co-ordinates 33°58'27.4"S, 23°53'15.8"E
Terrain Hiking and mountain-biking singletrack
Map At the Storms River Office
Access requirements Free self-issue permits available at gate for Garden Route National Park section; permit for SAPPI section from Storms River Adventures
Trail markings Hiking trail markers
Facilities Ablutions, parking at Tsitsikamma State Forest, Storms River office or Tsitsikamma Forest Inn
Cell reception Good coverage
Beware Forestry vehicles, hikers and mountain bikers
Time of year Year-round
Local info www.tsitsikamma.info and www.sanparks.org
More info www.stormsriver.com / Tel (+27 42) 281 1098

Two Oceans Trail Run (22km)

Province Western Cape
Region Cape Peninsula
Closest town Cape Town
Trail destination Devil's Peak and Newlands Forest
Contributed by Robyn Ferrar

THE DESTINATION The mother city hosts this event, starting from the iconic UCT Upper Campus.

THE TRAIL The most convenient starting point would be to park at Rhodes Memorial (GPS 33°57'08.57"S, 18°27'32.42"E) and head up one of the hiking trails until it intersects a jeep track, where you then turn right towards the first of the Devil's Peak trails.

One of the more technical trail runs in South Africa, it starts on jeep track but soon changes to rugged and exposed terrain on Devil's Peak. Mostly rocky and dry underfoot, the trail is overgrown in places, and anyone afraid of heights or scrambling should think twice before attempting the first half of this route. The second half, along the undulating forest trails and jeep tracks of Newlands Forest, is more forgiving.

FAST FACTS

Grading Intermediate to extreme
Duration 1.5–4hrs
Configuration Circular route
Start point UCT Upper Campus
GPS co-ordinates 33°57'27"S, 18°27'38"E
Terrain Mountainous and steep singletrack, jeep tracks and forest trails
Map Map of area available from Tourist Information Centres
Access requirements Free entrance
Trail markings Minimal markings – major trail junctions only
Facilities Toilets, showers, food and drink available at the start/finish; marshals and paramedics along the route; water table at ±5km mark
Cell reception Good
Beware Exposed sections of trail
Time of year Any time of year, but avoid high wind or bad weather on Devil's Peak
Local info www.trailrunning.co.za /Tel (+27 79) 558 3168
More info www.twooceansmarathon.org.za/events/trail-run/general

Virginia Farm Trails (2.5–26km)

Province KwaZulu-Natal
Region KZN Midlands
Closest town Eston
Trail destination Virginia Farm
Contributed by Pete Stainbank

THE DESTINATION Virginia Farm is situated in the vicinity of Eston, halfway between Durban and Pietermaritzburg. The farm focuses mainly on sugar cane, but also forms part of one of the oldest conservancies, namely the Beaumont Eston Conservancy. Due to the topography of this region, farming is not suited to all the areas, and pockets of undeveloped land exist. These are mostly in a pristine state, boasting rich plant, animal and bird life.

THE TRAIL A glorious farm trail network – with just on 8km of singletrack – makes Virginia Farm a trail-running paradise. The hills are enjoyable, even for beginners, as the trails are laid out to meander uphill using gentle gradients. Trails are safe, well marked and designed to accommodate all ages and fitness levels.

FAST FACTS

Grading Easy to intermediate
Duration 30mins to 3hrs
Configuration A network of loops
Start point Virginia Farm Homestead
GPS co-ordinates 29°59'27.7"S, 30°36'35.1"E
Terrain Farm trails; flowing, undulating singletrack and plantation roads
Map Available at www.virginiafarm.co.za
Access requirements Booking is essential
Trail markings Trails are well marked with clear signage
Facilities Runners must be self-sufficient during runs; ablutions, parking, coffee shop
Cell reception Intermittent reception
Beware Heat and the occasional plantation vehicle
Time of year Open year-round
Local info www.zulu.org.za
More info www.virginiafarm.co.za /Tel (+27 83) 781 1042

Voortrekker Monument (2–24km)

Province Gauteng
Region Gauteng North
Closest town Pretoria
Trail destination Voortrekker Monument
Contributed by Nicky Swanevelder

THE DESTINATION Voortrekker Monument, in a nature reserve on the outskirts of Pretoria, is an imposing granite structure. At 40m tall it dominates the surrounding urban landscape. Spectacular 180° views across the reserve will reveal savannah bushveld with plains game such as zebra, blesbok, reedbuck, springbok, impala and black wildebeest. The trails area is located within a safe, fenced reserve with adequate parking and most of the required amenities.

THE TRAIL Voortrekker Monument boasts a combo of technical singletrack and dual jeep track along the ridges of Schanskop Hill. The trails cover the full gamut, from rookie runners to top-end trail junkies. The trails are well marked and anything goes – from short loops to longer return routes – depending on your personal choice.

FAST FACTS

Grading Easy to difficult
Duration 1–3hrs, depending on route
Configuration Circular route with loops
Start point Voortrekker Monument picnic area
GPS co-ordinates 25°46'44.11"S, 28°10'13.49"E
Terrain Quartzite ridges, grasslands and woodland forest
Map Download at www.runtrail.co.za
Access requirements Paid entrance; open seven days a week from 08:00–17:00
Trail markings Signage as well as colour-marked stones
Facilities Shops, restaurant, art gallery and picnic areas
Cell reception Perfect reception along trail
Beware Mountain bikers, ticks, dehydration and falling; always carry a cellphone with you
Time of year Any time, but watch out for thunderstorms during summer
Local info www.voortrekkermon.org.za
More info www.runtrail.co.za

Walter Sisulu Botanical Gardens (2–5km)

Province Gauteng
Region Johannesburg
Suburb Ruimsig / Poortview
Closest town Krugersdorp
Trail destination Walter Sisulu Botanical Gardens
Contributed by Lisa de Speville

THE DESTINATION During the past decade these gorgeous gardens have regularly been voted Gauteng's favourite picnic spot, and it becomes obvious why every time you visit Walter Sisulu Botanical Gardens. This is a secure, fenced, pay-to-enter environment where you are completely safe, so it's the ideal spot for women running on their own.

THE TRAIL This is not a place where you run at breakneck speeds. Rather wind your way through the Bird and Butterfly Garden and the Succulent Section at a leisurely pace, taking in the scents, sights and diversity of your environment. There is no fixed route to follow, so mix it up and range free – every visit can be different, making for interesting and scenic runs.

FAST FACTS

Grading Easy to intermediate
Duration 30–90mins
Configuration Ultimately, a circular route
Start point Walter Sisulu Botanical Gardens, entrance gate
GPS co-ordinates 26°05'13.80"S, 27°50'40.68"E
Terrain A combo of paved walkways and footpaths
Map A photocopied map is available at the gate
Access requirements An entry fee is payable
Trail markings Signboards indicating the different sections of the gardens
Facilities Ablutions, drinking fountains, restaurant and shops
Cell reception Throughout
Beware Slower walkers, especially mothers and children
Time of year Year-round
Local info www.gauteng.net / Tel (+27 11) 085 2500
More info www.sanbi.org/gardens/walter-sisulu / Tel (+27 86) 100 1278

Welvanpas (8–18km)

Province Western Cape
Region Cape Winelands
Closest town Wellington
Trail destination Welvanpas Farm
Contributed by Jacques Marais

THE DESTINATION If you like to mix exploring the history of the area with pounding stunning singletrack trails, then the historic farm Welvanpas (the birthplace of legendary Voortrekker leader Piet Retief) is just the spot for you. Nestled between the beautiful Hawekwa and Groenberg mountain ranges near Wellington, this trail offers a stunning running treat amidst an abundance of fruit orchards, fynbos and forests.

THE TRAIL A range of well-marked trails, some with steep climbs, start from the farmhouse. Be careful where you cross the road to Bainskloof Pass, but for most of the run you will be soul running along handmade singletrack. The Yellow Route, perfect for novices, can be done at a sedate pace along relatively level terrain, while the higher routes will bang you onto more rugged terrain and vertigo-inducing ascents.

FAST FACTS

Grading Easy to difficult
Duration 2–5 hours (8–18km)
Configuration Circular
Start point Welvanpas Farm
GPS co-ordinates 33°39′51.59″S, 18°58′24.95″E
Terrain Mostly singletrack, steep uphills and fast downhills
Map Available on the web
Access requirements Day fee payable
Trail markings Trail is well marked
Facilities Coffee shop and craft sales
Cell reception 100% coverage
Beware Heat in summer; steep downhill sections on narrow singletrack
Time of year Year-round
Local info www.tourismcapewinelands.co.za / Tel (+27 21) 487 4800
More info www.wellington.co.za / Tel (+27 21) 873 4604/8

Wolfberg Cracks (19km)

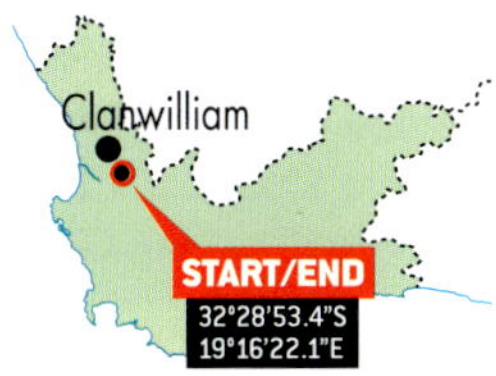

Province Western Cape
Region West Coast
Closest town Clanwilliam
Trail destination Cederberg Wilderness Area
Contributed by Jacques Marais

THE DESTINATION The Valley of the Red Gods welcomes you to the trail head of the Wolfberg Cracks and Arch, and this route arguably rates as one of the most beautiful you will ever run or hike within the Cederberg Wilderness Area.

THE TRAIL This steep hiking trail makes for a rugged run through spectacular rock formations, including an initially extreme ascent via the narrow Wolfberg Cracks. Once you have topped out onto the plateau, a glorious, circular run to the Arch and back down via the gravel pass (19km) is sure to blow your mind (and potentially your lungs). Sections are very wild and remote, and you might even see Cape mountain leopard spoor.

FAST FACTS

Grading Difficult
Duration 4–6hrs
Configuration Return or circular
Start point Wolfberg Cracks parking
GPS co-ordinates 32°28′53.4″S, 19°16′22.1″E (Wolfberg Cracks parking); 32°30′14.2″S, 19°15′27.0″E (Dwarsrivier Sanddrif)
Terrain Hiking trail singletrack, loose stones, scrambling
Map At Dwarsrivier office
Access requirements Permits at Dwarsrivier office
Trail markings SanParks signs on hiking trails
Facilities Shop, wine sales, wood, ablutions, camp site, self-catering cottages
Cell reception Poor coverage
Beware Snakes, dehydration in summer, snow in winter
Time of year Avoid summer and winter extremes
Local info www.cederberg.co.za
More info www.cederbergwine.com / Tel (+27 27) 482 2825

Wolwedans Off-road Run (6.4/14km)

Province Western Cape
Region Garden Route
Closest town Great Brak River
Trail destination Pepper Tree Restaurant and Great Brak River
Series Southern Cross Adventures
Contributed by Hano Otto

THE DESTINATION Great Brak River is a tranquil and scenic spot midway between George and Mossel Bay. Beautiful beaches, a lovely and safe lagoon, a quaint island with timber holiday homes, southern right whales and the widest pepper tree in South Africa give you enough reasons to stop here.

THE TRAIL The Wolwedans Hiking Trail to the dam wall and back is open to everybody and information can be obtained at the Great Brak River Tourism office or municipality. Run along the river on the beautiful hiking trail to the Wolwedans Dam, and back along the jeep tracks over the farms. The trail will take you through the most beautiful areas with the most fantastic views of Great Brak River, Mossel Bay and the Indian Ocean.

FAST FACTS

Grading Easy
Duration 30mins to 2.5hrs
Configuration Circular
Start point Pepper Tree Restaurant
GPS co-ordinates 34°02'28.4"S, 22°13'19.9"E
Terrain Singletracks, jeep tracks, rocky sections and grass tracks
Map Available from municipality, posted on website
Access requirements Race day only; Wolwedans hiking trail open to public (www.greatbrakriver.co.za)
Trail markings Marked on race day with arrows, marshals and bright orange ribbon
Facilities Toilets and restaurant at start; none en route
Cell reception Minimal coverage along remote sections of trail
Beware Heat
Time of year End December for the race; year-round for the trail
Local info www.visitmosselbay.co.za and www.greatbrakriver.co.za
More info www.southerncrossadventure.co.za

Wreck Challenge Trail Run (8.4km, 4km, 1.5km)

Province Western Cape
Region Garden Route
Closest town Great Brak River
Trail destination Glentana Beach Café
Series Trisport
Contributed by Sonja Terblanche-Otto

THE DESTINATION Great Brak River, situated halfway between George and Mossel Bay, got its name from the brackish water of the Great and Little Brak rivers. The lagoon mouth is divided into two sandy channels with a small island between them. The village boomed in 1859 as businesses expanded around an old toll bridge built across the Great Brak River at this time.

THE TRAIL The trail starts off along Glentana Beach past the famous 1902 wreck – a dock that stranded here in 1902 while on tow from London to Durban – before heading inland and uphill. Once you reach the top of the ascent it is reasonably flat before you again hit the downhill en route to the finish. A maximum altitude of 200m and non-technical surface makes it easy enough, even for novice runners.

FAST FACTS

Grading Easy
Duration 40–90mins
Configuration Circular
Start point Glentana Beach Café
GPS co-ordinates 34°02'54.4"S, 22°18'51.9"E
Terrain Rocks, singletrack, jeep tracks, sand and beach
Map Available at the start and posted on the website
Trail markings The race is marked with arrows, marshals and bright orange ribbon
Facilities Toilets and restaurant at start; none en route
Access requirements The section after the wreck can be run on race day only; map and information on the Glentana Wreck hiking route is available at the Great Brak River tourism office or at the municipality
Cell reception Minimal coverage along remote sections of trail
Beware Extreme temperatures and wind
Time of year Mid-December for the race; year-round for the trail
Local info www.visitmosselbay.co.za and www.greatbrak.co.za
More info www.trisport.co.za / Tel (+27 82) 579 7595

Glossary

Breathable mesh upper: Open-weave construction found in the upper part of a shoe's construction, allowing a relatively unrestricted movement of air to the feet, thereby keeping them cool.

Carbo-loading: A contemporary opinion whereby endurance athletes attempt to maximize stores of glycogen in their muscles. This strategy of generating 'muscle energy' is currently being reconsidered by leading nutritionists.

Dorsi-flexion: the movement which decreases the angle between the dorsum (superior surface) of the foot and the leg, so that the toes are brought closer to the shin. Movement in opposite directions is called plantar-flexion.

Genetically asymmetrical: Referring to the natural unequal alignment of the body, thus leading to a slight imbalance in each individual.

Glycogen: a molecule that serves as the secondary long-term energy storage in animal and fungal cells, with the primary energy stores being held in adipose tissue. Glycogen is made primarily by the liver and the muscles.

Heel strike: In minimalist running without a pronounced heel, the forefoot strikes the ground first to immediately transfer pressure via the ankles, knees, hips and spine. The calf muscle and Achilles tendon act as natural shock absorbers to prevent joint injuries.

Hydration bladder: A soft, pliable polythene reservoir, usually inserted into a backpack and used to store water or fluid.

Kinesiology: AKA muscle testing; a method by which the nerve reflexes of the body can be measured to ascertain imbalances in the body. Generally, an indicator muscle (such as the deltoid supporting arm movement) is tested for a specific weakness in the body.

Linear action: A continuous forward motion of the body through a single plane.

Minimalist shoe: Contemporary footwear approximating the feeling of running barefoot; exhibited in a new range of shoe models and styles with thinner soles, less cushioning and minimal underfoot protection.

Moisture-wicking: A technical fibre constructed in such a way that the individual conduits move perspiration away from the skin, thus enabling a garment to dry quickly.

Posture therapy: a technique (using kinesiology) used to align the body to reduce pain and prevent injury in running or other activities.

Pronation: A process initiated the moment the heel touches the ground and characterised by a distinctive, inward roll of the foot as the arch collapses.

Proprioceptors: receptors located in the muscles, tendons, joints and inner ear, which send signals to the brain regarding the body's position.

Racing flat: A reference to a specific style of minimalist footwear, featuring flat soles with minimal variation from heel to toe.

Trail running: Off-road running along a full gamut of terrain types, either along a clearly delineated trail, or navigating off-track through a landscape where no clear route exists.

Way Point: A specific compulsory checkpoint along any race route; generally during an orienteering race where athletes navigate a route along pre-determined, marked points.

Wedge: A support manufactured either from rubber, duct tape or similarly suited material, equivalent to the specific height required to re-align the body. Wedging counteracts these imbalances, thus resetting the body to a new posture to minimize pain and the tendency for recurring injury.

Yoga: An ancient Eastern practice which, at its root, refers to the inter-connectedness of everything in life, including body, mind, spirit and our immediate environment.

MAP KEY

Freeway/major road	Built up area	River
Main road	Point of interest	Marsh
Other road	Spot height	Race route
Railway		

List of Events

Date of Event	Name of Event	Town	Province	Organiser	Website
End of February	Bonitas Sunday Tribune 3 Cranes Challenge	Howick	KwaZulu-Natal	3 Cranes Challenge	www.3craneschallenge.co.za
March	Addo Elephant 76km / 44km Trail Runs	Kirkwood	Eastern Cape	Extreme Marathons	www.extrememarathons.com
March	Fynbos Trail Run	Stanford	Western Cape	Walker Bay Trails	www.walkerbaytrails.co.za
March	The Mole Rat Night Trail Run	Sedgefield	Western Cape	Southern Cross Adventure	www.southerncross adventure.co.za
End of March	Bokpoort Mountain Challenge	Clarens	Free State	Bokpoort Farm	www.bokpoort.co.za
Mid-March	ProNutro AfricanX Trail Run	Kleinmond	Western Cape	Stillwater Sports	www.stillwatersports.com
Spring and autumn	Diamond Dash	Cullinan	Gauteng	Diamond Dash Sports and Outdoor Events	www.diamonddash.co.za
End of March	Owl's Nest Pure Trail	Pretoria	Gauteng	WildTrail SA	www.wildtrail.co.za
April (Good Friday)	Two Oceans Trail Run	Cape Town	Western Cape	Two Oceans Marathon	www.twooceans marathon.org.za
April (Easter Sunday)	Goukamma Traverse	Sedgefield	Western Cape	Slow Festival	www.slowfestival.co.za
April	Merrell Xtreme – 3-Day Beach Stage Run	Port Alfred	KwaZulu-Natal	Backyard Adventures	www.backyard-adventures.co.za
April	Robberg Express	Plettenberg Bay	Western Cape	Magnetic South	www.magneticsouth.co.za
End of April	Stanley's Mountain and Trail Run	Ladismith	Western Cape	Quantum Adventures	www.quantumadventures.co.za
End of April	The Southern Cross 3-Day Trail Run	Sedgefield	Western Cape	Southern Cross Adventure	www.southerncross adventure.co.za
May (full moon weekend)	Jikeleza	Mazeppa Bay	Eastern Cape	Wild Trails	www.wildtrails.co.za
Early May	The Cradle Mayhem	Hartbeespoort	Gauteng	Mayhem Sports	www.mayhemsports.co.za
Mid-May	Mnweni Marathon	Bergville	KwaZulu-Natal	Bruce Arnett	www.trailrunning.co.za
Mid-May	Horse Whispers 24	Hazyview	Mpumalanga	Ilanga Trail Series	www.ilangatrailseries.co.za
May	Montagu Mountain Mania	Montagu	Western Cape	Mountain Mania	www.mountainmania.co.za
End of May	Oorlogskloof Mountain Trail Run	Nieuwoudt-ville	Northern Cape	Quantum Adventures	www.quantumadventures.co.za
Beginning of June	Sardine Mountain Bike Challenge and Trail Run	Port Edward	KwaZulu-Natal	Bundu Bashers Mountain Bike Club	www.bundubasher.co.za
June (first week-end during school holidays)	Katberg Eco Trail	Fort Beaufort	Eastern Cape	Kat Leisure Hotel Group	www.katleisure.co.za
June	Talbot Trail Run Winter Series – Cumberland	Pietermaritz-burg	KwaZulu-Natal	KZN Trail Running	www.kzntrailrunning.co.za
June	Talbot Trail Run Winter Series – Table Mountain	Pietermaritz-burg	KwaZulu-Natal	KZN Trail Running	www.kzntrailrunning.co.za
June	Old Fisherman's Trail Challenge	Fish Hoek or Hout Bay	Western Cape	Fisherman's Challenge	www.fishermans challenge.co.za
July	Iron Crown Trail Run	Haenertsburg	Limpopo	Haenertsburg Rotary Club	http://hbrotary.wordpress.com
Beginning of July	The Num-Num Trail Challenge	Machadodorp (eNtokozweni)	Mpumalanga	The Num-Num Trail	www.thenum-numtrail.co.za
July (Tuesday of the Knysna Oyster Festival)	Salomon Featherbed Trail Run presented by PETZL	Knysna	Western Cape	Magnetic South	www.magneticsouth.co.za
Mid-July	Mast Challenge	Cape Town (Tokai)	Western Cape	Trail Running	www.trailrunning.co.za
Mid-July	Rhodes Trail Run	Rhodes	Eastern Cape	Rhodes Run	www.rhodesrun.za.net

Mid-July	Bastille Day Trail Run	Franschhoek	Western Cape	Trail Running	www.trailrunning.co.za
July	Katberg Sky Trail	Fort Beaufort	Western Cape	Kat Leisure Hotel Group	www.katleisure.co.za
July	Grootvadersbosch Trail Run	Heidelberg	Western Cape	Quantum Adventures	www.quantumadventures.co.za
End of July	Hout Bay Trail Challenge	Hout Bay	Western Cape	Hout Bay Challenge	www.houtbaychallenge.co.za
End of July	Umdoni Park Challenge	Scottburgh	KwaZulu-Natal	Botha House	www.bothahouse.co.za
Beginning of August	Outeniqua Traverse	George	Western Cape	Mountain Runner	www.mountainrunner.co.za
August	The Save the Rhino 2-Day Trail Run	Great Brak River	Western Cape	Southern Cross Adventure	www.southerncross adventure.co.za
Second week of August	The Caveman Run	Jongensfontein	Western Cape	24-7 Adventure	www.24-7adventure.com
Mid-August	The Crazy Store Magaliesberg Challenge	Hartbeespoort	Gauteng	Energy Events	www.trailrunning.co.za
Mid-August	uMngeni River Run	Durban & Pietermaritzburg	KwaZulu-Natal	KZN Trail Running	www.kzntrailrunning.co.za
Late August	The Peninsula Ultra Fun Run (PUFfeR)	Cape Town	Western Cape	Fish Hoek Athletic Club	www.puffer.fishhoekac.com
Beginning of September	Bonitas Sunday Tribune Mont-Aux-Sources Challenge	Bergville	KwaZulu-Natal	Wildlands Conservation Trust	www.montauxsources challenge.co.za
Early September	Sunshine Coast Trail Run	Alexandria	Eastern Cape	Trail Adventures	www.trailadventures.co.za
Early September	Rooikat Trail Run	McGregor	Western Cape	Quantum Adventures	www.quantumadventures.co.za
Early September	Mountain Warrior Trail Run Festival	Stellenbosch	Western Cape	4x4 Team Building	www.4x4teambuilding.com
Beginning of September	Nagle Dam Trail Run	Pietermaritzburg/ Cato Ridge	KwaZulu-Natal	KZN Trail Running	www.kzntrailrunning.co.za
Mid-September	Baviaanskloof Trail Run	Patensie	Eastern Cape	Eastern Cape Parks & Tourism Agency	www.baviaansrun.net
Mid-September	4 Peaks Mountain Challenge	Ficksburg	Free State	Pure Adventures	www.pureadventures.co.za
Mid-September	Crazy Store Table Mountain Challenge	Cape Town	Western Cape	Trail Running	www.trailrunning.co.za
End of September	Nguni Classic MTB & Trail Run	Ladysmith	KwaZulu-Natal	Nguni Classic	www.nguniclassic.co.za
End of September / Beginning of October	Otter African Trail Run	Storms River Village	Eastern & Western Cape	Magnetic South	www.theotter.co.za
Beginning of October	Berg & Beach Stage Trail Run	Hermanus	Western Cape	Quantum Adventures	www.quantumadventures.co.za
Mid-October	The Hobbit 100	King Williams Town	Eastern Cape	Mountain Runner Events	www.mountainrunner.co.za
Mid-October	Laborie Paarl Rock Run	Paarl	Western Cape	Trail Running	www.trailrunning.co.za
Last weekend in October	Bonitas Radox Golden Gate Challenge	Clarens	Free State	Wildlands Conservation Trust	www.goldengate challenge.co.za
October / November (depending on full moon)	Kalahari Augrabies Extreme Marathon	Augrabies	Northern Cape	Extreme Marathons	www.extrememarathons.com
Early November	Hi-Tec Mystic Sable Stage Run	Pretoria	Gauteng	Vertical Horison	www.verticalhorison.co.za
Early November	Salomon Sky Run	Lady Grey	Eastern Cape	Pure Adventures	www.pureadventures.co.za
Early November	Fairview Dryland Traverse	Oudtshoorn	Western Cape	Dryland Traverse	www.drylandtraverse.co.za
November	Talbot Trail Run Summer Series – Cumberland	Pietermaritzburg	KwaZulu-Natal	KZN Trail Running	www.kzntrailrunning.co.za
November	Talbot Trail Run Summer Series – Table Mountain	Pietermaritzburg	KwaZulu-Natal	KZN Trail Running	www.kzntrailrunning.co.za
End of December	George Trail Run	George	Western Cape	Garden Route Trail Running	www.gardenroutetrail running.co.za

First edition published in 2012 by MapStudio™ South Africa

ISBN 978-1-77026-369-7

Production Manager John Loubser
Editor Thea Grobbelaar
Designer Nicole Bannister
Cartographers Genené Hart, Elaine Fick
Digital Compiler Anthony Davids
Researcher Abbygail Greybe
Proofreader Claudia dos Santos
Reproduction Resolution Colours (Pty) Ltd, Cape Town
Marketing Manager Sandy Christie (sandyc@mapstudio.co.za)
Feedback research@mapstudio.co.za
Photo credits © 2012 All images as credited on page
Printed and bound by Interpak Printers, South Africa

MapStudio™
Wembley Square, First Floor, Solan Road, Cape Town, 8001
PO Box 1144, Cape Town, 8000
Tel: 0860 10 50 50
www.mapstudio.co.za